CAPITAL SPECULATIONS

Becoming Modern: New Nineteenth-Century Studies

SERIES EDITORS

Sarah Way Sherman, Department of English, University of New Hampshire
Janet Aikins, Department of English, University of New Hampshire
Rohan McWilliam, Anglia Polytechnic University, Cambridge, England
Janet Polasky, Department of History, University of New Hampshire

This book series maps the complexity of historical change and assesses the forma-tion of ideas, movements, and institutions crucial to our own time by publishing books that examine the emergence of modernity in North America and Europe. Set primarily but not exclusively in the nineteenth century, the series shifts atten-tion from modernity's twentieth-century forms to its earlier moments of uncertain and often disputed construction. Seeking books of interest to scholars on both sides of the Atlantic, it thereby encourages the expansion of nineteenth-century studies and the exploration of more global patterns of development.

Stephen Carl Arch, *After Franklin: The Emergence of Autobiography in Post-Revolutionary America, 1780–1830* (2001)

Justin D. Edwards, *Exotic Journeys: Ex-ploring the Erotics of U.S. Travel Litera-ture, 1840–1930* (2001)

Edward S. Cutler, *Recovering the New: Transatlantic Roots of Modernism* (2002)

Margaret M. Mulroney, *Black Powder, White Lace: The du Pont Irish and Cultural Identity in Nineteenth-Century America* (2002)

William M. Morgan, *Philanthropists in Disguise: Gender, Humanitarianism, and Complicity in U.S. Literary Realism* (2004)

Piya Pal-Lapinski, *The Exotic Woman in Nineteenth-Century British Fiction and Culture: A Reconsideration* (2004)

Patrick H. Vincent, *The Romantic Po-etess: European Culture Politics and Gender, 1820–1840* (2004)

Betsy Klimasmith, *At Home in the City: Urban Domesticity in American Litera-ture and Culture, 1850–1930* (2005)

Sarah Luria, *Capital Speculations: Writ-ing and Building Washington, D.C.* (2005)

David L. Richards, *Poland Spring: A Tale of the Gilded Age, 1860–1900* (2005)

Angela Sorby, *Schoolroom Poets: Child-hood, Performance, and the Place of American Poetry, 1865–1917* (2005)

THIS BOOK WAS PUBLISHED IN ASSOCIATION WITH THE CENTER FOR AMERICAN PLACES, SANTA FE, NEW MEXICO, AND STAUNTON, VIRGINIA (WWW.AMERICANPLACES.ORG).

CAPITAL
SPECULATIONS

Writing and Building Washington, D.C.

SARAH LURIA

University of New Hampshire Press

Durham, New Hampshire

PUBLISHED BY
UNIVERSITY PRESS OF NEW ENGLAND
HANOVER AND LONDON

University of New Hampshire Press

Published by University Press of New England,

One Court Street, Lebanon, NH 03766

www.upne.com

© 2006 by University of New Hampshire Press

Printed in the United States of America

5   4   3   2   1

Library of Congress Cataloging-in-Publication Data

Luria, Sarah.

   Capital speculations : writing and building Washington, D.C. / Sarah Luria.

   p.   cm. — (Becoming modern)

Includes bibliographical references (p.) and index.

ISBN-13: 978–1–58465–501–5 (alk. paper)

ISBN-10: 1–58465–501–1 (alk. paper)

ISBN-13: 978–1–58465–502–2 (pbk. : alk. paper)

ISBN-10: 1–58465–502–X (pbk. : alk. paper)

1. American literature—Washington (D.C.)—History and criticism.   2. American literature—19th century—History and criticism.   3. Architecture and literature—History—19th century.   4. Washington (D.C.)—Buildings, structures, etc.   5. Washington (D.C.)—intellectual life.   6. Washington (D.C.)—In literature.   7. Architecture—Washington (D.C.)   8. Speculation—Washington (D.C.)   9. Washington (D.C.)—History.   10. Architecture in literature.   I. Title.   II. Series.

   PS253.D6L87 2005

   810.9'357—dc22   2005021673

Morals reformed — health preserved — industry invigorated — instruction diffused — public burthens lightened — Economy seated, as it were, upon a rock — . . . all by a simple idea in Architecture!

—JEREMY BENTHAM, Preface to *Panopticon*

What might have been is an abstraction
Remaining a perpetual possibility
Only in a world of speculation.
—T. S. ELIOT, "Burnt Norton" I, 6–8

Contents

List of Illustrations   xiii
Acknowledgments   xvii
Introduction   xxi

I. The Politics of Circulation

Chapter 1. George Washington's Romance: Plotting the Federal   3
            City, 1791–1800
Chapter 2. The Poetry of Internal Improvements: Abraham   38
            Lincoln and Walt Whitman in Civil War Washington

II. Models of National Domesticity

Chapter 3. A House United: Frederick Douglass's Interracial   71
            Domesticity during Reconstruction
Chapter 4. *Democracy*'s Church: The Hay-Adams Houses   99
            during the Gilded Age
Epilogue   143

Notes   157
Works Cited   179
Index   191

Illustrations

Fig. 1.1.   Thomas Jefferson's plan for the Federal City, 1791.   7

Fig. 1.2.   Pierre (Peter) Charles L'Enfant, *Plan for the City*   8
             Intended for the Permanent Seat of the Government of
             [the] United States, 1791.

Fig. 1.3.   Plan of the Town, Château, and Gardens of Versailles,   13
             France, 1746.

Fig. 1.4.   *A Map of the City of Washington in the District of*   15
             Columbia established as the permanent Seat of the
             Government of the United States of America taken
             from actual survey, as laid out on the ground, 1818.

Fig. 1.5.   Maison Quarrée, Nîmes, France, first century B.C.   23

Fig. 1.6.   Virginia State Capitol, Richmond. Thomas Jefferson,   24
             architect.

Fig. 1.7.   Edward Savage, *George Washington, Esq. President of*   26
             the United States of America, 1793.

Fig. 1.8.   *Geographical, Statistical, and Historical Map of*   28
             the District of Columbia. Engraved by Young &
             Delleker, 1822.

Fig. 1.9.   Robert Morris House, Philadelphia, 1800. Engraving   36
             by William Birch.

Fig. 2.1.   The Capitol, shortly before Lincoln's first inauguration,   48
             1861.

Fig. 2.2.   East front of the Capitol, c. 1870.   49

Fig. 2.3.   *Massachusetts Centinel* cartoon, 1788.   50

Fig. 2.4.   *Section through Dome of U.S. Capitol*, Thomas U.   51
             Walter, 1859.

Fig. 2.5.　Robert E. Lee residence, Arlington House, Arlington, Va.　54

Fig. 2.6.　Horatio Greenough, *George Washington,* 1832–41, marble.　59

Fig. 2.7.　Abraham Lincoln. Photo taken four days before his　60
assassination. Photograph by Alexander Gardner.

Fig. 2.8.　Armory Square Hospital ward.　65

Fig. 3.1.　The Douglass family in front of their house, 316–318　85
A St., N.E.

Fig. 3.2.　C. Becker, Othello engraving, c. 1880, Cedar Hill.　88

Fig. 3.3.　Cedar Hill, Anacostia, Washington, D.C.　89

Fig. 3.4.　Cedar Hill, street-level view.　92

Fig. 3.5.　The Growlery, Cedar Hill, c. 1893.　93

Fig. 3.6.　The Growlery, modern-day restoration.　94

Fig. 3.7.　East Parlor, front, Cedar Hill.　95

Fig. 3.8.　East Parlor, rear, Cedar Hill.　96

Fig. 3.9.　West Parlor, Cedar Hill.　97

Fig. 3.10.　Douglass in his study at Cedar Hill.　98

Fig. 4.1.　The Hay-Adams Houses, 1603 H St.–800 16th St.,　107
N.W., c. 1900. Photograph by Frances B. Johnston.

Fig. 4.2.　William Corcoran's "little White House," 1607 H St.,　108
N.W., c. 1907.

Fig. 4.3.　Augustus Saint-Gaudens, Adams Memorial, Washington,　109
D.C. Photograph by Jerry L. Thompson.

Fig. 4.4.　Pitch Pine Hill, the Adams house at Beverly Farms,　114
Massachusetts. Photograph by Marian Hooper Adams.

Fig. 4.5.　H. H. Richardson, Ephraim W. Gurney House,　123
1884–86.

Fig. 4.6.　St. John's Church, Lafayette Square. Photograph by　124
E. David Luria.

Fig. 4.7.　From Lafayette Square looking toward St. John's　125
Church. Photograph by E. David Luria.

Fig. 4.8.　Andrew Jackson statue, Lafayette Square, with White　127
House in background. Photograph by E. David Luria.

Fig. 4.9.　Adams House under construction. Photograph by　132
Marian Hooper Adams.

Fig. 4.10.　Adams House.　135

Fig. 4.11.　Mabel Hooper La Farge, *Henry Adams in His Study*.　137

Fig. 4.12. Cass Gilbert, rendering of Senate Park Commission's   140
            1902 plan for rebuilding Lafayette Square, c. 1917.
Fig. 4.13. The Hay-Adams Hotel. Photograph by E. David Luria.   141

Acknowledgments

As I look back and take account of all of the people who have helped me write this book, I am deeply moved by the generous sharing of expertise and support I have experienced along the way. My first debts are to George Dekker and Jay Fliegelman. Many budding Americanists at Stanford have thrived on their knowledge, acuity, and incredibly generous support, and I am one of them. George Dekker helped to ground the project with his impressive knowledge of American literary history, and the warmth of his friendship did much to sustain me. Jay Fliegelman was inspirational from the start: this book really began in his seminar on the American Enlightenment, when he held up one of Martha Custis Washington's dessert dishes (which he owned) to make a point about *The Federalist*. I have pursued the integral relationship between material, visual, and literary culture ever since. His intellectual enthusiasm and faith in my project renewed my energy for it more times than I can count. I am extremely grateful for his contribution.

In Boston, the manuscript continued to grow through the warm community of scholars and artists I have found here. I am particularly grateful for the comments, conversation, and friendship of Christine Coch, Renee Bergland, Allegra Goodman, Elizabeth Klimasmith, Joan Leegant, Nita Regnier, Augusta Rohrbach, Laura Saltz, Nancy Salzer, and Lynne Weiss. Not nearly so close to home but just as treasured has been the friendship, intellectual support, and critical feedback of Elizabeth Abrams, Adrienne Leveen, Charlotte R. Murphy, Marion Rust, and Bryan Wolf. Albert Gelpi, Robert A. Irwin, Jill Lepore, Carolyn Porter, and David Schuyler all read the manuscript at various stages in its development and gave important and timely advice. Conversations with Dell Upton, Thomas C. Hubka, and Alison K. Hoagland were inspirational as well as cautionary as I first ventured into the field of architectural history and criticism. All have contributed immeasurably to this book; any faults that might remain are my responsibility alone.

At Holy Cross I have found another talented and vibrant community of scholars, and I thank all of my colleagues in the English Department there. The college provided financial support through a Junior Research Leave, a summer fellowship, and funds for production costs. The Audio Visual Department and Media Lab at Holy Cross were unstinting in their technical expertise and resources. Joel Villa, who died before this book's publication, was a techie mastermind and a wonderful colleague who is sorely missed. Margaret Nelson led me through the production of the figures with friendly patience and impressive skill. Research for the project during its earlier phase was accelerated by generous grants from the Woodrow Wilson Foundation, the Stanford English Department, and the John B. Sias Fellowship of the Stanford English Department.

My research took me to various collections and sites, where I also received much assistance. I wish to thank, in particular, Cathy Ingram, Carnell Poole, and Douglass Stover at the Frederick Douglass National Historic Site for the generous sharing of their expertise and the archives located at Cedar Hill, for permitting me almost unrestricted access to the house, and for taking me to other sites useful to my research. I wish, too, to thank Megan Smith at the Maps and Prints Division of Houghton Library, Harvard University, as well as the staffs at the Massachusetts Historical Society and the Manuscripts Division of the Moorland-Spingarn Research Center at Howard University. Sonia Moss at Green Library of Stanford University has been crucial to countless research projects, and mine is no exception.

Earlier versions of chapter 1 appeared in *Prospects: An Annual of American Cultural Studies, Vol. 26* (2001), 1–34 (Copyright © Cambridge University Press 2001. Reprinted with the permission of Cambridge University Press), and in *Common-Place: Special Issue on Early Cities of the Americas* 3.4 (July 2003) <www.common-place.org>. I am grateful to Cambridge University Press and *Common-Place* for permission to republish them here. An earlier version of chapter 3 appeared in *The American Home: Material Culture, Domestic Space, and Family Life*, ed. Eleanor McD. Thompson (Copyright 1998 Henry Francis du Pont Winterthur Museum, Inc.). I am grateful to Winterthur Museum for permission to republish it here.

I am lucky to live in a community that functions like an extended kibbutz, where children flow in and out of houses and informal dinners are shared with life-saving regularity. For the warmth and joy they add to my and my children's daily lives, I would like to thank Randi Berkowitz and John Regosin, Audrey and Refael Cohen, Alisa and David Dolev, Dena and Jason Glasgow, Becky and Mark Leiter, and Nancy and Howard Smith. I get by with a lot of help from my friends.

This book is autobiographical insofar as I grew up in Washington, D.C., and the book in real ways has been a family affair. My father, Carlos de Lima Luria, is a gifted storyteller and writer, and I only hope some of his talent has been transmitted to me. My uncle, Washington photographer E. David Luria, tirelessly photographed sites that appear in the book. I am proud to be able to include his work here. My cousins Daniel O. Hirsch and Brenda Gruss provided a wonderful place to stay in Washington and key material about the city during the research phase of the project. The interests in history and art that I share with my brother, Scott Luria, and sister, Anne Luria Burg, make their friendship a real resource, upon which I draw again and again. My mother, Martha Reading Luria, died before I began work on this book, but it was inspired by her, a woman of letters and a true Washingtonian. I also relied on my husband, Thomas L. Schwarz, every step of the way. His humor and love, and his topnotch editorial skills, gave me just what I needed again and again (and again). And even though I had to keep my study door shut far more than I would have liked, my daughter, Martha Reading Schwarz, and my son, Theodore de Lima Schwarz, came in anyway, sat to my right and left, and so kept this from being a lonely venture. And as for the profoundest joy I have in life, well, I have them, and their father, to thank for that, too.

Introduction

Washington, D.C., has a long history of ambitious failure. Despite all of the plans to develop the national capital and the incalculable amount of money spent toward their fulfillment, Washington has always to a notable degree backfired. Visitors to the marble splendors of the National Mall may encounter prostitutes along New York Avenue just blocks away; those who travel to the city by train from the north are likely to get their first glimpse of the Capitol dome over the poor and rundown neighborhoods that surround it. Rather than providing an airtight patriotic experience, the capital has an uncanny habit of highlighting the nation's flaws with a kind of confessional zeal. How could a city so carefully planned go so wildly awry? This book is a reflection on that question. I focus on the capital during its most awkward phase, from its creation in 1791 until 1900.

While this book is about Washington during its first hundred years, it is by no means a history of the capital.[1] Instead, I take the opportunity offered by the capital's highly self-conscious landscape to interpret some particularly striking interactions between political visions and the built environment—through city space and architecture—that took place on its ground. I begin with the planning of the capital city in 1791. As historian Pamela Scott has argued, the street plan for Washington "embodied . . . the early organization of the federal government." James Sterling Young has gone so far as to suggest that the city's plan translates the Constitution into physical space; the capital "render[s] in a different language . . . the constitutional prescriptions for the structure and functions of the national government."[2] The close and intentional relationship between the capital's design and the Constitution poses a fascinating case for the further study of the interplay between the written word and material culture. That close relationship continues beyond the founding of the city, as the city remains a malleable space for the projection of political visions. I argue that Washington offers an extreme example of the way in which the literature of American political reform depends upon the built environment to fulfill the letter of its text.

Washington establishes an involved and dynamic relationship between architecture and literature. Critics tend to treat architecture and literature simply as metaphors for one another. It has become a commonplace in American and cultural studies to "read" cities and houses as "texts" and to "map" literature onto the spaces from which it emerges.[3] The texts I study here suggest that their authors are obsessed with architecture and city space precisely because houses *aren't* texts and cities *aren't* two-dimensional pages that can only be read. On the contrary, these writers depend upon architectural expressions of their visions so that their words can exceed the margins of their text and be experienced as a new physical reality. Together these spaces describe a dialectical relationship between the political imagination and physical space: political vision expresses itself through the city's built environment, and that space in turn promotes the vision and turns it into political fact. I argue that both Washington's successes and its failures can be traced in large part to the practice in which politics, literature, architecture, and urban planning intersect: speculation.

⁙

In 1774 there was a semantic revolution: "speculation," which had previously meant deep philosophical thought, came to mean a risky strategy of financial investment. Adam Smith referred to this new meaning several times in his *Wealth of Nations* (1776): "Sudden fortunes, indeed, are sometimes made . . . by what is called the trade of speculation."[4] This form of trade had long been in existence; in fact, it dates back to Roman times.[5] But its new name in 1774 is significant, because it signals the very merger of political theory and marketplace psychology that would help underwrite the development of the United States. That this revolutionary partnership was pivotal for the launching of a new nation is nowhere more clearly seen than in the planning in 1791 of a grand new capital city, Washington, D.C.

Speculation, from "specula," or watchtower, and "speculere," to look, to look at, is the grounding of reality in the future. You invest in real estate now because you think it will be worth more in the future. You back your candidate now because you think she or he will win in the next election. You plan a magnificent capital city—rivaling those of Europe—because you imagine that your nation will surpass such nations in time. The earlier you buy into the vision, the more you stand to gain when (and, of course, if) that vision comes true. Speculation is thus in part about how fiction— imagined grand scenarios, often the grander the better—helps to sell things. In this book it is about how fabulous political visions help to sell personal political agendas. But just as a real estate speculator might build a road and a few impressive buildings and dwellings to attract investors to, and to get them to *believe* in, the new town he wishes to develop, so too the political speculators I study here engage and even build physical models of their ideas in order to promote them and lure investments in their vision.

At the time of the capital city's founding, political theorizing always risked the charge of being "mere" speculation—utopian scheming that would never amount to anything real. As Alexander Hamilton noted of one idea in 1777, "I expect it will do better in speculation than in practice."[6] The planning of Washington, D.C., however, suggests that financial speculation became a way to turn political theories into practice; in the new capital, Federalists such as George Washington used financial speculation to get their political speculations built. The city was designed to help fulfill the Constitution, ratified just four years before: not only would the city serve as home to the national government, it would provide a site where the abstract concept of the nation could be experienced as a physical reality—something a citizen could point to, visit, and admire. The capital's design in fact translates the Constitution into physical space; the city's dazzling network of avenues makes self-evident the dynamic connections between the separate branches of government, as Pennsylvania Avenue connects the Capitol to the White House and, at other intersections, to plazas originally intended to represent the various states.[7] How could a fledgling nation pay for such a fabulous plan? A handsome engraved map of the city, showing its numbered lots for sale, was circulated among the populace, who were invited to invest in the capital (and hence the nation) by buying land within it. Thus the capital, shaped by the political speculation of a new, rational relationship between citizen and government, would be achieved through real estate speculation. Pragmatists such as Hamilton acknowledged that such investments would tie the citizens' hearts to the nation through the much stronger bond with their pockets.[8] Washington seemed to promise the perfect blend of public interest and self-interest: by investing in the nation's capital, citizens stood to increase their own capital. By appealing to human nature—the attraction to grand visions and the desire for wealth—financial speculation offered a savvy strategy by which "mere" political visions might be turned into fact.

Despite the logistical reality that, as Benedict Anderson notes, "the members of even the smallest nation will never know most of their fellow-members, meet them, or even hear of them," this nation's framers betray an anxiety that it would not be enough for citizens to imagine their new, artificially formed community; they had to be able to experience it physically.[9] Discussions surrounding the design of the nation's capital suggest that the planners saw the city as a strategic opportunity for the bodily education of citizens in new political behaviors. Within the city's orchestrated space, citizens would physically experience a federal organization of government and so be acclimated to its political mindset. They would adopt a *national* view rather than the local, disjointed view that was all citizens had had any cause to know. To further imprint the nation's rational order, avenues in the city's plan are named after states and streets are numbered and alphabetized. Those personally investing in the city would go so far as to make the nation's city literally their own home. Washington's remarkable street plan thus materializes a narrative whereby individual citizens are brought into the national fold. The city bears out Angela Miller's claim that "nationalism was at root a substance, a thing, and not merely a social process. It existed in the 'everlasting hills,' in the broad rivers and the sweeping plains, as the very substance of nationalist rhetoric."[10]

That Washington, as it was originally planned, was to be developed through financial speculation has been well documented.[11] My research goes beyond the founding of the city to show how financial and political speculation continued to shape the city's space. Indeed, I argue that Washington remains a speculative space, the projection of a grand vision that is never quite realized.

Washington brings to our attention a whole category of speculative literature that not only designs but builds its vision as a way to promote investment in its ideas. Once established, Washington became a stage for expressive architecture through which subsequent reformers could promote their visions of how the nation should change. I study four such cases here. Abraham Lincoln, Walt Whitman, Frederick Douglass, and Henry Adams all lived for a time in Washington, and their Washington writings imagine new political landscapes that are realized physically in the capital. For example, Lincoln envisions a transcendent Union made possible by technological innovation, and that vision is materialized by the huge new Capitol dome. In Whitman's accounts of the capital during the Civil War, the new pavilion-style hospitals appear to actualize the incredible, unified national landscape that Whitman conjures in his poetry. In his Washington home, Frederick Douglass builds a model of the interracial landscape he advocates during Reconstruction. Lastly, Henry Adams redefines political power on his own terms through the double house on Lafayette Square that H. H. Richardson designs for Adams and his friend, the statesman and author John Hay.

The spaces and texts studied here are best described as speculative. The spaces constructed by the texts are as fantastic as they are real, as rhetorical as they are concrete—vanguard environments that seek to change the political world. These speculative structures attract investment to their ideas through their novelty—they tend to be not just unconventional but anti-conventional. Most compelling is their use of an unusual scale, which includes structures both huger than huge (the Capitol dome) and strikingly small (the diminutive entrance of Henry Adams's home). These pairs of spaces and texts all suggest that the longstanding attraction between literature and place—both city space and architecture—has often been more fully consummated, and on a much more literal level, than any metaphoric relationship would allow.

Thoreau's tiny "cabin for one" is perhaps the most famous example of this interplay between the architecture and the literature of political reform. When Thoreau built his cabin by Emerson's pond, he laid the foundation for *Walden*. *Walden* in turn provides exact directions for how to build such a cabin or, preferably, design one's own. But cabin and book do more than that. The cabin promotes the book's ideas, and it fulfills them—it proves the book's claim that its philosophy is practical, buildable. It is a fantasy realized, and this no doubt accounts for much of its staying power.[12] Thousands of *Walden* readers still make the pilgrimage to Walden Pond and the replica cabin that stands nearby, and it is wonderful to see just how compact, how simple yet well-planned, his tiny cabin must have been. Yet what would Thoreau's cabin be without *Walden,* and vice versa? The authors I analyze do not necessarily take hammers and nails and build a model of their political visions as explicitly as Thoreau. Instead, their texts describe a range of strategic interactions between words and architecture.

The following four chapters have on the whole little to do with the monuments for which Washington is most famous. Instead, the authors studied here focus on two everyday spaces that were far more central to late-eighteenth- and nineteenth-century political thought: routes of communication—such as streets, canals, and railroads—and the home. The book is thus divided into two larger sections. "The Politics of Circulation" (which includes the planning of Washington, D.C., and the city during the Civil War) shows how pivotal the issue of physical infrastructure—or what was termed "internal improvements"—was to bringing about a connected, national landscape. Washington served as a testing ground for the feasibility of such ambitious projects, and here I draw upon the analyses of this nation's obsession with internal improvements so richly described in the work of D. W. Meinig, John W. Reps, and John Seelye.[13] The second section, "Models of National Domesticity" (which includes Douglass's and Adams's domestic experiments), shows how the home became a crucial testing ground in Washington for whether the new political ideas represented in the capital had taken hold. Here I draw upon the large field of scholarship, including that of Gillian Brown, Amy Kaplan, Lora Romero, and Dell Upton, that has helped to delineate the ways in which domestic space is always political space.[14] I hope here to contribute to this increasingly rich analysis of the political landscape. This study is particularly interested in the way in which physical infrastructure and domesticity—roads and houses—are inseparably linked: routes of circulation (both inside and outside of the home) create routes of access and as such are channels through which political power can flow. Lincoln imagines a national network of railroads, telegraph lines, *and* "mystic chords of memory" that reaches to every "heart and hearthstone"; Henry Adams's enlarged domestic circle establishes its own private routes of political influence into the center of national power.[15]

In chapter 1 I show that the plan for the new capital was preoccupied with the idea of circulation. The city's network of avenues and streets modeled the ideal national landscape prophesied by *The Federalist,* connected through a network of rivers, canals, and roads. George Washington's vision for the city showed the collaboration between marketplace and politics that he felt would make the nation secure. Washington speculated that the Potomac River would be developed into an important trade route to the nation's interior, making the city not just a capital of the nation but of trade as well, an Albany and a New York all in one.[16] Accordingly, Washington hoped not just statesmen but many citizens would make the nation's capital their home. From this national domesticity the elusive emotional link between private citizen and federal government would be forged.

In chapter 2 I analyze Lincoln and Whitman's presence in the capital during the Civil War. Lincoln lobbied tirelessly for technological infrastructure, particularly railroads and the telegraph, as a means of tying the Union together. But such "internal improvements" were highly controversial—they not only gave citizens mobility and access to government but also gave the national government access to citizens and state territory. To counter suspicions that the nationalists would exploit the need for infrastructure to infringe upon state sovereignty, Lincoln perfected a well-established rhetoric of internal improvements that provided a poetic, transcendent imagery to ennoble the effort toward union. That imagery comes to a climax in both of his inaugural addresses and in the Capitol dome under which they were delivered. Lincoln's inaugural addresses, and Whitman's accounts of the Civil War hospitals in his poetry and prose, bring fantastic national domestic infrastructures to life. In Washington's new pavilion hospitals, Whitman walks into the world of his poetry as he circulates through the corridors lined with men from all parts of the Union, touching them, dressing their wounds, writing to their families, bestowing his kiss. Both authors materialize an ideal network of relations forever moving between the national and the local, one that is no longer hemmed in by actual geographical constraints.

In chapter 3 I analyze Frederick Douglass's materialist politics during Reconstruction. The legislative victories won during Reconstruction were too vulnerable, Douglass argued, as the repeal of the Civil Rights Act in 1883 would show. Douglass's insistence throughout Reconstruction that African Americans accumulate property suggests a more solid strategy to shore up these vulnerable gains. Black property and respectable homes—these would lead white Americans to view black citizens as more like themselves. Douglass himself invested heavily in real estate, and his Washington homes provided a place where he could model his materialist politics. His last and most impressive home resembled a small slave plantation, with its big house and several outbuildings, including a strange slave cabin–like structure in which Douglass liked to write. The main house had an impressive approach and prospect overlooking the Capitol. Here Douglass, the ex-slave, was now master, living in perfect middle-class respectability with his second wife, who was white. His arrangement of his home deconstructs the very notion of racial difference as it frustrates the desire, which Douglass criticized among whites, to categorize everything in terms of race.

In chapter 4 I tell the story of how Henry Adams reestablished his family seat in the capital and used his Washington home to materialize the point of view he adopted in his writings as critic of the national political scene—that of an eternal outsider at the center of things. In 1880, Adams published a novel, *Democracy,* the heroine of which lives on Lafayette Square, directly across from the White House. That same year Adams essentially moved into his heroine's house, a house that was known as the "little White House" and was located at 1607 H St. N.W. The symbolism of Adams living there after, as he claimed in *The Education of Henry Adams,* having considered the president's house to be his family home, is rich. Several years later Adams bought the lot next door to the little White House and worked with architect H. H. Richardson to design a double house for Adams and his friend John Hay. Adams's domestic alliance with Hay, biographer of Lincoln, poet, and two-time secretary of state, reunifies moral, intellectual, and artistic life with politics. Through his home, Adams models an alternative, higher political ground to rival the corrupt political machine that he described in *Democracy* as residing in the big White House across the way.

The four case studies presented here do not attempt to account for the entire nineteenth century. Instead the book is guided by particularly striking examples of the concrete ways in which political discourse engages the built environment; indeed, architecture emerges as a crucial protagonist in the national narratives that speculation describes. To provide continuity between the chapters, I begin each with a short discussion of the way in which speculation retained its political potency, and volatility, in that chapter's particular historic moment.

We know the value of asking when a text was written; we are now beginning to understand the value of asking where. The past two decades have seen a tremendous interest in the meaning and function of space and place, and this has helped to redress what Wayne Franklin and Michael

Steiner have charged is the "spatial amnesia" of American and cultural studies, and what geographer David Harvey cites as the "overwhelming pre-
disposition to give time and history priority over space and geography."[17]
Washington, D.C., suggests several ways in which we can "reground" the
study of American literature and culture, as studies of the city by Katherine Kinney and Lauren Berlant both show.[18] Washington's fertile ground
expands the possible connections between a text and the space in which it
was written or performed and shows how those sites might be of instrumental importance.

By lifting texts out of their physical context we miss the important ways
in which texts are site specific—how they engage the political, cultural, and
economic landscapes from which they emerge. The texts and spaces studied here are rightly considered together. One may, of course, read Lincoln's inaugural addresses without considering the setting in which they
were delivered, but by doing so one might miss the source of both his imagery and the physicality of his language in the transcendent rhetoric of internal improvements, a source shared and highlighted by the Capitol dome.
As a physical backdrop, the dome acts as an architectural chorus whose
voice resonates throughout Lincoln's tragic addresses. Considering setting
and speeches together lets us not simply read but better experience Lincoln's addresses as performances in their full and complex theatricality.
Such juxtapositions thus can lead to new appreciations of both literature
and architecture. Douglass's career during Reconstruction has under-
standably been criticized as a time when Douglass moved away from the
radicalism of his earlier years. But Douglass's analysis and use of domestic
space gives a new way in which to understand his accumulation of property. Similarly, from an architectural historian's point of view, the Hay-
Adams House was not a cutting-edge Richardson building. But viewing
the house through Adams's writings makes his collaboration in its design
no longer an encumbrance upon Richardson's genius, instead revealing
the house's depth and meaning.

Washington, D.C., suggests that it may be time to rely less upon language that describes cities or buildings as things that can be "read"; while
such metaphors might be attractive and even serviceable, they risk flatten-
ing the built environment into a "text" and hence may be unnecessarily
limiting. We encounter a built environment not just by seeing it but by
moving through it and experiencing it. We need a language that registers,

as fully as possible, the encounter of ideas, perception, the body, and physical space. While we may want to go beyond reading spaces as texts, we
might well think of texts as invoking, promoting, and even sometimes
building physical spaces. Thoreau's *Walden* is an obvious case in point, but
consider too the sheer physical mass of Whitman's extensive colonizing
line, or the carefully constructed paths of Lincoln's arguments, which fun-
nel our thoughts so that his conclusion seems the only possible destina-
tion. The insistent materialism of the literature of American political reform behooves cultural critics to explore the interaction between verbal
and material culture without dissolving the difference of each. The play between the imagination and the three-dimensional built environment has
always been crucial to the reforming of the political landscape, which is always a physical as well as a metaphoric space.

Washington, D.C., reminds us that Henry David Thoreau and Thomas
Jefferson were not the only American authors who were obsessed with architecture. Indeed, any number of authors might be pointed to as ex-
pressing themselves both through words and through architecture and domestic design. Consider how the blueprint for a model home offered by
Catherine E. Beecher and Harriet Beecher Stowe in *American Woman's
Home* (1869) cannot be divorced from Stowe's working through of such
ideas in Rachel Halliday's house in *Uncle Tom's Cabin;* or how the cultural
aesthetic of American realism is implemented in Edith Wharton's treatise
on interior design, *The Decoration of Houses.*[19] Such examples remind us
that there is no fast boundary between verbal and material culture and instead suggest a spectrum from words to buildings where spaces are constructed more or less concretely. At the verbal end of the spectrum, to pick
an example from Adams, lies his heroine Mrs. Lee's house on Lafayette
Square, and at the material end lies Adams's house on the lot next door.
All of these spaces reside on the speculative plane of architecture and letters, where the social, political, and cultural landscape can be more easily
reformed. The grassy expanse of today's National Mall, which forms the
heart of monumental Washington, presents a particularly clear example of
a speculative plane where new national visions are forever being staged,
and it is there, in a brief epilogue, that I conclude this study.

In what follows, I describe what might be termed a relatively high
ground of speculation, one that is primarily grounded in political idealism.
But there is a dark side of speculation, based on blatant self-interest, that

was brought out most humorously in Mark Twain and Charles Dudley Warner's searing portrait of Washington, D.C., in their novel *The Gilded Age* (1876): "I never push a private interest if it is not justified and ennobled by some larger public good," boasts the corrupt Senator Dilworthy.[20] But we cannot so easily dismiss the political visions studied here as mere window dressings for their authors' self-interests, and therefore their speculations, both built and written, demand to be taken seriously. That said, the idealism of their work is open for criticism, and to some extent I suggest ways in which this is so. But my main interest here is that of a speculator—to open territory in the hope that others will develop it further, and in unpredictable ways.

I. THE POLITICS OF CIRCULATION

Chapter 1

GEORGE WASHINGTON'S ROMANCE

Plotting the Federal City, 1791–1800

HEADNOTE: *"The Land of Speculations"*[H1]

Speculation, the life of the American, embraced the design of the new city. Several companies of speculators purchased lots, and began to build handsome streets, with an ardor that soon promised a large and populous city. Before they arrived at the attic story, the failure was manifest; and in that state at the moment are the walls of many scores of houses begun on a plan of elegance.
—CHARLES JANSON (1807)[H2]

The significance of speculation to the planning and early development of the Federal City, as Washington was first called, has been well documented by Bob Arnebeck and John W. Reps. Arnebeck notes that "understanding what the speculators did to the city [of Washington] is as crucial to understanding the city as studying what L'Enfant did or how the White House and Capitol were designed and built."[H3]

Speculation was the way of the land in the late eighteenth century, a fact Edward Chancellor ties to the "vast wilderness" that still lay waiting to be turned into real estate. Benjamin Franklin, Patrick Henry, and George Washington are, as Chancellor points out, just some of the nation's visionary statesmen who invested heavily in "back lands."[H4] But these men would not have called themselves speculators. That term was typically reserved for people who invested in land simply for the purpose of making money. They were not, as a rule, interested in its development but aimed to sell it as quickly as possible and so to turn a fast profit. In order to find people who might have the cash and interest to invest in the rural land where George Washington wanted to build the nation's capital, however, the president was forced to depend to some degree on such men. The same would be true in the coming decades in the development of the public lands: "The Federalists had opposed the liberal sales terms for the public land in part on the ground that it would encourage speculation. Government policies, however, only contributed to speculation."[H5]

James Greenleaf was a case in point. Arnebeck calls Greenleaf "one of the best salesmen of the 1790s," the man who "seduced" George Washington into letting him buy lots in the Federal City for less than a third of the projected asking price.[H6] Washington later defended his decision, stating that while he felt "repugnance" at the too low price, he nevertheless felt forced into it: "matters at that time seemed to be in a stagnant state and something was necessary to put the wheels in motion again."[H7] Washington wrote a letter to the commissioners overseeing the capital's development that recommended Greenleaf to them. In it one can hear the way in which Washington tries to link Greenleaf's private interests to those of the nation:

This Gentlem[a]n . . . has it in contemplation to make certain proposals to you for building a number of houses . . . provided he can have lots upon such terms & conditions as *may correspond with his interest in the undertaking while it tends, at the same time, to promote the great object of the City.*—I am persuaded, Gentlemen, that you will listen with attention and weigh [with] candour any proposals that may *promise to promote the growth of the City.*[H8]

A happy marriage of public interest and self-interest is indeed what the Federal City seemed to promise. This is surely how George Washington must have understood the fact that he sited the new capital near his own estate, Mount Vernon, on the Potomac River, which he was working to improve, through his Patowmack Company so as to create a major route of trade into the nation's interior. George Washington, therefore, is also a speculator by my definition, although one arguably motivated by interests both "noble" and less so.

Greenleaf attracted more investors to the capital, including Thomas Law, John Nicholson, and Robert Morris (more of whom later). Greenleaf claimed "that Washington was the New Jerusalem where real estate fortunes awaited the bold."[H9] George Washington, meanwhile, seeking to sell off some of his capital in "back lands" in order to enrich his retirement, offered Greenleaf "'23,216 acres along the Kanawha and 9,744 acres along the Ohio' Rivers."[H10] Greenleaf declined the sale. Eventually, Washington notes that he realized that in the Federal City Greenleaf was "'speculating deeply—was aiming to monopolize deeply and was thereby laying the foundation of immense profit.'" The volatility of any project that was forced to depend upon speculation became clear as Greenleaf, Nicholson, and Morris were unable to fulfill their pledge to develop their numerous landholdings in the city. In a letter to the commissioners Washington wrote, "the continual disappointments of Messrs. Morris & Nicholson are really painful," then observing, "One would hope that their assurances are not calculated for delay and yet they seem to admit of hardly any other interpretation."[H11]

What the landholdings and dealings of all of the speculators treated in chapter 1 emphasize, whether they were motivated by interests we might view as noble or base, is the degree to which the Federal City's development was tied to the nation's westward expansion. Greenleaf and his partners were able to present themselves as solid investors in the Federal City because of their reputed successes in earnings from the sale of American back lands to primarily foreign investors. The landholdings and dealings of all of these men, totaling in the many millions of acres, staggers the imagination today.

Tied to this fantastic growth was a speculative domesticity where national visions could be made concrete. Dell Upton has argued that Jefferson used his home to portray himself as a republican and an aristocrat. The curious political economy of Monticello shares many of the traits that I identify as inimical to speculative design: the commanding prospect, the involvement of the owner (a political reformer) in the house's design, the weird scale (as Upton explains, Monticello is a huge house that looks much smaller than it actually is), and its anti-conventionalism, which nevertheless works within many conventions.[H12] I conclude chapter 1 with another speculator's house, that of Robert Morris, the investor who hazarded his own fortunes (while trying to increase them) by purchasing numerous lots in the Federal City in an effort to help the fledgling capital through its "financial crisis."[H13] Located on the edge of developed Philadelphia, Morris's house shows how speculators routinely position themselves on the political and financial verge of their world.

o o o

Designed in 1791 and officially established in 1800, the Federal City spans the decade that Gordon Wood has called the "most awkward in American history." The "age of Federalism," marked by the presidencies of George Washington and John Adams, was the period when, Wood argues, this nation came closest to creating a "European type of fiscal-military state."[1] Critics charged the Federalists and "King George" Washington with having monarchic aspirations. The creation of a permanent capital for the nation was taken as concrete proof of a counterrevolution.[2] Most perturbing of all, George Washington chose a surprisingly ambitious plan for the new capital, which suggested his Federalist Party's sly attempt to use economic incentives and outright fantasy to lure a hostile citizenry toward a centralized state.

George Washington could have chosen the much more modest plan proposed by Thomas Jefferson for a capital based upon a traditional grid of streets, beautifully exemplified, in Jefferson's opinion, by Philadelphia, but shared by many other American cities as well (fig. 1.1). But Jefferson's simple proposal was upstaged by a plan for a city such as the world had never seen.[3] This plan, proposed by the French military engineer Peter Charles L'Enfant, featured an irregular grid of streets overlaid by a dazzling network of avenues that shot across the city in every direction (fig. 1.2).[4] These avenues in turn were studded by statues of national heroes, each crowning a square representing a particular state. The Capitol was to be built upon the highest point of land, over a manmade cascade forty feet wide that emptied into a canal bordering the grand mall and leading toward the president's residence a mile and a half away.[5]

L'Enfant's grandiose plan, I shall argue, appealed to George Washington because it offered a concrete model of that ambiguous political structure called an "extended republic" drafted in the Constitution and defended by *The Federalist*.[6] L'Enfant's highly successful remodeling of Federal Hall in New York City had already been lauded for the way it served as "'an allegory of the new constitution'"; when Jefferson saw L'Enfant's plan for the Federal City, he was not pleased with the way it "glowed with an iconography of federal supremacy."[7] In contrast, L'Enfant considered Jefferson's grid plan, which was rooted in more traditional republican values, too static to accommodate the centralized and dynamic vision of a "commercial republic" that men such as L'Enfant's friend and ally Alexander Hamilton had determined the nation should adopt.

The discussions surrounding the layout of the Federal City show that it was seen not only as an emblem of that vision but as a means of implementing it. As C. M. Harris has argued, George Washington "put his hopes in the physical world of architecture and monuments and institutions, believing they offered the best means to regulate the popular will and induce a national identity and character." L'Enfant and Washington designed a city that looked like the Constitution; L'Enfant explained and justified the controversial plan in terms that suggest he believed that people's political behavior would be changed by putting them in this new physical environment. For example, the proposed national university "would attract the best

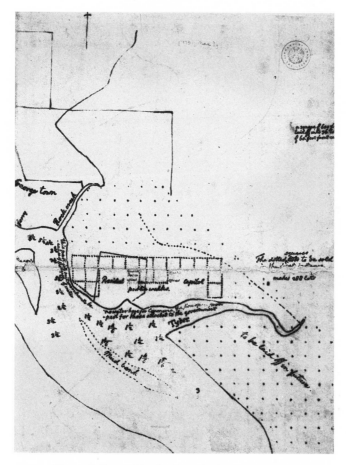

FIG. 1.1. Thomas Jefferson, Plan for the Federal City, 1791. *Manuscripts Division, Library of Congress.*

and brightest of the next generation and tie their loyalties and their careers to the national center," hence ridding them, L'Enfant claimed, of "'those jealousies and prejudices which one part of the union had imbibed against another part.'"[8] No "extended republic" had ever existed before, and people were naturally tied to their immediate locales. The idea of being attached to a nation that was both new and huge was without precedent. A visit to the nation's capital, it was hoped, would help convert citizens to a new national perspective.

The correspondence and papers regarding the Federal City's design describe what amounts to a dialectical relationship between Washington and

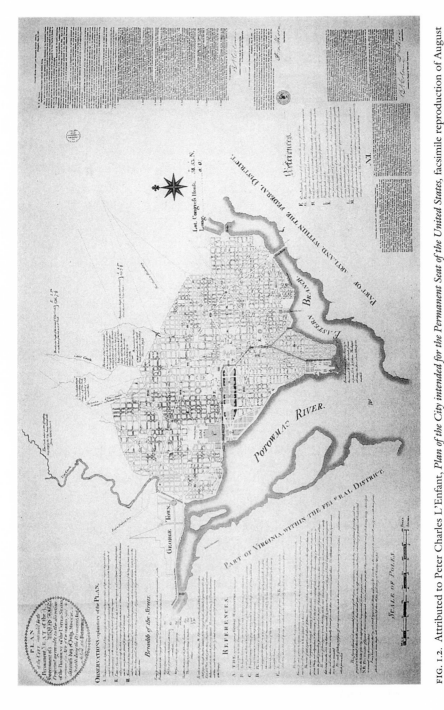

FIG. 1.2. Attributed to Peter Charles L'Enfant, *Plan of the City intended for the Permanent Seat of the United States*, facsimile reproduction of August (?) 1791 map by the United States Coast and Geodetic Survey, 1887. *Library of Congress. Published with the support of the National Geographic Society.*

L'Enfant's radical, future-oriented political vision and their ambitious plan for a new capital city. The city would help to fulfill their political vision just as their bold vision would help to generate interest and investment in the city's development. This dialectical relationship was particularly ingenious because it used marketplace psychology to displace a strong centralizing authority onto the landscape itself: dazzled by the plans for a beautiful capital, an "American Rome," citizens would buy up its empty lots and make the nation's capital their home. As the city caught on, its investors could hope to get rich; thus, the capital city itself would help to reorient citizens toward a strong national government and a national identity. These bold projections were thwarted when lots in the Federal City failed to sell. Worse still, insufficient funding derailed L'Enfant's plan to develop the entire city all at once. But despite these setbacks, George Washington's belief in the project remained steadfast, as architect Benjamin Henry Latrobe noted in 1806: "It has been said that the idea of creating a new [capital] city—better arranged in its local distribution of houses and streets—more magnificent in its public buildings, and superior in the advantages of its site to any other in the World, was the favorite folly of General Washington."[9]

Historians have offered many sound explanations for what David Schuyler calls the "abysmal failure" of the efforts to develop the capital. The commercial success of the city was founded upon only vague and unrealistic schemes. "For members of the government," Schuyler notes, "the new city was notably lacking in urban form and in the amenities of urban life."[10] Stanley Elkins and Eric McKitrick contend that Washington, D.C., from the start was never more than "imaginary," because its baroque aesthetic was so out of sync with the nation it sought to represent that it could not get itself built.[11] Yet it is also true that the reasons for Washington's failure—its anomalousness and its impracticality—were also reasons for its success.

Because Washington was a new kind of city, both in idea and in fact (however disappointing the latter), it did foster new political relationships and in turn a new national landscape. While citizens were not in a hurry to buy lots and move to the capital city, a fairly permanent Washington community did evolve that was instrumental in clearing a path toward a new national political culture. With something of the freedom enjoyed in frontier towns, Washington evolved its own particular domesticity that was distinct from other East Coast cities, where congressmen enjoyed greater fraternity in their boarding houses and women more political influence in and beyond their drawing rooms. As Catherine Allgor has shown, the awkward business of learning how to negotiate matters on the new national level was made easier by Washington's social scene, greased so to speak by its unique social contact and strategic dinners.[12]

Ultimately, if L'Enfant and George Washington's plan was thwarted by its being so fantastic—a magnificent city on paper only—it also proved the resilience of an enticingly grandiose political vision, once it was in print and widely circulated. This vision has had an inordinate influence over the development of Washington, especially during the twentieth century. Although city planner Elbert Peets demonstrated in 1932 the many ways in which that first plan was altered, so that "L'Enfant would say that *his* city of Washington was never built," L'Enfant's plan still dominates our discussion and understanding of Washington, D.C., despite the fact that many other subsequent plans have had a more cumulative impact on the present city.[13]

In the following sections, I will trace the way in which George Washington and Peter Charles L'Enfant used land, imagination, and domesticity to promote their radical vision. Karl Marx later recognized America as "a fictive state"; the planning of the Federal City was a crucial step in how it got to be so.[14]

Political Designs

Modeling the Federal City upon the Constitution reflects the Enlightenment reformer's faith in the physical environment as a powerful tool for the reconfiguration of society. In the late eighteenth century, Jeremy Bentham made large claims for his Panopticon, a structure that controlled its inhabitants through surveillance: *"Morals reformed — health preserved — industry invigorated — instruction diffused — public burthens lightened . . . — all by a simple idea in Architecture!"*[15] In his geopolitical description of America, J. Hector de Crèvecoeur similarly ties political and social behavior to its physical environment: "Men are like plants; the goodness and flavour of the fruit proceeds from the peculiar soil and exposition in which they grow": "Those who live near the sea feed more on fish than on flesh and often encounter that boisterous element. This renders them more bold and enterprising," while "those who inhabit the middle settlements . . . must be very different; the simple cultivation of the earth purifies them." Under the influence of the American landscape, and the country's social customs and laws, the European becomes "naturalized" into an American; once "the slave of some despotic prince," he "become[s] a free man."[16]

In his humorous descriptions of Philadelphia and New York City, Washington Irving ties each city's street plan to the political and moral behavior of its citizens. His exaggerated descriptions suggest a spectrum of eighteenth-century political landscapes—one with too much government, and one without any at all—against which it will be useful to consider the plans for the Federal City:

The philadelphians boast much of the situation and plan of their city, and well they may, since it is undoubtedly, as fair and square, and regular, and right angled, as any mechanical genius could possibly have made it. I am clearly of opinion that this hum drum regularity has a vast effect on the character of its inhabitants and even on their looks, "for you will observe" writes Linkum, "that they are an honest, worthy, square, good-looking, well-meaning, regular, uniform, straight forward, clockwork, clear-headed, one-like-another, salubrious, upright, kind of people, who always go to work methodically, never put the cart before the horse, talk like a book, walk mathematically, never turn but in right angles, think syllogistically, and pun theoretically, according to the genuine rules of Cicero, and Dean Swift;—whereas the people of New-York—God help them—tossed about over hills and dales, through lanes and alleys, and crooked streets—continually mounting and descending, turning and twisting—whisking off at tangents, and left-angle-triangles, just like their own queer, odd, topsy-turvy rantipole city, are the most irregular, crazy headed, quicksilver, eccentric, whim-whamsical set of mortals that ever were jumbled together in this uneven, villainous revolving globe, and are the very antipodeans to the philadelphians."[17]

At one end of Irving's spectrum is Philadelphia, the birthplace of American republicanism and the nation's second capital city. The classical tradition upon which the city is based (geometry, logic, Cicero, and so on) shapes the thoughts, patterns of speech, movements, and even demeanors of its citizens. The city's right angles, regularity, and levelness make their mark on the Philadelphians, who are likewise "fair and square," "salubrious and upright." On the other end of Irving's spectrum, the "topsy-turvy," "crooked" alleys and lanes of old New York characterize the deviousness of its capricious citizens.

There is more than a hint in Irving's portrait that Philadelphia's layout is to be associated with republicanism through its classicism and the lack of mystery of its self-evident plan. Its hyperrational space makes people comically serious and "hum-drum," whereas New York is a model of anarchy, which its citizens either suffer from or exploit. Philadelphia and New York had both fought hard, and almost succeeded, to serve as the nation's permanent capital; Irving's portraits implicitly disqualify both cities as unfit models for the national government. The hope of both cities, and especially Philadelphia, to prevail over the fledgling and beleaguered city of Washington persisted well beyond 1806, when Irving published his portrait.

The new Federal City provided a third alternative to the labyrinthine New York and gridlike Philadelphia by combining attributes of both. L'Enfant's network of avenues only appears to go every which way, while actually being precisely orchestrated. The plan stresses movement, flow, energy, and diversity (of prospects, of directions, of sites, of landscape) to create a space where, in the terms of eighteenth-century spatial analysis, the citizen might feel both liberated and controlled. The "grand scale" of the city, for example, in contrast to the contained scale of Philadelphia, might leave a person feeling overpowered, or empowered; L'Enfant's commentary suggests that both responses were his intent. If Philadelphia's plan can be characterized as self-evident, the Federal City's plan must be characterized as ambiguous. Likewise, the nature of the government it embodies lies between republicanism and monarchism, in that chameleon-like space called "federalism."

The extent to which the "framers" believed that the physical landscape could alter political behavior might seem incredible to us today, but, as historian Mona Ozouf has pointed out, the environmental determinism of the Enlightenment flowed irresistibly from seventeenth-century utopian thought. Utopianism had left a "legacy of a whole century concerned with showing the influence of spatial configuration on public happiness. . . . A new political arrangement seemed to involve a new arrangement of urban space."[18] Hence while the founders of the nation may have at first referred to themselves metaphorically as "framers" and "architects," by the constitutional period they were literally building a new national "edifice."[19] This strategy was as ingenious as it was vexed.

Speculation and Romance

John W. Reps once remarked upon the "irony" of L'Enfant basing his plan for the new republic's capital city upon imperial capitals such as Versailles, London, Paris, and Karlsruhe (fig. 1.3).[20] More recently, however, Pamela

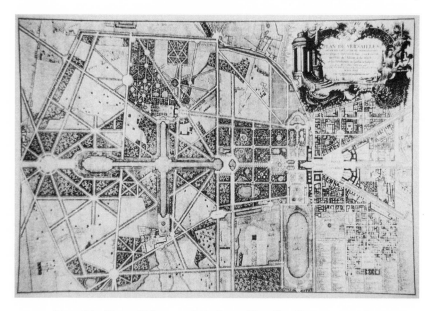

FIG. 1.3. Plan of the Town, Château, and Gardens of Versailles, France, 1746. *John W. Reps.*

Scott has shown how L'Enfant altered royal planning in subtle and complex ways, and the result, I wish to argue, is a politically ambiguous urban design. L'Enfant created a slippery space where charges against the monarchist bent of federalism could still be evaded.[21]

This political sleight of hand was achieved by locating the plan for the Federal City, as Benjamin Latrobe claimed, "far above the nation then present."[22] In doing so, its planners opened up a whole new plane upon which to build, one that precisely embodies what Nathaniel Hawthorne described as the "neutral territory" of a literary romance, somewhere between "the Actual and the Imaginary."[23] On that new plane, as we shall see, historically insurmountable conflicts are easily resolved: republicanism and federalism, empire and democracy, north and south, east and west, all become melded into one political whole. Most strategically, L'Enfant's plan fuses the scope of the national government with the energy of the marketplace. Whereas Jefferson's plan maintains an antagonistic relationship to mercantilism by planning not a city but simply a seat of government where officials could temporarily convene for the required two short sessions a year, L'Enfant's plan instead draws a new kind of city, whose main industry would be government and trade. While critics are right to see such a "city" as artificial, L'Enfant's plan seems to be a pre-cursor to the still more "modern conception of community" that Hauss-man would pursue in the re-creation of Paris, a community unified not by historic ties but by the city's spectacle and display concentrated along its boulevards. Haussman achieved the deindustrialization of Paris, pushing its working class communities and factories out from the city proper, so that, as David Harvey explains, "the city center was given over to monu-mental representations of imperial power and administration, finance and commerce, and the growing services that spring up around a burgeoning tourist trade."[24]

L'Enfant's city was dominated by the idea of circulation: it depicted what *The Federalist* called an "energetic" government and similarly relied upon an energetic marketplace. Detailed plans of the city were widely disseminated—they were even printed on handkerchiefs—for display in the hinterlands.[25] Figure 1.4 shows "an authentic plan of the Metropolis of the United States," advertised as an accurate guide for the prospective pur-chaser of lots but also as "a very handsome ornament for the parlor or counting room."[26] Such images, L'Enfant predicted, would lure pilgrims to the capital, whose splendors would in turn lead them to invest in its real estate and eventually move there, in the process making the nation their true home. Thus, the logistics of realizing L'Enfant's incredible city were worked out to the utmost degree, on paper. It was an entirely speculative venture, conceived in the period when the term "speculation" shifted from its purely philosophical meaning to that of a financial investment strat-egy.[27] By inventing a fantastic space that synchronized political and com-mercial relations, Federalists such as Washington, Hamilton, and L'Enfant hoped to wean American citizens from their local ties and attach them to a capital, nation, and riches that could rival their counterparts in Europe. After Tobias Lear bought a lot in the capital, L'Enfant "urged him to in-terest his fellow New Englanders in investing in the [Federal City] and moving [there] rather than to the West."[28]

The construction of an imagined capital was fueled, as Latrobe claimed, by the "revolutionary enthusiasm" of men such as Washington, L'Enfant, Hamilton, and Robert Morris.[29] All but L'Enfant were framers of the Constitution and were perhaps still flushed with their narrow success in se-curing its ratification. The creation of a new capital city offered another risky venture whereby the Federalists would attempt to overrule social and

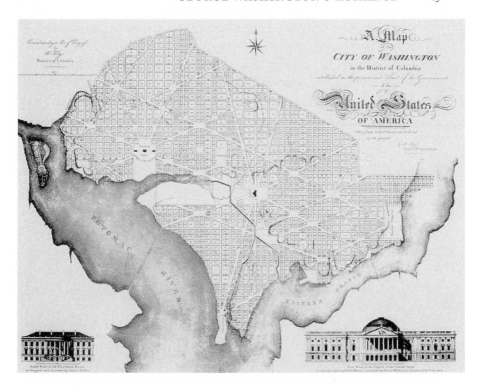

FIG. 1.4. *A Map of the City of Washington in the District of Columbia established as the permanent Seat of the Government of the United States of America: taken from actual survey as laid out on the ground.* Drawn by Robert King, 1818. *Geography and Maps, Library of Congress.*

political convention. When George Washington adopted the plan, the nation was little more than a disheveled confederation of townships with a small and unstable economy.[30] The Federal City's beleaguered start exposed just how quixotic his vision was. Congress refused to grant all but the most minimal funds, so that the capital, which had been confidently touted as the "city of magnificent distances," became instead a poorly developed town whose muddy streets and empty lots invoked endless satire. One early visitor's response typifies the way in which L'Enfant's vision failed to elicit the intended admiring response: "Being told that we were entering Washington city, I continued looking for the houses for some little time; but seeing none, I thought I had misunderstood the gentleman who made the remark, and turning round for an explanation, he told me, laughing, that we were almost in the very middle of it."[31]

Why did George Washington risk his good name on such a speculative venture? Historians generally echo Latrobe: Washington's "enthusiasm" for the nation led him to choose an overly ambitious design.[32] But the new city *had* to be overly ambitious. Enlightenment thought on the political uses of the landscape suggests that only by offering an unconventional political design that coupled the potential for huge profits with a fantasy of America's future global importance could the city hope to prevail against the forces of political habit and alienation.

Paper, Land, and the Legitimacy of Government

The possibility for reform to create a new yet stable political landscape was debated by Enlightenment thinkers such as Edmund Burke and Thomas Paine, as well as Jefferson and Hamilton. Could political theories redraw complex situations that had evolved over centuries in Europe, or alter those which had already taken root in the United States?

For Burke, political stability depended upon property. Handed down through generations, land was the proper basis for political power, since it was by nature static or, in Burke's words, "sluggish" and "inert." Any attempts to redraw the political landscape—especially those based upon "wicked speculations" about the theoretical "rights of man"—were not only naive but dangerous. As was evident in the purchase of British estates by the increasingly powerful bourgeoisie, such political speculations led to real estate speculation, the redistribution of land through the more democratic marketplace. In this way, Burke charged, the land, and hence the political order, became "volatized": "the spirit of money-jobbing and speculation goes into the mass of land itself, and incorporates with it," assuming "the worst and most pernicious part of the evil of paper circulation, the greatest possible uncertainty in its value."[33]

As land becomes more like paper and historical landscapes become rewritten, the people lose their primary attachment to the political order. Burke argues, "To be attached to the subdivision, to love the little platoon we belong to in society, is the first principle (the germ, as it were) of public affections. It is the first link in a series by which we proceed towards a love of our country and mankind."[34] Citizens cannot bond emotionally and psychologically to a written constitution. The authority of Britain's government, Burke maintains, is attested by the fact that it does *not* have a written constitution; instead, its laws are inscribed in the "customs, manners, and habits of [British] life." These

have more than the force of treaties in themselves. They are obligations written in the heart. They approximate men to men without their knowledge, and sometimes against their intentions. The secret, unseen, but irrefragable bond of habitual intercourse holds them together, even when their perverse and litigious nature sets them to equivocate, scuffle, and fight about the terms of their written obligations.[35]

It is precisely against this mystification of government, which was epitomized by Britain's lack of a written constitution and the reliance instead upon "secret, unseen . . . bonds" of origin long forgotten, that "wicked speculators" such as Thomas Paine protested.[36] Through obscure royal writs, centuries old, monarchies had created confusing physical landscapes with labyrinthine cities and crazy-quilt countrysides that left its inhabitants unempowered. Paine rejected the "vast distances" and "succession of barriers" (kings, parliaments, magistrates, bishops, nobility, and so on) that the British government had generated between man and God—man's only ruler: "The duty of man is not a wilderness of turnpike gates, through which he is to pass by tickets from one to the other. It is plain and simple, and consists but of two points. His duty to God, which every man must feel; and with respect to his neighbor, to do as he would be done by."[37] In her study of the French Revolution, Mona Ozouf shows just how literally its early festivals targeted such barriers: "the beating down of gates, the crossing of castle moats, walking at one's ease in places where one was once forbidden to enter: the appropriation of a certain space, which had to be opened and broken into, was the first delight of the Revolution." Ozouf describes one fantastic festival where an "aeronaut" was launched on a gondola into the sky over the streets of Paris: "his was the overwhelming excitement of someone crossing the city without having to follow a complicated network of narrow streets . . . it was the sheer ease of the crossing, the ability to take in [as he put it] the 'whole of assembled Paris.'"[38] Republican space, as first conceived by the Revolution, would be open and offer straight lines of access to political power.[39]

Burke argued against the geometric abstraction evident in republicanism's straight lines and Paine's "two points" and charged that it could never compete with the complex history that tied people to their political and emotional homes.[40] Jefferson shared this belief in the organic nature of political behavior and hence sought to naturalize republicanism. Mitchell Breitweiser has shown the degree to which Jefferson acknowledges the force of history over political design in *Notes on the State of Virginia*. Jefferson, observes Breitweiser, draws attention to the fact that "Virginia . . . does not exist except as a political construct, . . . the map is not a representation of something that is *there*. An obvious point, perhaps, but in Jefferson's Virginia, unlike Barbé-Marbois's France, the sense of abstract boundary had not blended with the experience of the land."[41] It was through cultivation, through farming, that Jefferson sought to blend republican theory with a physical, first-hand experience of the land.

The Federalists were equally anxious to ground their paper constitution as quickly as possible in political habit. As James Sterling Young has noted, the Constitution and the city plan "are renderings, in a different language, of the constitutional prescriptions for the structure and functions of the national government."[42] L'Enfant's avenues create the paths legislated by the Constitution between the branches of government and dramatize the balance of power that yokes them together. Pamela Scott further notes how the carefully distributed avenues, named after the fifteen states and leading to state squares, "would function as separate yet interrelated entities, symbolizing the distinct nature of the states within the nation of united states."[43]

But while the republican grid of streets and farms relied upon cultivation, the federalist avenues relied upon circulation, speculation, and the imagination to mix their theory into the land itself. The avenues reached out to the future; they let citizens think big and imagine they could see there, off in the distance, the vision that had been inscribed in their minds in its built, fulfilled form. So, too, the grand vistas leading to the state squares decorated with national heroes would cause the citizen to exchange what L'Enfant considered to be too "local [a] view" for one of national scope.[44] Those statues, in turn, of "such individuals whose usefulness hath rendered them worthy of general imitation," L'Enfant maintained, would "invite the youth of succeeding generations to tread in the paths of those sages or heroes whom their country had thought proper to celebrate."[45] L'Enfant's avenues thus helped to literalize the paths that he hoped youths would be inspired to follow. Rather than being contradicted by historic landscapes, in other words, L'Enfant invented a new physical space to speed up the process of writing the government into the hearts and habits of the citizenry. Such a built environment would help to give the speculated nation the crucial thereness it otherwise lacked.

The advantage of dealing with a futuristic rather than a historic landscape was demonstrated to George Washington in his negotiations with the original owners of the land where he wished the Federal City to be built. Two neighboring communities—Georgetown and Carrollsburgh—were fighting over the chance to have the capital in their district. Washington settled the dispute by arguing that the landholders' "fears and jealousies" were contrary to the "public purpose." Instead, he maintained that

neither the offer from George-town or Carrollsburgh, separately, was adequate to the end of insuring the object. That both together did not comprehend more ground nor would afford greater means than was required for the federal City; and that, instead of contending which of the two should have it they had better, by combining more offers make a common cause of it, and thereby secure it to the district; other arguments were used to show the danger which might result from delay and the good effects that might proceed from a Union.[46]

On this fictional plane of the nation's speculated future greatness the differences between landholders, and between their private interests and those of the public at large, can be easily resolved. As long as the nation and its capital are perceived as vast, then the different interests can unite in one common interest. Suddenly, instead of having to fight over where the capital should be, the landholders together cannot provide enough land for the large city. Equally deftly, the private interests of the landholders, and of George Washington himself, whose own plantation was not far away, are quickly united under the cause of union, of creating a secure capital city, and hence are aligned with the public good.[47] As long as we are dealing on this fictional plane, the public good can be represented as unified and made to corroborate any point of view. And as a final push toward union, Washington reminds the landholders that other locations might win the capital if they do not move quickly. His successful "management" of the jealous landholders through the irresistible mechanics of fantasy and competition underscores the practicality of federalist speculation.

With a stroke of the pen, the Federal City's planners converted the backwater plantations on the Potomac into an opportunity for wide-scale real estate speculation. What set speculation apart from "regular trade" was risk. In regular trade, prices were set according to present market value rather than an imagined future value. As a result, Adam Smith noted in *The*

Wealth of Nations (1776) as he introduced the still-new term, "Sudden fortunes, indeed, are sometimes made . . . by what is called the trade of speculation."[48] The best way to tempt citizens, Hamilton and his allies gam-
bled, was to offer the possibility of a glorious future beyond imagination,
where such "sudden fortunes" might be made. Hence, the Federal City *had*
to be big, unconventional, and risky in order to compete with the forces
of political habit and of nature itself.[49] Political allegiance was being constructed, in other words, on what Burke warned was the shakiest of grounds.
But from Hamilton's perspective, once the citizen had been lured by the
romance of the nation's greatness to actually invest in it, the hook was in.
By targeting their pockets, Hamilton gave less chance for citizens to escape. Through his invasive political economy, which would seek to regulate commerce, manufactures, banking, and agriculture, Hamilton hoped
to control "those objects which touch the most sensible chords and put
into motion the most active springs of the human heart."[50]

Rather than the land itself, the Federalists made the marketplace the
first tie to government. It should be remembered that most of the Constitutional framers were not large landholders but mercantile men, whose
business was in trade, not agriculture.[51] Speculation led to a heightened
trade in land as a commodity—freed up from its local, historic, and often
contentious roots, land was represented through words, images, and maps,
and hence circulated on a national plane of geographic interconnected-
ness. On this speculative plane between "the Actual and the Imaginary," a
greater elasticity was achieved, where the unimaginable became possible—
a national city that would nevertheless suggest itself as a desirable home for
citizens, and that could close the gap between nation and citizen by offering a model of domesticity that yoked the nation to the hearth. Most crucial to this national domesticity is the Federal City's fantastic scale.

The Politics of Scale

Montesquieu had argued that republics had to be small in order to ensure
full political participation and contact.[52] But this, Hamilton, as Publius,
argues, is precisely why republics fail: the loose confederation of small sovereign states that existed under the Articles of Confederation posed a constant threat to the Union, creating an "infinity of little, jealous, clashing,

tumultuous commonwealths, the wretched nurseries of unceasing dis-
cord." Only by creating more physical distance between citizens and the
branches of government could the natural "friction" between them be al-
leviated, the voices of all be heard, and a government be established based
upon "reflection and choice" rather than "accident and force."[53] James
Madison then continues, "Extend the sphere and you take in a greater variety of parties and interests; you make it less probable that a majority of
the whole will have a common motive to invade the rights of the other citizens; or if such a common motive exists, it will be more difficult for all
who feel it to discover their own strength and to act in unison with each
other."[54] They therefore make scale a primary cause: "extend the sphere,"
and "factions" will be physically discouraged. People will have more room
to spread out and less chance to unite locally, thereby having a better
chance to unite nationally. The result for the writers of *The Federalist* is an
"extended republic" that is as elastic as it is stable.

That the republic would be "extended" was hence of pivotal importance, and we see this dramatized by the debates surrounding the political
aesthetics of the new capital. Both Jefferson and George Washington saw
scale as a determining political force, though in opposite ways. When asked
for his opinion on a proposed design for a new state capitol building for
Virginia, Jefferson replied by sending his own plan, drawn to a smaller
scale: "tho I suppose there is more room in the plan begun, than in that
now sent, yet there is enough in this for all three branches of government
and more than enough is not wanted."[55] Jefferson uses scale as a means by
which to check the tendency in government toward tyranny. The "natural
progress of things is for liberty to yield and government to gain ground,"
Jefferson observed, and his plan for the Federal City similarly shows a de-
termination to resist that governmental expansion.[56] In contrast, for
George Washington, as we saw with his negotiations with the landholders,
"more than enough" was precisely what *was* wanted. For both Washington and Jefferson, scale would make or break the new political landscape's
success.

At issue behind the question of scale was whether the national government would be based more upon an imagined or an experienced relationship. Federalists desired more room among citizens and clearly preferred
the imagined political relationships made possible through the print culture; Jefferson, on the other hand, demanded a closer experience with po-

litical life. This debate is registered by Jefferson and L'Enfant's contrasting political aesthetic. In questions of design, Jefferson is wary of relying too much upon one's imagination. He describes instead how he arrived at a plan for the new Virginia State Capitol:

In the execution of those orders [to procure drafts for the capitol building] two methods presented themselves to my mind. The one was to leave to some architect to draw an external according to his fancey, in which way experience shews that about once in a thousand times a pleasing form is hit upon; the other was to take some model already devised and approved by the general suffrage of the world. I had no hesitation in deciding that the latter was best.[57]

Imagination is tainted for Jefferson because, like monarchy, it is guided by individual whim. He impatiently dismisses designs based on the "fancey" of "some architect." What is wanted, in the case of the Virginia State Capitol, is "not the brat of a whimsical conception never before brought to light" but a design modeled upon classical architecture. To counter the arbitrariness of the individual will and imagination, Jefferson appeals to a democratic history and seeks a model that is "approved by the general suffrage of the world." Jefferson's design closely resembles the Roman temple, the Maison Quarrée, at Nîmes, France, which he greatly admired (figs. 1.5 and 1.6).[58] Jefferson protects republican government by eliminating the problem of individual choice, instead determining all choices through experience and history. Imitation becomes the best safeguard against the tyranny of arbitrary leadership.[59]

L'Enfant rejected Jefferson's qualms with equal force. "I would reprobate the Idea of Imitating," L'Enfant wrote Jefferson; "it . . . shall be my Endeavour to delineate on a new and original way the plan [for the Federal City]."[60] Indeed, in first choosing the actual site for the city, L'Enfant wrote to Hamilton that he felt compelled to exceed the orders given him by George Washington and to give "imagination its full Scope." Swayed by the grandiose vision of local real estate promoter George Walker, L'Enfant drew up plans for a city that would be much more "extensive" than originally intended.[61] L'Enfant seems to enjoy an almost physical relief at being able to extend his imagination, a relief that echoes the claustrophobia of *The Federalist*—the visceral quality of its arguments against the "infinity of little, jealous, clashing, tumultuous commonwealths" under the Articles of Confederation. At the same time, L'Enfant's decision to do

FIG. 1.5. Maison Quarrée, Nîmes, France. *Author photo.*

"more than I am bid to do" and go against his orders demonstrates Jefferson's concern that imagination was dictated by "individual whim" and hence had to be cautiously managed in a republic.

Whereas L'Enfant's aesthetic craves the extra room offered by expanded notions of the possible, Jefferson's aesthetic seems to crave equally the inspiration that comes from the constraint of an accurate representation of what is actually there. When a statue of George Washington was being planned, Jefferson rejected the conventional taste for gigantic statues, complaining that they "all appear outré and monstrous." "A statue is not made," Jefferson advised, "like a mountain, to be seen at a great distance. To perceive those minuter circumstances which constitute its beauty you must be near it." Statues should strive for as accurate a representation as their genre would allow; in scale they should be "so little above the size of the life, as to appear actually of that size from your point of view."[62] Such a "life-sized" statue would draw viewers to it and offer a more engaged experience with and examination of it.

Jefferson acknowledged the possibility of a large republic; indeed, his own expansionist program demanded it, and his plan for the capital city

FIG. 1.6. Virginia State Capitol, Richmond. *Virginia Historical Society, Richmond, Virginia.*

reflects this.[63] Jefferson composed his city out of "squares" surrounded by rows of dots (see fig. 1.1).[64] These dots describe an already colonized space beyond the core village, signifying the village's contained size but also its eventual expansion. We have, then, a model of extended republican design. The nation's capital retains its small scale, while it can be at the same time extended, or enlarged, as required. Expansion is expected and planned for, but it will occur only in response to the nation's growth. The city takes its grid layout from already established republican forms. Jefferson's expansionism, then, merely continues the traditional, contained, republican scale of its core—nothing new is introduced, rather simply more of the same. Jefferson envisioned the expansion of the entire national landscape in the same way. The vast nation should be composed of smaller units that would facilitate citizens' personal, physical experience with the government.

Jefferson's plan for the Federal City almost revels in its limitations. Not only is the city bound by its classical form, but Jefferson's plan lingers equally long over the limits to his design established by the Potomac River itself. He carefully records the river's shallow depth in diverse places: "no water here for commerce," he writes at the opening to the "Tyber" River. (In contrast, representations of L'Enfant's plan emphasize the mighty surge of the Potomac and hence the city's commercial potential.) Jefferson's dots thus suggest the future expansion of the city, while his soundings advertise the limits to that expansion. His sketch is as much a plan as a map; in this way it registers the discordance revealed by Mitchell Breitweiser in Jefferson's *Notes on the State of Virginia:* "There are two parallel tensions running throughout these replies: between the commercial exploitation of the land and the land's resistance, and between the mental appropriation of the land and its resistance to comprehension. This is not a univocal measured appraisal, but two voices, as it were—a planner, and an empirical observer who knows the limits and frailties of plans." Breitweiser goes on to suggest that it is in fact the up-close recording of local detail that Jefferson finds most compelling of all.[65]

L'Enfant rather breathlessly rejects a grid plan precisely because it fails to meld with the natural landscape:

Such regular plans indeed, however answerable they may appear upon paper or seducing as they may be on the first aspect to the eyes of some people must even when applyed upon the ground the best calculated to admit of it become at last tiresome and insipid and it never could be in its origin but a mean continuance of some cool imagination wanting a sense of the real grand and truly beautiful only to be met with where nature contributes with art and diversifies the objects.[66]

L'Enfant's design instead "combines" his art with the sublime power of nature, making the two practically indistinguishable.

A portrait of George Washington with the plan for the Federal City, engraved in 1793 by Edward Savage, shows how the delineation of a new and grand city lent credence to the image of Washington as "King George" while celebrating the originality of Washington's vision and its power to bend nature to his political design (fig. 1.7).[67] The plan is presented as Washington's brainchild (and not the "fancey" of "some architect"); he calmly gazes into the magnificent future prescribed by his design and echoed by the open sky in the background. While Jefferson gazes in adoration upon the classical past, Washington is equally transfixed by the future—he appears even to be looking at his city, already built. It is there, he can see it, and we are invited to see it too. This confident expectancy is further suggested by the way Washington supplements the classical past, as represented by the column. He turns his back to it and yet subsumes it by the uprightness of his posture; he becomes a pillar himself of the future state. Contrary to Jefferson's dark view, this portrait suggests that it is no crime to have "the vision thing."

The inevitable success of this vision is suggested by the rest of the en-

FIG. 1.7. *George Washington Esq. President of the United States of America. From the Original Portrait Painted at the request of the Corporation of the University of Cambridge in Massachusetts.* Drawn, engraved, and published by E. Savage, 1793. *John W. Reps.*

graving, which points to the power of the mind to turn nature into art: flowers are transformed into the floral motif on the chair, drapery, lace cuff, hair ribbon, and bow resting upon the plan; they are echoed even in the petal-like quality of Washington's hair. The flowerlike bow, hovering over the plan, hints at how nature inspired the radiating intersections of avenues. The engraving further imposes Washington's very person upon the land itself: the Eastern Branch follows the course of his knee, his fingers are compared to the avenues, his pants buckle serves as a template for the city blocks—the very paper of the plan, then, becomes a landscape that bends to Washington's hand.

An engraving of the entire District of Columbia from 1822 echoes this Federalist confidence in the power of the imagination to evolve nature into an idealized political state (fig. 1.8). The engraving emphasizes the Potomac River and Eastern Branch, swelling their watery masses in a way that suggests their future importance as routes to the western interior. At their juncture lies the Federal City. It seems to grow out of their energy, channeling it in its vivid infrastructure, which is not rigidly bounded but reaches out as if it must by its nature spread, taking over the unincorporated regions of "Washington County." Indeed, the land surrounding the Federal City shows the barely organized nation, with its winding roads and tiny towns, waiting to be brought into the federal system of energetic circulation and strong, decentralized government. In one sense, then, the mighty rivers show the course of progress from an unorganized state of nature to the modest and limited town-grid of Alexandria (in the bottom right corner of the engraving), where government and landscape are still alienated from one another, and, finally, to a climactic merging of flow and order, energy and reason, diversity and unity—a kind of naturalized irresistible force as the crooked is made straight and the hinterlands are brought into the national marketplace. Jefferson's "insipid" republican grid, the engraving predicts, will succumb to the energy of "truly grand" federalist design.

The Politics of Avenues

No single feature of Washington's city is more instrumental to this Hamiltonian vision than its controversial network of radiating avenues. Each avenue, with autocratic sweep, superimposes the idea of the "federal" over the city's more localized grid. Even George Washington felt L'Enfant's first plan (which no longer exists) had "too many avenues," and he demanded that some of them be "suppressed."[68] Lewis Mumford faults this most notable feature of L'Enfant's plan: "By any criterion that apportionment between dynamic and static space, between vehicles and buildings, was absurd." L'Enfant's "extravagant intersections" were a "wastage of precious urban land."[69] Yet for L'Enfant they were indispensable to the city's success.

The avenues presented an idealized image of the marketplace that would promote the nation to its citizens and attach them to it. L'Enfant

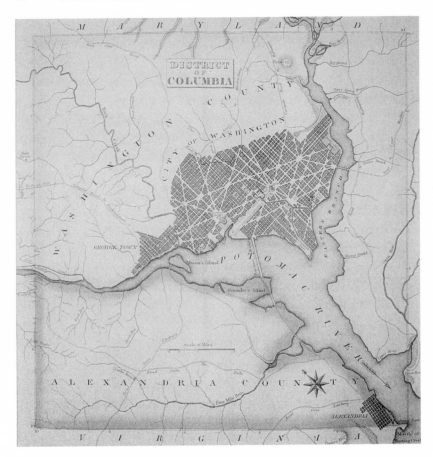

FIG. 1.8. *Geographical, Statistical, and Historical Map of the District of Columbia.* Engraved by Young & Delleker, 1822. *Library of Congress.*

reasoned that his huge city would lure citizens to invest in its lands "by necessitating a constant going in every direction whether for Spending the Social after noon or for transacting morning little business—the paths beaten through all avenues would to the eyes of all visitors best have depicted the grand feature of the city plan . . . the ride over accidentally to have discovered a variety of Situation more pleasing and convenient for houses than are describable."[70] Jefferson designs a walking city, L'Enfant a driving one. Jefferson's citizens tread and retread the capital city's paths of regular government and so, like the plow, dig their way into the groove of the nation's politics. L'Enfant's citizens are, by the very span of their nation, more passively wedded to their carriage and the spectator's role of watching the "grand features" of their political system. The carriage at once distances them from government and draws them intimately to it, as the political economy whose routes they follow "invites" them into personally investing in the vision—into tying themselves financially to the national city, by buying land within it and perhaps even making it their home.

Crucial to the political conditioning implicit in the street plans are where the streets lead. Jefferson's streets simply point to the open lands beyond. Such unspecified vistas are called "weak," but in Jefferson's republican aesthetic they point to where the strength of the nation lies; they give immediate reassurance that the government is still surrounded by "vacant lands," a factor Jefferson claimed was key to the nation's integrity: "our governments will remain virtuous for many centuries; as long as they are chiefly agricultural; and this will be as long as there shall be vacant lands in any part of America. When they get piled upon one another in large cities, as in Europe, they will become corrupt as in Europe."[71]

While Jefferson's roads end in the inconclusiveness of open space, L'Enfant's avenues lead to a defined future; the word avenue itself comes from the French word for the future, *avenir*. L'Enfant punctuates each vista with art—a statue, a national hero, or a national edifice, such as the "Presidential Palace" or the proposed National University. L'Enfant explains in a memorandum the way in which he arrived at the city's street plan, combining a republican grid with a federalist network of avenues:

Having determined some principal points to which I wished to make the others subordinate, I made the distribution regular with every street at right angles, North and South, east and west, and afterwards opened some in different directions, as avenues to and from every principal place, wishing thereby not merely to [contrast] with the general regularity, nor to afford a greater variety of seats with pleasant prospects, which will be obtained from the advantageous ground over which these avenues are chiefly directed, but principally to connect each part of the city, if I may so express it, *by making the real distance less from place to place, and by giving to them reciprocity of sight, and by making them thus seemingly connected,* promote a rapid settlement over the whole extent.[72]

Through his "reciprocity of sight," L'Enfant creates a fantastic effect. He unites the city, actually shrinking its monarchic scope to a more republican scale by "making the real distance less from place to place." So, too, his artful merging of grid plan and radiating avenues suggests the structural compatibility of republican and federalist design.

The political innovation behind L'Enfant's plan is clear in the way in which its sightlines do not converge on one single point. Instead of the centralization of power figured by baroque city form, L'Enfant's reciprocity of sight creates a decentralized network of participating viewers. Drawing perhaps upon his experience as a military engineer during the Revolutionary War, L'Enfant literally materializes a capital, and hence a nation, that is held together more by vision than by physical contact. The *Regulations, Order, and Discipline for the Troops of the United States* (1779), for which L'Enfant drew the illustrations, calls for an encampment to be defended by posting a "complete chain of sentinels," to be placed as far apart as possible but still within sight of each other around the camp.[73] In this way, the entire space around the camp will be covered; while no one sentinel can see the entire camp as a whole, their combined visions will produce just such a picture. Any disturbances on any front, including within the camp, will be reported to a superior officer, with whom the complete vision is thus held. The Federal City models a dynamic relay between representatives and citizens, officers and sentinels, to produce a national community held together by views. L'Enfant's avenues solve the logistical problems of an imagined community. From its various focal points, the Federal City produces the corporate vision through which the nation can be extended indefinitely. As such, L'Enfant's plan ultimately asserts the physical possibility of the impossibly romantic creed *E pluribus unum.*

In ascribing his name and reputation to L'Enfant's grand city, George Washington took an extraordinary risk. His vision of the capital as a thriving port and gateway to the west was stymied by prolonged debates over the internal improvements, such as the Chesapeake & Ohio Canal, necessary to realize it.[74] Washington's city soon became "Washington's folly." Surely this vulnerability, and the irreverence it inspired, confirmed that "King" George was no Louis XIV or Napoleon III. Unlike those men, Washington could not get his city built. And so the charge of monarchy was deflated, as was suggested by Albert Gallatin in 1797: "We have had a government of individual will instead of that of the people . . . The aim is to assimilate our government to a monarchy. Every measure seems to squint towards this darling object, and hence irredeemable debts, excise systems, national banks, loans, federal cities."[75] The disdain implied by "squints" echoes the derision of "folly" and suggests again that critics saw the Federalists as mere speculators—not so much monarchs as monarch wannabes. Monarchs gaze; speculators squint. And yet it may be that pre-cisely by disarming their critics, by enabling them to enjoy so many laughs at their expense, L'Enfant and Washington were able to save the last laugh for themselves. The capital city's unconventional national domesticity shows one last way in which the Federalists' plan led to "folly" and yet managed to persist and even succeed.

National Domesticity

Behind the federalist grand scale was a radical revision of domesticity—one rooted not in the local "little subdivisions" of Burke's political landscape but in the very idea of circulation itself. Jürgen Habermas has linked the rise of the marketplace during the late eighteenth century to the in-troduction of a central hallway system or circulation plan into domestic ar-chitecture, and to the rise of the modern novel, with its omniscient narra-tor serving as a coordinating force to link the story's many parts and characters.[76] The new American capital was also a laboratory for the re-configuration of private and national life, and a new kind of domesticity evolved there. This national domesticity confirmed the primary impor-tance of circulation, although in ways that L'Enfant and Washington could not have foreseen.

The new capital did in fact inspire patriotic settlers. In 1799, John Tay-loe III and his wife, Anne Ogle, bought land near the president's house—Lot 8 on Square 170, bordered by New York Avenue and Eighteenth St., N.W. There they built the "Octagon House," which still stands today, to fit their odd-shaped lot, one of the many such created by L'Enfant's diag-onal avenues. The Tayloes' home modeled the marriage of domestic and national life envisioned by Washington and L'Enfant. The Tayloes were one of Virginia's most prominent families, and Tayloe had run, though un-successfully, for Congress. Their choice of the capital for their in-town winter residence signaled their support of the national government. They hired the architect of the Capitol, William Thornton, to build their private home. There they entertained members of official Washington, including Thornton and his wife and their friend Harrison Gray Otis, congressman from Massachusetts. The Tayloes even fulfilled L'Enfant's dream by mak-ing the capital their first, and not second, home when some of the family eventually chose to live there year round. Best of all, the Tayloe home seems to have encouraged others to invest, as L'Enfant had hoped. By 1800 six houses stood on Square 170, three built of brick and three of wood.[77]

The Tayloes' model of national domesticity relied upon slavery, as did the development of the capital itself. Their home was supported by profits made on their large tobacco plantation, Mount Airy in Richmond County, and on their other estates. They owned close to fifteen thousand acres of land and one thousand slaves.[78] Each fall they brought as many as twelve slaves with them to Washington to serve their large family (which eventually included fifteen children) for the four months they remained in town. The house itself was built in part by slave labor, hired from local slaveholders. This was a common practice in the new capital; slaves provided the bulk of the labor to build the Capitol and other buildings, to clear the city's avenues and streets, and to rebuild the city after its destruction during the War of 1812. While slave trading was relatively rare during the city's first decade, by 1812 the capital was an important junction for it. It was not uncommon to see slaves in chains as they walked toward one of the holding pens in the city, or toward its docks to be shipped further south. President James Madison's secretary complained in 1809 of the "revolting sight" such "gangs of Negroes" presented in the streets of the capital of a nation that prided itself on its democracy and freedom.[79]

Despite early successes in the development of the city, progress was frustratingly slow. Although there were periods of great building activity, such as after the War of 1812, by 1820 the government was still left with many of its lots unsold. The city's population in 1820 was listed at 13,117, up from only 3,201 in 1800. In 1820 the city had 9,376 white residents, 1,796 free black residents, and 2,330 slaves. In 1800, slaves had outnumbered free black residents five to one.[80] The city's growth remained tied to the growth of the national government. Artisans came to build the new city, lawyers, doctors, and storekeepers to attend to its community's needs, servants and slaves to serve in its hotels, boardinghouses, and private homes.

The fact that everyone in the city helped to build or run the new government led to a new kind of domesticity that was literally shaped by national politics. The Supreme Court justices, for example, not only deliberated together but often lived together in boardinghouses, as did the members of Congress. The private homes of Washington's official and non-official community naturally fostered a conversation about national politics and an accelerated schedule of entertainments and social calls that made the Washington home noticeably different from homes in other American cities. This national domesticity was crucial to the city's and the national government's success. As historian Catherine Allgor has shown in her study of Washington's "parlor politics," it was one thing to draw up a Constitution with a set of laws by which the government would function and quite another to evolve a national political culture of manners and negotiating practices that would make that government work.[81] The "inside the Beltway" mentality that we are now so familiar with did not exist; on the contrary, elected representatives were wary about wheeling and dealing on the national level. The more informal setting of the home became the site where such a culture could most naturally and even innocently evolve. We know that national policy is, as often as not, brokered around the Washington dinner table instead of the House or Senate chambers. The logic of that custom was already becoming evident in the parlors and dining rooms of early Washington, D.C.

The women who resided in the Federal City have in the past been overlooked by scholars, but recent research has shown their instrumental role in fostering the national domesticity.[82] Allgor specifies the many ways in which women demonstrated the importance of social circulation to a smoothly functioning political system. The paying and receiving of social calls was one of the main jobs of affluent women, and it did much to grease Washington's political wheels. Women such as Louisa Catherine Adams, Dolley Madison, Hannah Gallatin, and Floride Calhoun all used their "female network" of influence toward political ends, whether to support a particular piece of legislation, to secure a government post for a relative or friend, or to improve the city through the creation of a hospital or orphanage. Allgor goes so far as to credit Margaret Bayard Smith with being the very first "Washington insider."[83]

Bayard Smith, wife of the editor of the *National Intelligencer*, established a particularly powerful circle of influence. Through it she secured a government position for the son-in-law of Martha Jefferson Randolph, the only living daughter of Thomas Jefferson, whose family, by 1828, was nearly impoverished. Smith had been a staunch supporter of Jefferson, and thus her lobbying on his daughter's behalf was not only a compassionate but a political act. Allgor argues that it was this fuzziness between the personal and the political that gave women a wider scope for action than men enjoyed. Just as the national culture was still anti-power, it was also anti-patronage, but women were able to avoid this charge. Since women were not "in" politics, they could claim to work from purer motives of affection and compassion, and this gave them the leverage and innocence that men lacked. Another attempt by Smith to help her brother-in-law become a Supreme Court justice shows how this "parlor politics" worked. Smith recounts in a letter how she called upon the wife of a man whose influence Smith needed to court. Her friend "with her usual kindness immediately asked me to stay to dinner, which invitation I accepted, having found gentlemen more good humored and accessible at the dinner table than when alone." On another occasion Smith managed to get a young Mr. Ward a spot on the sofa next to Representative Henry Clay. The two men enjoyed their conversation, a correspondence ensued, and Mr. Ward secured himself a valuable ally in Washington. Through their social rituals, Washington's women created a trust and informality that forged the personal networks so crucial to government. Allgor concludes that as the capital's first and largest group of lobbyists, the Washington women helped pave the way for the rise of the patronage and eventually the party system, organizations that would in turn make it less necessary, and hence less common, for women to play such an active political role.[84]

In addition to being more engaged in political debate, white affluent women enjoyed a greater degree of personal freedom in Washington than in other American cities. It was more acceptable for women to go about the city unaccompanied by men. They went to the Capitol in order to watch Congress or the Supreme Court in session (three hundred women crammed into the galleries, and even onto the Senate floor, to hear the Webster-Hayne debates). In addition, Washington parties were often very crowded, and women therefore had to stand. Margaret Bayard Smith noted that this simple fact alone gave women more social mobility, because they did not have to sit, as was the custom, and wait for men to come to them. While Washington society was still structured rather rigidly according to class, a "respectable" woman could take advantage of the fact that in Washington one could be "decently aggressive" and push her case. The fact that the president's house was still the people's house made Washington's official and non-official homes more open than those elsewhere.[85]

Coda

While the Federal City's political and domestic life evolved along its own paths, L'Enfant realized his vision of a speculative domesticity tying a citizen's interests to the nation's success in a house he designed for Robert Morris. Morris was George Washington's financial wizard during the Revolution and a framer of the Constitution.[86] By the 1790s he was on his way to becoming one of the richest men in the country through speculation in real estate; he and his partners had amassed over six million acres of western land. This grand confidence in the nation's expansion was registered in Morris's enthusiasm for a grand capital city: he and his partners were among the Federal City's largest investors.[87] In 1794, at the height of his success, Morris engaged Peter Charles L'Enfant to build him a magnificent house in Philadelphia.

Morris's house is the perfect speculator's house (fig. 1.9). Located at the frontier of the city where its street ends, it emphasizes diversity of access and movement, while maximizing its angles of vision. The house has at least two main entrances. Its wings extend from the main body of the house, permitting more windows, and even the corners are rounded off by another window to offer an almost 360-degree view. The house was to be paid for by other properties that Morris expected to sell. Conceived by L'Enfant's speculative imagination on speculated rather than real funds, the house could be in every way excessive. It was to be of marble; its basement had three levels. It was a house such as Philadelphia had never seen. One townsman called it "a very uncouth and expensive edifice."[88] Finally, the house was featured as one of William Birch's exquisite engravings of Philadelphia, to celebrate and attract investment to the city.[89] Such a magnificent house would help establish the city's elegance, as the fashionable people in the engraving who have come to see it attest.

By 1798, Robert Morris was in debtor's prison. Thomas P. Cope, a local Quaker merchant, attributed Morris's failure to "overgrasping and inconsiderable speculations."[90] A more modern account says that Morris was "overextended."[91] Cope estimated Morris's debts to amount to more than twenty million dollars. In his diary, Cope cites Morris as an instance of "the versatility of human affairs and the folly of inordinate ambition": "Had they [Morris and his partners] confined their views to narrower limits they

FIG. 1.9. *An Unfinished House in Chestnut Street, Philadelphia.* Engraved by William Birch, 1800. *Rare Book Department, The Free Library of Philadelphia.*

would in all probability have been among the foremost of our citizens in wealth, state and consequence, especially Robert Morris, whose talents as a statesman and financier are universally acknowledged and seldom exceeded."[92] Cope's criticism suggests the danger of attempting to see too far: one should not own more than one can personally superintend. Morris's overextension meant that he could no longer maintain direct contact with all of his business prospects, and this, according to another biographer, also led to his demise. "He undertook more than any single man could look after," and so "could not avoid the necessity of reposing confidence in other persons."[93] Morris's reliance upon representatives whose activities he could not personally witness made him vulnerable to being misled. What men, entrusted with power and money, can be sure to act in their constituents' best interests? Reading Morris's misfortune as a metaphor for the citizen and the nation, we can conclude that to exchange one's personal control and perspective for the hope of extending one's properties and power is a risky business indeed.

The Federal City, however, tempted citizens to believe that the opposite was true. Like Washington's prized city, Morris's house became known as Morris's "folly." It was razed and its materials sold off to help pay Morris's debts. Yet even though Morris's house wasn't really *there,* as Jefferson might have protested, it continued to exist in print through Birch's engraving, and so, ironically, helped to promote rather than discourage confidence in the city. Similarly, L'Enfant's plan survived in print. Since the capital's centennial in 1900, his grand vision has been defended and championed so that his plan has become a familiar justification for spending countless dollars on the city's development, especially its monumental National Mall. Both Morris and Washington's follies thus suggest ways in which a speculative political landscape is made less stable, but also more resilient, by its dependence upon excess, romance, paper, and circulation.

Chapter 2

THE POETRY OF INTERNAL IMPROVEMENTS

Abraham Lincoln and Walt Whitman in Civil War Washington

HEADNOTE: *The Civil War and Speculation*

The civil war in America, with its enormous issue of depreciating currency, and its reckless waste of money and credit by the government, created a speculative mania such as the United States, with all its experience in this respect, had never before known.
— HENRY ADAMS, "The New York Gold Conspiracy" (1871)[H1]

As Eric Foner notes, the Age of Capital (1848–75) saw "unprecedented economic expansion presided over by a triumphant industrial bourgeoisie" and led to "the consolidation of the capitalist economy." Technological infrastructure, including the railroad and the telegraph, was the underpinning of this expansion: "If the cotton mill symbolized the early industrial revolution, the railroad epitomized the maturing capitalist order."[H2]

In this chapter on Washington, D.C., during the Civil War, I will continue to analyze the love-hate relationship between political reformers and financial speculation. Lincoln derided speculators who sought to profit from the war, but his policies and political vision often depended upon those who speculated in the railroads, and the two groups of investors were often the same.[H3] As an attorney, Lincoln had often represented railroad companies.[H4] As president, Lincoln wanted a strong Union and that would require a fully developed network of communication via the railroad and the telegraph. Financial speculation seemed to be the only way to motivate such risky undertakings as the Union Pacific Railroad.[H5] It wasn't until Lincoln's first term as president that

Congress finally agreed upon a highly controversial appropriations bill that would let construction on the long-discussed railroad begin.[H6]

The most obviously base level at which speculation was practiced during the war was the practice of trading upon Union victories and losses on Wall Street. Investors took advantage of the increase in production (of clothing, food, munitions), and the printing of more money to pay for it, that was generated by the war. The defeat of the Union Army at Chancellorsville, Virginia generated a flurry of trading, because it meant the war would continue and more paper currency would have to be issued. As one trader admitted, "Along with ordinary happenings, we fellows in Wall Street had the fortunes of war to speculate about and that makes great doings on a stock exchange. It's good fishing in troubled waters." While Abraham Lincoln sat by the telegraph machine in the War Office in Washington and listened to the latest reports from the battlefront, J. Pierpont Morgan sat in his office on Wall Street doing the same thing, but for different reasons: Morgan wanted to be the first to direct his investments according to the news. Lincoln tried to curb war-related speculation but failed.[H7]

Before, during, and after the Civil War the railroad generated its own speculation fever. As William H. Vanderbilt commented: "The railroads are not run for the benefit of the dear public. That cry is all nonsense. They are built for men who invest their money and expect to get a fair percentage on the same."[H8] Railroad construction heated up speculation in land as well: "Would you make money easy?" a typical booster tract from the mid-nineteenth century asked. "Find, then, the site of a city and buy the farm it is built on! How many regret the non-purchase of that lot in New York; that block in Buffalo; that acre in Chicago; that quarter section in Omaha." Land abutting the railroads was described as "a vast wilderness waiting like a rich heiress to be appropriated and enjoyed."[H9]

Political speculators such as Whitman and Lincoln acted as boosters as well for their own envisioned national landscape. Lincoln's succinct prose, which Garry Wills aptly describes as "telegraphic," creates shortcuts to a national feeling as Lincoln works to establish a higher moral ground for the war—a nation guided by the "better angels of our natures" and "dedicated to the proposition that all men are created equal."[H10] Lincoln is a speculator in the sense I develop here because he describes a moral national plane and promotes investment in it through his persuasive rhetoric, *and* he seeks to realize that vision by promoting the physical infrastructure on which it relies. While Whitman was not in a position to promote government policy that was friendly to speculators, his poetry and even his prose clearly depended upon and promoted the technological infrastructure that Lincoln lobbied hard to create. Whitman, for his part, almost seems to follow the railroad tracks themselves, appropriating mile after mile of poetic views. I describe the sprawling line of Whitman's poetry and prose as speculative, reaching out as it does and colonizing just about everything into his "song of America."

The national landscapes Whitman and Lincoln promote find their fullest expression in the capital during the war. I place Whitman and Lincoln's war writings in relation to the Washington sites that inspired them or in which they were delivered. Their rhetoric lets us see how during the war the National Mall in particular was a stage where several buildings (the Capitol, the Smithsonian Institution, Robert E. Lee's mansion, and the Armory Hospital, located where the National Air and Space Museum stands today) modeled rival speculations as to the direction the nation should take.

◦ ◦ ◦

It is impossible to describe the truly fearful condition of [Washington's] streets. They are seas or canals of liquid mud, varying in depth from one to three feet, and possessing as geographical features conglomerations of garbage, refuse, and trash.   —NOAH BROOKS, Feb. 28, 1863[1]

As in 1800 and 1850, so in 1860, the same rude colony camped in the same forest, with the same unfinished Greek temples for workrooms, and sloughs for roads.   —HENRY ADAMS[2]

Mud, mud and more mud . . .   —UNION SOLDIER[3]

In the previous chapter, we saw how Peter Charles L'Enfant considered the new capital's elaborate network of avenues to be pivotal to the city's success. The avenues would tie the city together and display its charms, so as to lure citizens to invest in its lots. The capital would serve as a model for the nation as a whole. A national infrastructure of roads, canals, and eventually railroads was seen as the first and crucial step to forming ties to the new nation that had not had time to evolve more naturally: to introduce members and regions of the Union who otherwise would most likely never meet, and, most importantly, to bridge the gap between what was termed the nation's interior and its "external" (or federal) government. In 1808, Treasury Secretary Albert Gallatin warned of "'the inconveniences, complaints, and perhaps dangers'" inherent in trying to form a nation of such as "'vast extent of territory'" and urged the "'opening [of] speedy and easy communication through all its parts' in order that such 'dangers'" could be 'radically removed, or prevented.'"[4] Yet a national infrastructure of interstate roads was highly controversial because it epitomized the contest between state and federal authority. Defenders of state sovereignty protested the incursion such an infrastructure would represent of federal influence into every locale. They would lead in the words of one congressman to the "consolidation" of the states, "chain[ing] them together . . . at the price of their independence." As Representative Barbour from Virginia put it, no one doubted the benefit of "internal improvements" (such as canals) but this was a question of "a different complexion—it [was] a question of power."[5]

From the beginning, the capital's streets had been controversial, and Congress had refused the necessary funds for their improvement. The extent to which L'Enfant's vision had deteriorated was highlighted by his ambitious Tyber Canal. According to L'Enfant's plan, the canal was to flow from the Potomac River past the White House and the Capitol, where it would form a forty-foot-wide cascade emerging from beneath the Capitol before continuing down past the Navy Yard to empty out into the Anacostia River. A tribute to eighteenth-century ideals of circulation, the canal would have modeled how easily nature could be shaped to Federalist design, as Madison predicted for the nation as a whole: "The communication between the Western and Atlantic districts, and between different parts of each, will be rendered more and more easy by those numerous canals with which the beneficence of nature has intersected our country, and which art finds it so little difficult to connect and complete."[6] By midcentury, the fetid waters of the Washington City Canal bred mosquitoes that carried malaria and plagued the city, including those individuals living in the White House.[7] The Tyber had come to suggest just how difficult it might be to tie the various regions of the nation together. Intended to promote the city to its would-be investors, L'Enfant's plan of circulation instead betrayed just how tenuous that union was. Washington's avenues dramatize the attempt, however vexed, of a modern nation-state, based upon a written constitution, to make itself concrete.

That said, the antebellum era was marked by intense technological development nationwide: it saw the construction of the Erie Canal (1825), the trans-Atlantic cable (1858), and the nation's first telegraph and railroads. Critical to these successes was the marriage of rhetoric and technology that characterized the times. The "turnpike era," as that period has been dubbed, was also America's "golden age of oratory," which turned the Union into a religion—among others, Henry Clay spoke passionately on behalf of his "American System" of internal improvements, while Daniel Webster tied the nation together with his speeches, passages of which were memorized and repeated by schoolchildren and citizens everywhere. The concurrence of these technological and oratorical developments demonstrates a dialectical relationship whereby an impassioned rhetoric paved the way for controversial projects such as the transcontinental railroad to be approved, and the new railroads in turn gave proof that the glorious Union such nationalistic rhetoric envisioned could actually come true. As Isaiah Berlin has noted, new technologies spawned a "new race of propagandists— artists, poets, priests of a new secular religion, mobilising men's emotions, without which the new industrial world could not be made to function."[8]

This partnership between technology and rhetoric is most clearly demonstrated by Abraham Lincoln and Walt Whitman, in different ways both poets of internal improvements. They shared an almost religious enthusiasm for them. Lincoln had lobbied aggressively for improved waterways and the railroads and was an attorney for the railroad interests in the 1850s. This physical infrastructure was central to Lincoln's vision of a networked nation that would promote freedom and prosperity through the rapid circulation of goods and ideas.[9] Whitman's poetry celebrated the nation through circulation of all kinds—strolling down Broadway, riding the horsecars, crossing by the Brooklyn ferry. His own body, in fact, became a fantastic bridge: "my elbows rest in sea gaps,/I skirt the sierras . . . my palms cover continents."[10] Both men were so closely tied to such technologies that they became in turn inseparable from their rhetoric. Through such galvanizing language, Lincoln and Whitman served as boosters for the Union as they sought to strengthen citizens' affective bonds to the nation by giving it poetic force.

Both men continued to promote these fantastic, concrete landscapes in Washington, and this essay looks at how their visions and the capital interact. At first glance it would seem that Washington would only undercut Whitman and Lincoln's positive, hopeful view of the Union. By all accounts, the capital during the war amounted to a public relations disaster. Due in part to its proximity to the front, the city became the chief headquarters and hospital for the Union Army. Soldiers marched out L'Enfant's avenues to the front and returned on stretchers to be housed anywhere space could be found—in hotels, in the Patent Office museum, in the Capitol itself. As Katherine Kinney has argued, Washington was indeed an "uncanny" space, where the repressed surfaced as the violence it would take to preserve the Union became horrifically clear.[11] But Washington did provide, at times, a perfect ground for the selling of both Lincoln and Whitman's visions; certain texts by each author and the city sites they engage reinforce each other in such a way that the men's visions improve the city and the city strengthens the claim of their visions. For example, Lincoln's inaugural addresses engage the huge Capitol dome in a way that the dome adds emphasis to what Lincoln argues, while his speeches in turn help the dome—whose scale and design were controversial—to appear in its best light. Whitman, for his part, presents scenes from Washington's hospitals to the public as both awful and transcendent—ideal spaces whose long corridors of men, like indoor avenues full of misery and life, suggest not the breakdown of the Union but its ultimate, intimate fulfillment. John Seelye has argued that by the mid-nineteenth-century internal improvements had "become associated with political expediency," and, indeed, in *Walden* Thoreau derides the nation's "so called internal improvements" as being "all external and superficial."[12] In Washington, Whitman and Lincoln suggest a revived rhetoric of internal improvements, one where the capital's very uncanniness—the wounded and dead soldiers, even its muddy streets—testifies to the Union's sublimity and depth: "Before I went down to the Field and among the Hospitals, I had my hours of doubt about These States; but not since," Whitman famously wrote, "The War, to me, proved Humanity, and proved America and the Modern."[13]

The Poetry of Internal Improvements

The importance of circulation toward implementing a political system comes down to the fundamental issues of movement and access. In France, as Mona Ozouf reminds us, "walking at one's ease in places where one was once forbidden to enter . . . [had been] the first delight of the Revolution."[14] The storming of spaces of power, such as the Bastille, let citizens fulfill their theories about the rights of man. This suggests that movement itself might be seen as a conversion experience, whereby political theory could become experienced fact. This emphasis upon the instrumental importance of movement was only further enlarged during the romantic era,

an age that Cornel West has argued was dominated by a "telos of movement and flux," due in part to the ever-expanding marketplace.[15] Men of
letters put down their pens, left their studies, and went out into nature:
"Crossing a bare common," Emerson writes, "I have enjoyed a perfect exhilaration. Almost I fear to think how glad I am."[16] Movement comes first
here—man's altered state is triggered by his footsteps.

On a larger scale, the nation's system of roads, canals, and railroads was
seen as the first practical step toward implementing a new form of government. In his "Second Reply to Hayne," Daniel Webster reports this exchange: "'What interest,' asks [Hayne], 'has South Carolina in a canal in
Ohio?' Sir, this very question is full of significance. It develops the gentleman's whole political system." Because South Carolina wanted a loose con-
federacy of independent states, joined only by "some slight and ill-defined
bond of union," Webster argued, it opposed a system of federal internal
improvements. The North, on the other hand, favored a strong Union, so
it pushed for a highly developed infrastructure of explicit connections,
whether it be a railroad in South Carolina or a canal in Ohio.[17]

It is perhaps no accident that the golden age of oratory—the age of Calhoun, Webster, and Clay—coincided with the "turnpike era." Internal improvements seemed to encourage and generate an inspired rhetoric of national connectedness. In *The Federalist,* James Madison insisted that they
would echo and strengthen the "chords" and " bonds of affection" that
"knit together" the "people of America" into an "American family."[18]
Abraham Lincoln acknowledged there was something in the railway that
"heated . . . our imaginations."[19] D. W. Meinig has traced the "extravagant
rhetoric" that was "rehears[ed] year after year" in support of a transcontinental railroad. Indeed, with that railroad, the imagination seemed to know
no bounds, as its proponents made increasingly large claims in its support:
it would create "a great thoroughfare between two oceans"; it would
"[link] by a great federative bond the whole political fabric from ocean to
ocean"; it would form an "American road to India."[20] In a speech given in
support of the Cumberland Road, which would go through Maryland,
Pennsylvania, and Virginia, Henry Clay uses his rhetorical arts to suggest
and reinforce new connections between citizens' private lives and the national government. Clay argues that the road was needed so that "we
should be able to continue and maintain an affectionate intercourse with
our friends and brethren—that we might have a way to reach the Capitol

of our country . . . to consult and mingle with yours in the advancement of the national prosperity."[21] A nation crisscrossed by numerous routes inspired, and helped to fulfill, a visionary rhetoric of a unified nation.

This rhetoric of internal improvements can be detected even in the letter that Daniel Webster wrote in Congress while listening to Henry Clay give the aforementioned speech. Webster marvels that such a "dry" subject as roads could inspire such a compelling rhetorical performance. "Mr. Clay speaks well. I wish you were here to hear him," Webster writes.

> The highest enjoyment, almost, which I have in life, is in hearing an able argument or speech. The development of *mind,* in those modes, is delightful. In books, we see the result of thought and of fancy. In the living speaker, we see the thought itself, as it rises in the speaker's own mind. And his countenance often indicates a *perception* before it gets upon his tongue. I have been charmed by observing this operation of minds which are truly great and vigorous; so that I sometimes am as much moved, as in reading a part of Milton and Shakespeare, by a striking and able argument, although on the dryest subject.[22]

A theme of connections operates here on several levels. Webster recounts the drama of the scene as Clay searches for just the right words: his ideas emerge first upon his forehead, as signs of what is coming, and then finally take shape as speech. Clay's performance thus bridges the interior of his mind with its public external expression, and Webster suggests that such a journey of thought—from private life to public life—is as moving as great poetry. Perhaps Clay's enthusiasum for internal improvements generated his inspiring performance; Webster's account at least makes even the "dryest" congressional debate seem like something not to be missed. His letter itself creates a direct path to the Capitol, opening it up to view and enticing his reader from her home in the hinterlands to Washington, D.C.: "I wish you were here to hear him."[23]

As a statesman and orator, Lincoln was directly descended from Webster and Clay. He drew upon Webster's speeches when writing his own and called Clay "the man for whom I fought all my life."[24] Lincoln's first announcement of his candidacy for political office began with a detailed discussion of measures that could be taken to improve the navigability of the Sangamo River and hence the prosperity of the surrounding county; as a young state representative, Lincoln boasted that he "would have his limbs ripped off before he would violate his pledge" to promote internal improvements. Lincoln was the first president to succeed in getting funds allocated for a transcontinental railway; his own interest in the railroad was reflected by his son Willie, who committed railway schedules to memory.[25]

Lincoln's rhetoric imitates the very technology that so engaged him. From his intense interest in the telegraph, Lincoln developed what Garry Wills calls a "telegraphic eloquence," with a "monosyllabic and staccato beat" that gave Lincoln a means of "say[ing] a great deal in the fewest words," a skill he refined until "his *message* [itself] was telegraphic." At the same time, Lincoln adheres to well-established classical rhetorical form. Lincoln "perfected a new classicism," Wills asserts, one suited to modern times. In contrast to Webster's "Second Reply to Hayne," which was delivered over three days and took up seventy five pages in print, Lincoln's Gettysburg Address was only 272 words long. Wills explains, "Lincoln took the formal ideals of the past into the modern era, where the pace of life does not allow for the leisurely style of Lincoln's rhetorical forbears."[26]

If the rhetoric of internal improvements seeks to make the nation more organic, to create a fluid connection from the political Union to the personal lives of its citizenry, Lincoln's rhetoric excels in this regard. Lincoln worked as a surveyor when he was a young man. He was also inordinately fond of logic and worked hard on how to best order the points of arguments he overheard among his father and friends.[27] Those early experiences resonate in his rhetoric as he lays out paths of thought his listeners have no choice but to follow: "If we could first know where we are, and whither we are tending, we could better judge what to do, and how to do it."[28] He displaces his authority onto these landscapes—the paths he simply surveys as a historian, the irresistible conclusions to which his "stream" of thought tends.[29] In his first inaugural address, Lincoln argues: "Physically speaking we cannot separate. We cannot remove our respective sections from each other, nor build an impassable wall between them. A husband and wife may be divorced, and go . . . beyond the reach of each other; but the different parts of our country cannot do this. They cannot but remain face to face; and intercourse, either amicable or hostile, must continue between them."[30] We are held together, Lincoln asserts, not by an artificial and tyrannical federal authority but by the very landscape itself.

Naturalizing his arguments in this way lets Lincoln be disarmingly passive. Wills argues that Lincoln's best prose "'flows always like a limpid stream'" and proceeds "quietly closing door after door": "The points are advanced like series of theorems in Euclid, as clear, as sequential, as compelling." Lincoln "sounds deferential rather than dogmatic" as he creates "a rhetorical trap" whereby the reader must come to Lincoln's own conclusion, while Lincoln appears innocent of any such manipulation. "This," Wills maintains, "is the highest art, which conceals itself."[31]

Harriet Beecher Stowe deduced Lincoln's strength when she described it as being "of a peculiar kind: it is not aggressive so much as passive, and among passive things, it is like the strength not so much of a stone buttress as of a wire cable . . . swaying to every influence . . . yet tenaciously and inflexibly bound to carry its great end."[32] Lincoln's multilayered ties to internal improvements help him to communicate his vision of a representative, even passive, Union that at the same time cannot be destroyed. The effectiveness of this physical rhetoric becomes particularly evident in his two inaugural speeches delivered beneath the gigantic Capitol dome.

Passive Wire

Lincoln delivered both inaugural addresses from the eastern steps of the Capitol. At his first inauguration, the dome was still under construction (fig. 2.1). At his second inauguration, the dome was complete (fig. 2.2). Speech and dome offer a climactic image for the poetry of internal improvements, and it is their association with this physical rhetoric that arguably makes them particularly impressive and memorable. For both of Lincoln's inaugural addresses, the dome helped him by lending visual support to his startling claims—the dome gave them an eerie sense of being literally true.

The dome's enormous height is made possible by its technological innovation. It was made of pig iron, the same metal used in railroad tracks, and was really a double dome—the external facade with its three tiers of columns supported by a hidden interior truss structure. Climbing the half-finished dome for the view in the days before Lincoln's first inauguration, John Hay, Lincoln's private secretary, described "this light, aerial gallery, iron-railed" dome as the focus point for the capital's network of avenues: the "broad avenues, which converge upon the capitol as the roads of the Roman empire converged upon that golden milestone by the Pincian gate."[33] Hay imagines that all roads lead to Washington. With the capital as an idealized map of the nation as a whole, the completed dome, and its inner structure of iron trusses and spans, would offer a climax to the vision

FIG. 2.1. The Capitol, February 12, 1861, shortly before Lincoln's first inauguration. *Architect of the Capitol.*

of a national infrastructure of internal improvements, of accelerated communication and trade leading to prosperity and political freedom: in this sense the dome would appear to be organic, the result of the energy from a hundred roads, canals, telegraph and other connections converging at the nation's political center in one great upsurge of force. The dome's height is the measure of that force. At the top of the dome would stand the statue of Freedom by Thomas Crawford.[34]

The new dome was part of a larger project to expand the Capitol in order to accommodate the increasing size of Congress and to reflect the nation's expansion. But the dome's inordinate size and innovative design were deemed by critics to go too far. Architect Robert Mills, who had himself proposed a smaller, more traditional masonry dome, complained, "We must ever regret the innovation here made upon the original design of the

FIG. 2.2. East front of the Capitol, c. 1870. *Architect of the Capitol.*

Capitol by the introduction of an immense dome."[35] Another critic faulted "the extreme height of the dome," "elevated as much as possible," for the "violence" it would do to the rest of the building. It was 287½ feet high, the largest dome of its kind ever built.[36]

The dome raised the same conflict between state and federal sovereignty that dogged internal improvements. Historically, the dome and its columns signified the relationship between the states and the nation. The famous cartoon of 1788 shows how it is the states (pillars) that by ratifying the Constitution will "swell" "the great National DOME" (fig. 2.3). The nation's existence clearly depends upon the power of the states. The power relationship between the thirty-six pillars (to represent the then thirty-six

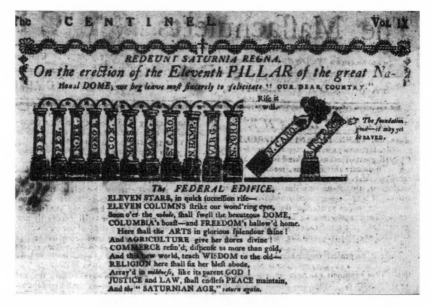

The CENTINEL. Vol. IX.

REDEUNT SATURNIA REGNA.

On the erection of the Eleventh PILLAR of the great National DOME, we beg leave most sincerely to felicitate OUR DEAR COUNTRY.

The FEDERAL EDIFICE.

ELEVEN STARS, in quick succession rise—
ELEVEN COLUMNS strike our wond'ring eyes,
Soon o'er the whole, shall swell the beauteous DOME,
COLUMBIA's boast—and FREEDOM's hallow'd home.
Here shall the ARTS in glorious splendour shine!
And AGRICULTURE give her stores divine!
COMMERCE refin'd, dispense us more than gold,
And this new world, teach WISDOM to the old—
RELIGION here shall fix her blest abode,
Array'd in mildness, like its parent GOD !
JUSTICE and LAW, shall endless PEACE maintain,
And the " SATURNIAN AGE," return again.

FIG. 2.3. *Massachusetts Centinel* cartoon, August 2, 1788. *Newspaper Division, Library of Congress.*

states) and the new Capitol dome is more ambiguous. In fact, the visible columns are only symbolic; the dome's internal trusses provide its actual support (fig. 2.4).[37] The decorative columns might suggest the way in which state power has been absorbed by the nation, an idea echoed by the gradual diminishment of the first tier's columns into the third tier's ribs. Critics faulted the design for its duplicity: "The construction of the new dome is a violation of the principles of design. Iron is to be used in precisely the same form of construction as if it were stone; of course, the pillars will be cast hollow, and they will be painted to imitate the marble."[38]

As the Capitol dome forms a climax to the debate on internal improvements, so too does Lincoln's first inaugural address. Lincoln makes several legalistic arguments against secession but then switches to a personal tone at the end, when he announces "I am loth to close." With this he introduces his now famous closing image: "Though passion may have strained, it must not break our bonds of affection. The mystic chords of memory, stretching from every battle-field, and patriot grave, to every living heart and hearth-stone, all over this broad land, will yet swell the chorus of the Union, when again touched, as surely they will be, by the better angels of our nature."[39] Lincoln shapes his rhetoric with the familiar imagery of the

FIG. 2.4. *Section through Dome of U.S. Capitol,* Thomas U. Walter, 1859. *Architect of the Capitol.*

poetry of internal improvements. In fact, the passage is not original to Lincoln but is his reworking of a passage proposed to him by William Seward.[40] Like the dome behind him, Lincoln's rhetoric is notably concrete.

Garry Wills points out the physical quality of Lincoln's words. For example, the phrase "I am loth to close" does what it says—the "lingering monosyllables" of "loth" and "close" physically slow down Lincoln's speech; they "seem to cling to the occasion, not wanting to break off the communication on which the last hopes of union depend." Similarly, Lincoln's final image gains power from its vividness: "the bonds and the strings are equally *physical* images," "chords" that later, Lincoln says, will be "touched" "by the better angels of our nature." These are "geometric" and "electric cords," Wills maintains—Lincoln used both spellings of "cord" "indiscriminately." Lincoln's image hence describes the Union as a land crisscrossed by cords—be they heartstrings or telegraph wires— whose combined messages will "swell the chorus of the Union," just as a circle is crossed by chords or, as Wills notes, "the cord on a tortoise shell gave Apollo his lute."[41] With these various resonances, Lincoln summons a transcendent network of emotional bonds tying citizens' hearts right to the nation itself. Lincoln's image clarifies connections in the Union that had been only vague—citizens' hearts and homes to each battlefield and grave; the North to the South—and hence makes the nation more visible. It is this section that students still memorize, not only because it forms the concluding climax of the speech but also, surely, because of its concrete, tangible imagery.

In his account of Lincoln's first inaugural, John Hay suggests a correspondence between the event and its setting: "To the imaginative spectator there might have been something emblematic in the architectural features of the scene. The construction of the great dome of the Capitol was in mid-progress, and huge derricks held by a network of steel ropes towered over the incomplete structure."[42] Lincoln's emotional and transcendent imagery is echoed by the dome's physical presence. We have the same idea being expressed in two different ways, and this physical/rhetorical expression is right in line with the main argument of Lincoln's speech. Lincoln insists that the Union cannot be dissolved. It is by now a physical historical fact, a fact that does not come from some political authority above but is rooted in the landscape and in the citizens themselves—in their hearts, their memories, their homes, their "better natures." In this way, Lincoln naturalizes the Union; it is not artificial but organic. In its own language, the dome confirms Lincoln's claim, perhaps making that fantastic union he described seem still more real: it is right there; you can see it. Even the futurity of Lincoln's claim, that the "mystic chords of memory . . . will *yet* swell the chorus of the Union, when again touched, as surely they *will* be," is echoed by the not yet finished dome. That Lincoln was sensitive to the symbolism of the dome and its visibility is suggested by the claim that Lincoln ordered construction to resume on the Capitol when it had stopped because of the war: "It is a sign," he said "we intend the Union shall go on."[43]

If we pull back our focus from just the Capitol dome and consider Lincoln's inaugural address within the larger field of the National Mall in which it took place, we can appreciate how the Mall served as a stage for rival speculations as to the direction the nation should adopt. The extension of the Capitol and the dome, which began in the mid-1850s under the administrative direction of Jefferson Davis, then secretary of war, was itself a speculation that the nation would remain intact, and so too was Lincoln's reputed insistence that the dome's construction be continued as a "sign" that the Union would survive and win the Civil War. As if in direct opposition to that view stood the home of Robert E. Lee, known as Arlington House, which lay at the other end of the National Mall, high on a hill directly across the Potomac River.

As Alan Gowans notes, Arlington House "was very deliberately sited on a bluff on the Virginia side of the Potomac, to overlook the new federal city. Its forms are as ideological as its siting."[44] If the Capitol's most prominent feature is its overpowering dome, then Arlington House's most prominent feature is its overpowering columns (fig. 2.5). The home, which belonged to Lee's wife, Mary Custis, was built by her father as a shrine to his father by adoption, George Washington. Lee made his decision to resign from the U.S. Army from this site. He had been in the army for over thirty years. Lincoln offered him command of the Union forces, but as Lee explained in letters to his family, "With all my devotion to the Union, and the feeling of loyalty and duty of an American citizen, I have not been able to make up my mind to raise my hand against my relatives, my children, my home." Mary Custis Lee, who became a fiercely loyal secessionist, wished to stay and defend the home against the violation of her liberty, and that of Washington's beloved home state of Virginia, by the unconstitutional aggression of the North.[45] When Lincoln delivered his first inaugural address, Lee had already left Arlington House and Jefferson Davis had been inaugurated as president of the Confederate States of America. During the Civil War, the Capitol with its exaggerated, Roman-style dome and the Greek-style temple of Arlington House with its exaggerated columns (built so that they could easily be seen from the river and the federal city) presented, in the enlarged scale so typical to visionary

FIG. 2.5. Arlington House (Robert E. Lee Residence), Arlington, Virginia, c. 1871. *Virginia Historical Society, Richmond, Virginia.*

spaces, two rival speculations as to the direction the nation would ulti-mately take: with the nation or the states having established their ultimate relative authority.[46] Lee suggests that the nation has asked him to put it be-fore his own family and his first home. In his second inaugural address, Lincoln resolves that tension, as he may be said to have in his first address, by fashioning the Union as itself an ideal home.

Lincoln's second inaugural address again interacts with the Capitol and its wider setting. The Union Lincoln invokes is forgiving, nurturing, and sanctioned by God. He does not portray the Union as nearly victorious, nor does he acknowledge that the Union forbade the South to exercise what many considered its right to secede. The dome in a sense says this for him: it conveys the victory of the federal government over regional identifi-cations and establishes itself as indivisible, as irreversibly real. In one sense, the dominating presence of the dome counteracts, and perhaps even makes room for, the disarmingly passive and gentle tone of Lincoln's speech. In-deed, both the first and the second inaugural addresses suggest that a pri-mary use of technological rhetoric is to help the nation-state insist that political authority is not centralized in an autocratic body but is dispersed throughout the community. In the first inaugural Lincoln's "mystic chords of memory" naturalizes the force that holds the nation together; in the second inaugural Lincoln spiritualizes it. Both speeches help Lincoln to evade charges that he proved himself a dictator by refusing to let the South secede.

The reversal of power suggested by the dome, in which the nation, rather than the states, has primary control, is never acknowledged by Lincoln in his address. The first part of his speech explains how "the war came." In his first inaugural address, Lincoln claimed that the cause of the war lay in the citizens' hands and not the government's: "In *your* hands, my dissatisfied fellow countrymen, and not in *mine,* is the momentous issue of civil war. The government will not assail *you*" (emphasis original).[47] So, too, in Lincoln's second address the Union is on the defensive; it did not attack, but was attacked by, "insurgents."

In a second explanation he gives for the war during his second inaugural address, Lincoln suggests that it is not the national government, the states, or even the insurgents that are to blame. Instead, Lincoln poses the possibility that God has "given" "this terrible war" to "both the North and South" as punishment for the sin of slavery. He poses this ultimate cause in a way that is as assertive as it is passive by putting his proposition in the conditional form:

If we shall suppose that American Slavery is one of the offences which, in the providence of God, must needs come, but which, having continued through His appointed time, He now wills to remove, and that He gives to both North and South, this terrible war, as the woe due to those by whom the offence came, shall we discern therein any departure from those divine attributes which the believers in a Living God always ascribe to Him?

If, Lincoln says, God gave us this war as punishment, should we be surprised? In other words, if this is a judgment of God, then we must accept it. He repeats this idea again. He notes that while we hope that "the mighty scourge of war may speedily pass away," "*if* God wills that it continue . . . still it must be said 'the judgments of the Lord, are true and righteous altogether.'" God's decree is all powerful, and we can do nothing but fight the war until God deems our sins to have been adequately repaid. Keeping this explanation in the conditional form, however, Lincoln leaves some uncertainty as to whether God really is the author of this war. But at the same time he repeats his claim that we have no choice but to accept the righteousness of that, if it is indeed the case. Lincoln is able to make his point, and even to insist upon it, while still keeping it in the more passive conditional form.[48] As a silent echo, the white, transcendent, heavenly dome at the top of the republican house of government, a dome inspired most directly by St. Isaac's cathedral in St. Petersburg, implies that the fate of the Union is ultimately beyond our control and rests in the hands of God.[49]

Lincoln's second inaugural address again leads to a climax resonant with the domestic imagery we encountered in the first: "Let us strive to finish the work we are in; to bind up the nation's wounds; to care for him who shall have borne the battle, and for his widow, and his orphan."[50] Lincoln's words again invoke a "big tent" under which all citizens can dwell; in the first inaugural that affective structure was made from the "mystic chords of memory"; here it is made by "binding up the nation's wounds," which will unite the nation as a family. Lincoln overlays the technological infrastructure to which he dedicated so much of his political life with sentimental, domestic ties.

The Patent Office, which honored and gave incentive to the nation's technological development, was built in the place L'Enfant had set aside for a National Church. That the poetic imagery of the Capitol dome and Lincoln's speech has its source in technology repeats the point implied by that substitution: unifying technology *was* the church; it would be the source of an improved political home, such as had only been dreamed of. The Capitol dome almost literalizes Lincoln's national home; "dome" comes from Latin *domus,* or dwelling, from which we get "domestic." One soldier responded in this way to the completed Capitol dome: "As I approached the Capitol . . . and caught sight of the new dome . . . it seemed . . . in utter defiance of the rebellion. . . . Then as never before I felt that my first loyalty was to the DOME—rather than that of Michigan, Pennsylvania, or any other state—to that dome in the mighty shadow of which all other domes could safely rest."[51] The hypervisibility of the dome overshadows the states and closes the gap between the citizen and the nation by winning his "first loyalty."

Despite the soldier's warm response, the appropriateness of the dome's use of classical style to inspire national feeling had come under criticism. This argument was dramatized on the National Mall. At the time of Lincoln's speeches, the Mall was dominated by two structures—the white sandstone Capitol and the red sandstone Smithsonian Institution (1846–55)—and these two edifices were often seen as architectural rivals. For Senator Robert Owen, who oversaw the design of the Smithsonian, the building's style, which was based roughly upon twelfth-century Norman architecture, was much more suitable to the nation than the extravagant classicism of the Capitol. In his *Hints on Public Architecture* (1849), Owen praises the Norman style for its implicitly democratic nature—it is infinitely variable, far cheaper, and easily applied to modern needs in both domestic and public architecture. From it we can evolve an architecture of *"our own"*: "Its entire expression is less ostentatious, and, if political character may be ascribed to Architecture, more republican." Owen's *Hints* suggests an indirect attack on the Capitol itself. Owen's prime example of the wrongheadedness of applying classical style to American buildings is Philadelphia's Girard College, which was ornamented with rows of costly, purely decorative columns and suffered from poor light and an unsuitable floor plan. Girard College was designed by Thomas U. Walter, the architect for the new, extended Capitol dome.[52]

Sculptor and aesthetic critic Horatio Greenough, on the other hand, rejected the Smithsonian building—that "dark pile—that castle of authority"—as decidedly *un*-republican. The building's "gothic" (read European) "towers and belfries" lent an un-American air of secrecy to the Mall. Greenough describes the jarring contrast the castle makes with the stately Capitol: "Suddenly, as I walked, the dark form of the Smithsonian palace rose between me and the white Capitol, and I stopped. Tower and battlement, and all that medieval confusion, stamped itself on the halls of Congress, as ink on paper! Dark on that whiteness—complication on that simplicity! It scared me . . . It seemed to threaten. It seemed to say, I bide my time! Oh, it was indeed monastic at that hour!"[53]

If we view the Capitol dome through its association with the rhetoric of internal improvements, we can see how it may have appeared to achieve the organic relation between classicism and American republicanism that Greenough asserts and Owen denies. Garry Wills defines Lincoln's "new classicism" as the way Lincoln's technological rhetoric observed the rules of classical oratory, while bringing these "formal ideas of the past into the modern era."[54] So too, the dome appears modern, inventive, and continuous with the nation's interior—it seems to almost arise directly from it. Norman architecture's ultimate failure to dethrone classicism is registered by today's National Mall, where the Smithsonian building still sticks out incongruously in the national lineup of monumental structures.

What the contest between these two styles for the heart of the nation suggests is not that either style is more closely related to some unifying

view of the national spirit, but rather that these buildings are best understood when reconnected to the rhetoric that promoted and critiqued
them. Laden with such politicized interpretations, the Smithsonian and
Capitol become rival speculations, each asserting its own wager as to the
political and cultural direction the nation should take.

One last feature of Lincoln's inaugural landscape suggests the central
importance of a dynamic sense of movement to a successful "organic" use
of classical design. Horatio Greenough's own attempt to model an organic
classicism in his statue of George Washington makes an informative contrast to Lincoln's adept fusion of high classicism with a modern democratic
style. Greenough's statue was located outside the Capitol building, facing
its eastern side. Lincoln would have confronted it as he delivered his inaugural addresses (fig. 2.6; see also fig. 2.2). Greenough remarks that the goal
of this statue was to present the first president so as "to convey the idea of
an entire abnegation of Self and to make my hero as it were a *conductor* between God and man."[55] Washington's foot extends out toward the viewer,
while his arm and finger point upward; the statue draws the viewer in and
becomes a bridge to the divine.

Greenough's modeling of Washington uses, art historian Vivien Fryd
notes, a "surface classicism" that models itself after examples from antiq-
uity; one source is a famous ancient Greek rendition of Zeus. The statue
had many critics who faulted it for not being suited enough to the father
of the nation. Greenough's Washington looked too much like an em-
peror, and people were certainly not used to seeing the first president half-
naked; in short, one person complained, "it is not *our* Washington that he
has represented.'" The elite iconography of the statue made it *too* speculative, too above, or outside of, the popular conception to be integrated to
it. The statue accordingly spent an unhappy life being moved from location to location around the Mall; it now resides inside the National Museum of American History.[56]

Greenough's statue fails to make an emotional, concrete connection. In
contrast, a late photograph of Lincoln, taken shortly after his second inauguration, offers an example of how a presidential image could become a
"conductor," in this case to national feeling (fig. 2.7). Lincoln, too, is
seated. When he was photographed as a candidate during his first election,
Lincoln took the much more traditional statesman's posture and stood. In
this portrait, Lincoln offers a more unconventional presidential view. He

FIG. 2.6. Horatio Greenough, *George Washington*. *Smithsonian American Art Museum, Transfer from the U.S. Capitol.*

adopts a nonauthoritative, frank, and surprisingly intimate pose. The photograph lets Lincoln use technology to create a short cut to personal, familial attachments—here, to the president, even—without which the federal government might not survive. Lincoln appears to rely upon what Whitman would call "personal magnetism" to bind up the nation's wounds. The photograph illustrates Whitman's description, in a "Washington Letter" to the *New York Times,* of Lincoln as he returned down Pennsylvania Avenue after delivering his second inaugural address:

[Lincoln] was in his plain two-horse barouche, and looked very much worn and tired; the lines, indeed, of vast responsibilities, intricate questions, and demands of life and death, cut deeper than ever upon his dark brown face; yet all the old goodness, tenderness, sadness, and canny shrewdness, underneath the furrows. (I never see that man without feeling that he is one to become personally attached to, for his combination of purest, heartiest tenderness, and native Western even rudest forms of manliness.)[57]

FIG. 2.7. *Abraham Lincoln: Last sitting four days before his assassination at Ford's Theater on April 14, 1865.* Photograph by Alexander Gardner. *Prints and Photographs Division, Library of Congress.*

That the nation is improved only, ultimately, through the violent sacrifice of its youth, and of the president himself, is registered by Lincoln's deeply lined face. It is a liminal face, as Whitman describes it, whose contrasts are what make it so moving. Lincoln was a "hoosier Michel Angelo, so awful ugly it becomes beautiful, with its strange mouth, its deep cut, cris-cross lines, and its doughnut complexion."[58] Through this strange face and tired body, the president becomes, in Whitman's view, "our" Lincoln.

Whitman's New Roads

Walt Whitman's views of Lincoln and Washington during the Civil War suggest an extreme conclusion to the poetry of internal improvements, one

where technological infrastructure serves not as a means to a union between the nation's interior and its external government but as an end.

Like Lincoln's poetic prose, Whitman's language is extremely physical
and inextricably tied to internal improvements. His poetic line is perhaps
best described as "extended," in the sense of the Federalists' use of that
word as they envisioned an "extended republic." Whitman's line reaches
out, and like the proposed Federalist network of internal improvements, it
ties any number of diverse objects together and so binds vast reaches of territory into one whole.

In his study of what he calls Whitman's "processional mode," Alan Trachtenberg clarifies the involved relationship between Whitman's poetry
and roads, his fascination with Broadway and street life, and the "passage
from street to poem." A poem like "Crossing Brooklyn Ferry" itself becomes a "capacious vehicular structure," "a form of movement."[59] Whitman pushes the rhetoric of internal improvements this far. The new roads
created by his new poetic line, whose "capacious" scale makes it cohere
with what we have seen of speculative form so far, seeks to create his vision
as a reality, to make it physical and concrete; Washington, D.C., during the
Civil War provided Whitman with a particularly fertile ground.

Whitman moved to Washington in 1863, initially to search for his
brother, who had been wounded in the war, and he remained there ten
years. From the start, Whitman was concerned by the gap he perceived between the capital and the nation: "the city, the spaces, buildings, &c. make
no unfit emblem of our country, so far, so broadly planned, everything in
plenty, money & materials staggering with plenty, but the fruit of the
plans, the knit, the combination yet wanting—Determined to express ourselves greatly in a capital but no fit capital yet here."[60] Through his Washington writings, Whitman seeks to resolve this tension by establishing
paths between citizens and their capital. By the end of the war, he sees the
"knit" between them begin to form.

To bridge this gap, Whitman seeks to establish an immediate connection via the numerous reportorial accounts he wrote during the war. Some
of these, he explains, he wrote simply as notes to himself.[61] Others he published in the *New York Times* and elsewhere. In these eyewitness reports,
Whitman takes Lincoln's telegraphic prose to the next level, as he lets his
readers feel as though they are themselves right there: "No prepared picture, no elaborated poem, no after-narrative, could be what the thing itself

is," Whitman maintained. "You want to catch its first spirit—to tally its birth. By writing at the instant the very heart-beat of life is caught."[62] In his plans for a "yearbook" of 1863, the city and the war come to life:

> this book, with its frame work jotted down on the battle-field, in the shelter-tent, by the way-side amid the rumble of passing artillery trains or the marching of cavalry, in the streets of Washington, the gorgeous halls of gold where the national representatives meet, and above all in the great military hospitals, . . . amid the ashy face, the bloody bandage, with death & suffering on every side . . . —a book of the spirit & fact of the events we are passing through . . . full of the blood & vitality of the American people.[63]

Whitman draws citizens to the nation by bringing them to the places where that nation is most intensely felt—in the capital and in the scenes of the war. Here we can see Whitman's primary interest in comings and goings, so that even the events are something "we are passing through." The entire passage conveys an intense sense of movement—this is writing on the go. Whitman's emphasis on movement naturally leads him to focus his vision upon Washington's streets.

Whitman's plan for his yearbook drafts a blueprint for several successive views he offers to his readers of the capital city during the war. He commits to showing the "death & suffering" on every side and signals his conviction that the "great military hospitals" give the most accurate picture of the war. At the same time, he offers views that are "processional"; they keep us moving through the war, enabling us to take the violence of nation-making in stride. Whitman's journalistic images let us see the value of internal improvements as a way of organizing, and giving a shape of progress to, the national sprawl, and to the violence that results from the incursion of the nation's contests into the personal lives of the citizens who must fight its wars. The roads cut across regional identities and let Whitman not create but make manifest, or photograph, the national family he always sees as already there. In her study of Whitman's response to Washington during the war, Katherine Kinney points out that the big problem is "what is to be done with all the bodies" of men, dead, wounded, and alive, that flooded the capital. Kinney points to Whitman's ambivalence about the huge sacrifice of men needed to win the war.[64] But included in Whitman's wide response to Washington are repeated views of its hospitals that suggest that those men are just what the capital needs, because they lead inexorably to the nation's awful but sublime internal improvement.

Washington's avenues become for Whitman a main site where one can evaluate whether or not the capital has achieved a successful "knit" with its citizens. In chapter 1 we saw how Lewis Mumford pointed to the inordinate amount of Washington's space used for circulation as opposed to buildings.[65] We might assume that this is precisely what appealed to Whitman about the capital. But an early image that Whitman provides of the city after the Union army's defeat at Bull Run (1862) offers a dramatic picture of this conflict between circulation and dwelling space. The capital's emphasis upon avenues and grand marble edifices leaves its exhausted soldiers with no place to go: "They drop down anywhere, on the steps of houses, up close by the basements or fences, on the sidewalk, aside on some vacant lot, and deeply sleep. A poor seventeen or eighteen year old boy lies there, on the stoop of a grand house. . . . Some clutch their muskets firmly even in sleep . . . —and on them, as they lay, sulkily drips the rain."[66] Eventually Washington was ringed by forts and had over fifty hospitals, but well into the war, troops, wounded and healthy alike, were crammed into whatever public buildings could house them, including the Capitol and the Patent Office.

The capital city's inherent tension between circulation space and interior space is resolved for Whitman in Washington's new military hospitals. There scientific knowledge and invention combine to create the right setting for the men. The hospitals were built according to the new "pavilion plan," which prevented the spread of disease by classifying men in modular wards that permitted a much greater degree of air circulation. As Dell Upton points out, "an ideal hospital of the nineteenth century was . . . an 'edifice built up out of pure air.'"[67] Whitman shows us an example in this account: "Fancy to yourself a space of three to twenty acres of ground, on which are group'd ten or twelve very large wooden barracks, with, perhaps, a dozen or twenty . . . small buildings, capable altogether of accommodating from five hundred to a thousand or fifteen hundred persons." For Whitman it seems an almost model world, where everything needed has been planned for and provided in a well-ordered manner to insure smooth functioning: "Sometimes these wooden barracks or wards . . . are ranged in a straight row, evenly fronting the street; others are planned so as to form an immense V. . . . They make altogether a huge cluster, with the additional tents, extra wards for contagious diseases, guard-houses, sutler's stores, chaplain's house. . . . These wards are either lettr'd alphabetically, ward G, ward K, or else numerically, 1, 2, 3, &c." These mini-cities when filled contain "a population more numerous in itself than the whole of the Washington of ten or fifteen years ago."[68] The hospitals provide an improved Washington. It is as if someone blew a whistle in the city and shouted "Fall in!" No longer are sick soldiers crammed between glass display cases at the Patent Office museum or parked in the halls of the Capitol; there is now a system that can endlessly expand and bring order to the entire city. We can guess that Whitman's aesthetic was particularly attracted to the hospitals because of their huge scale and democratic organization, as they gathered men of all ranks from all over the Union in the nonhierarchical order of Ward A or B and Bed 5 or 6.

The pavilion hospitals succeed because they combine circulation with dwelling; one might conclude from Whitman's interior view of Armory Square Hospital, which Whitman called a "model" hospital, that they resemble avenues that have been brought indoors (fig. 2.8). In this description, Whitman creates a path for his readers, bringing them into the scene and letting them feel as though they are there: "Let us go into ward 6. It contains to-day, I should judge, eighty or a hundred patients, half sick, half wounded. The edifice is nothing but boards, well whitewash'd inside. . . . You walk down the central passage, with a row [of beds] on either side, their feet towards you, and their heads to the wall."[69] An emphasis upon circulation can be seen as well in even more elaborate hospitals, such as that in Jeffersonville, Indiana, which took the shape of an urban étoile of avenues.

Down these corridors Whitman moves, tying the Union together as he encounters "representatives from all New England, and from New York, and New Jersey, and Pennsylvania—indeed from all the States and all the cities."[70] The order of the hospitals offers something not unlike what Alan Trachtenberg sees in Whitman's "processional form": "Processional form signals a hope of unity at the site of difference and conflict: it is Whitman's crowd control, we might say, his way of subduing and containing recalcitrant particulars within his dream of an American oneness."[71] As Whitman proceeds, making his rounds, he stops to bind the men's wounds, write letters to their families, and share a fraternal kiss.

The above passage and photograph of the hospital wards are fairly sterile, and as Kinney and others have noted, Whitman felt ambivalent about publishing the horror of what he saw during the war: the "interior history [of the war] will never be written, perhaps must not and should not be."[72] But

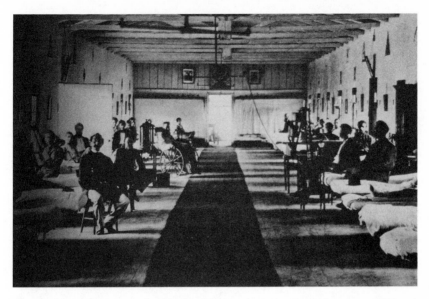

FIG. 2.8. *Washington, D.C. Patients in Ward K of Armory Square Hospital. Prints and Photographs Division, Library of Congress.*

Whitman gives many glimpses into that history, and his unwillingness to go any deeper creates all the more interest in it. For instance, after the war Whitman makes a much-noted claim that he has many "blood smutch'd notebooks," sheets of paper he fastened with a pin and kept in his pocket so he could make notes while he was circulating among his patients. On these "lurid . . . little note-books" he scribbled details of the soldier's cases. These might seem to represent his most successful attempt at recording the "interior of the war," combining as they do his notes, the men's blood, and his hands-on involvement with circulation through the wards.

Like a speculator opening up a new territory for investment, Whitman practices expert market psychology here: he suggests a path to the "real interior" of the war—and then says he is not sure he really wants to take us there. Whitman shows us his bloody notebooks, for instance, and then tells us, "I leave them there just as I threw them by after the war."[73] He claims that his *Specimen Days* includes a "verbatim copy" of those notes, but many a reader, including this one, has no doubt wished she could see those bloody, pinned pages for herself.[74] In the "Wound Dresser" (1865) Whitman excites our interest in a similar way as he takes us through the doors of his memory into the hospital wards and does not flinch from showing us "the bloody stump" of a soldier's amputated arm and the "refuse pail,/

Soon to be fill'd with clotted rags and blood, emptied, and fill'd again." At the same time, he does not let us linger but keeps us moving through his relatively short poem: "On, on I go, (open doors of time! Open hospital doors!)"[75] These glimpses into the horror of the war make the sacrifice of the men and the nation they suffered for all the more compelling. Such promotionalism, however ambivalent, invites the reader to share's Whitman's sense of awe. The hospitals, Whitman says, "open a new world somehow to me, giving closer insights, new things, exploring deeper mines than any yet, showing our humanity."[76]

Whitman's faith in the restorative power of circulation is seen in his portrait of Pennsylvania Avenue on the day of Lincoln's second inauguration, March 4, 1865. Whitman's account appeared as a "Washington Letter" in the *New York Times* (March 12, 1865). For Whitman, the street scene is so exciting that it overshadows the most important events of the day, such as the inauguration where Lincoln delivered his second most famous speech. In Whitman's view, the "show" on Pennsylvania Avenue was "to me worth all the rest." In order to get it all down as accurately as possible he uses one of his signature lists, which form so much of his poetry: "Mud, (and such mud!) amid and upon which streaming crowds of citizens; lots of blue-dressed soldiers; any quantity of male and female Africans, (especially female), sometimes a dead lock; more mud, the wide street black, and several inches deep with it." First on his "list," the mud does not in fact repel but becomes a magnetic medium that "absorbs all"; citizens, soldiers, and "Africans" alike are taken into the Union, as they "stream" "amid and upon" the avenue. For Whitman, "the effect was heterogeneous, novel, and quite inspiriting," as the avenue benignly collects the anarchic spontaneity of the crowd.[77] Like Lincoln, Whitman took what was most embarrassing for the city and turned it to national advantage. Mud, which had been the avenue's shame, is now its unifying element.

Whitman's portrait accords Pennsylvania Avenue the highest praise when he claims its "oceanic crowd" makes it "equal almost to Broadway." In its resemblance to New York's great thoroughfare, Pennsylvania Avenue fulfills its purpose: it brings citizens together, creating a spatial union in place of a historic one. At last the tension between Washington's architectural grandeur and the spirit of the citizens is resolved: "the wide Avenue, its vista very fine, down at one end closed by the capitol, with milky bulging dome, and the Maternal Figure [of Freedom] over all . . . at the other, the western end, the pillared front of the Treasury Building." The tension between circulation and domesticity is resolved here as the avenue funnels directly toward the "maternal" dome, which hovers protectively "over all." The outdoor avenue becomes roomlike, a fantastic space where all can dwell; the prevalence of such scenes in Whitman's writing suggests that this for Whitman was his ideal national home: "altogether quite a refreshing spot and hour, and plenty of architectural show with life and magnetism also."[78]

Whitman's vision of a unifying human infrastructure reaches its most sublime expression in "When Lilacs Last in the Dooryard Bloom'd," with its haunting image of Lincoln's funeral train: "Over the breast of the spring, the land, amid cities . . . Carrying a corpse to where it shall rest in the grave/ Night and day journeys a coffin." Lincoln's body is so closely identified with the railroad that the train is not even mentioned; it is as if the coffin floats through the nation on its own: "Coffin that passes through lanes and streets,/Through day and night with the great cloud darkening the land." So, too, the long processions and the women veiled and cities draped in black form a black meandering trail through the nation that mirrors the path of the funeral train itself: "With the pomp of the inloop'd flags with the cities draped in black,/ With the show of the States themselves as of crape-veil'd women standing/ With processions long and winding and the flambeaus of the night." Technology and humans merge in this poem, as Lincoln's body becomes, once again, a "passive wire cable" tying the nation together, and the black crepe forms a train, as on a dress of mourning, that follows the tracks. At the same time the speaker begins his own journey in the poem from "an old farm-house," carrying a lilac from the bush in its dooryard, to the coffin: "Here, coffin that slowly passes,/I give you my sprig of lilac."[79] We do not see exactly how the speaker gets there. The poem simply asserts a fantastic infrastructure in which home, nation, death, and poetry all flow together and achieve a perfect fit.

Coda

I went to Washington as everybody goes there, prepared to see everything done with some furtive intention, but I was disappointed—pleasantly disappointed.   —WALT WHITMAN[80]

The poetry of internal improvements provided a fantastic, as well as essential, means of expression for the survival of the "extended republic," and it reminds us of the extraordinary attempts, however vexed, at that imagined community's literal fulfillment. Washington's streets made the tension between the nation's vision and its reality keenly felt. They generated scenes beyond imagination, during the Civil War especially but at other times in the capital's history as well. Streets offer perhaps the most condensed site where political theory and experience meet, where the visions of urban planners run up against what Michel de Certeau cites as the unpredictable, infinite, and "illegible" paths of the city-walker, or what Jane Jacobs calls the "ballet" of the street.[81]

As grand as Washington has become, its irrepressible confession of the gap between national vision and experience remains. Washington has never had a Baron von Haussman to accomplish a complete makeover of its space. While different groups and commissions have gained the upper hand for periods of time to pursue specific projects, the city's space remains beyond the control of any one body. This tension between competing national visions and experience is built right into Washington's speculative design, and its most famous street, the National Mall. The Mall's limits were settled with the completion of the Lincoln Memorial in 1922. Robert E. Lee's mansion, there in the near distance and in direct view of the mall, made the job of designing the Lincoln Memorial all the more difficult. In the end the memorial's temple was opened only on the Capitol side, and Lincoln gazes, appropriately enough, upon the tremendous dome. The back of the memorial is closed and hence seems to suggest that the nation has turned its back on its deep involvement with the South, and slavery, and Robert E. Lee. But at the same time, the mall was extended, via Memorial Bridge, across the Potomac, establishing a direct path of travel to Lee's mansion and the graves of the Civil War soldiers, and those soldiers buried after, at Arlington Cemetery. As part of this improvement, Peter L'Enfant's grave was moved from obscurity in a private cemetery in Maryland and placed directly in front of Lee's house. It is marked with a table upon which is engraved L'Enfant's plan for the Federal City. And such has the lineup evolved, partly by coincidence, partly by design, to make a national road that celebrates the nation's glory, while highlighting its troubled past.

II. MODELS OF NATIONAL DOMESTICITY

Chapter 3

A HOUSE UNITED

Frederick Douglass's Interracial Domesticity during Reconstruction

HEADNOTE: *Racial Equality and Capital*

As Eric Foner notes, Reconstruction coincided with the "heady final years" of the "age of capital" (1848–75); as slavery ended, new commercial centers in the South developed, industrial production accelerated in the North, and the West opened "to mining, lumbering, ranching, and commercial farming."[H1] Many reformers during Reconstruction argued that racial equality would only be achieved if African Americans could take their place in this economic rise by accumulating wealth and most importantly property. African Americans did improve their economic positions to a remarkable degree, but that progress was significantly jeopardized and retarded by the extent to which whites refused to sell land to them and blocked efforts to force the redistribution of land in the South. Despite all the progress African Americans made, this "failure to provide ex-slaves with property comparable to that of landed whites" was a significant cause of the "failure of Reconstruction."[H2]

This economic program toward racial equality formed the mission of the Freedman's Savings and Trust Company, a private bank chartered in 1865 to advance the social position of freedmen. By preaching thrift and economy, the bank sought to "mold ex-slaves into middle-class citizens."[H3] Frederick Douglass, who during Reconstruction exhorted his black audiences to "accumulate property," gave his full support to the bank: "the more millions accumulated there, I thought, the more consideration and respect would be shown to the colored people of the whole country."[H4] Douglass himself served briefly as the bank's president, to help foster confidence in it. "The belief that the Freedman's Savings and Trust Company was an institution essential for the progress of black people," Carl Osthans notes, "was central to its existence."[H5]

Within ten years of its opening, the bank had failed. The bank's leadership in Washington, Douglass reported, defied bank policy and "turned to a pursuit of profit through speculative investment in real estate and business loans." During the Panic of 1873, when depositors sought to retrieve their funds, the bank was unable to fulfill their requests; in the end, depositors were lucky to get back sixty cents for every dollar they had invested.[H6] Douglass accused the bank's largely white officers of essentially stealing their black client's hard-earned savings: "'It [was] the black man's cow, but the white man's milk.'"[H7]

In his definitive history of the Freedman's Bank, Carl Osthaus writes, "to a certain degree then, the Bank provides a case study in the perversion of a philanthropic crusade into a speculative venture."[H8] While Osthaus here defines speculation in its narrow financial sense, the broader definition of speculation invoked in this study identifies the "philanthropic crusade" as itself a speculative venture and makes apparent the connection between its radical political reform and its risky economic tactics—even before the bank started speculating in real estate and business ventures. Even the bank's decision to exceed the rules of its charter and invest in real estate (and the Union Pacific Railroad) was presented as part of the bank's original philanthropic crusade. The bank would seek to invest in and "aid the poor, industrious freedmen by providing loans when other banks refused. Many freedmen had houses and some real estate which could serve as collateral, and they would benefit by 'small but judiciously made' loans."[H9]

The Freedman's Savings and Trust was from its start a speculative venture. It was unconventional, no "ordinary savings bank" but one that "would save men as well as money." Fueled in part by political idealism, it "grew phenomenally" and quickly became "over-extended." It was promoted aggressively, and its "propaganda" was at times downright fictitious: the Washington-based bank was falsely advertised as being under the aegis of the government; branches put pictures of Lincoln and the American eagle on their passbooks. The bank's officers insisted upon the bank's solidity: "It is safe. It can not fail, for it is founded on the United States Government. . . . There is no speculation, and consequently no risk in this Bank."[H10] As Frederick Douglass put it, "Like snowflakes in winter, circulars, tracts and other papers were, by this benevolent institution, scattered among the sable millions, and they were told to 'look' to the Freedman's Bank and 'live.'"[H11]

Douglass did his own share to promote the bank. To one audience, who had paid him an honorarium, he said:

There are ways opening up for all of you. Let every colored man see to it that if he gains five dollars per week that he will lay up one dollar of it; if he makes ten dollars lay by two of them—put them in the Freedmen's Savings Bank where it will breed some more. There one thousand dollars at the end of the year will gain sixty more. Put it in there where it is safe. I believe in it. I have got a little money up there, and I am going to take some from here and put it there.[H12]

Significantly, the bank's speculative ventures started soon after the bank moved its headquarters to Washington, D.C. Osthaus notes that this "change in the Bank's nature" had already begun before the bank moved to Washington, however, and was often pursued with the "best of intentions." The influence that the monumental capital had upon the bank might be detected in one of its most risky ventures—the construction of a handsome new building on some of the city's most expensive real estate to help promote and inspire confidence in the bank. In 1871, the bank began building its new "four-story stone headquarters" at 1507 Pennsylvania Avenue, on Lafayette Square across from the White House.[H13] Douglass testifies to the powerful impression the new building made. It was

one of the most costly and splendid buildings of the time, finished on the inside with black walnut and furnished with marble counters and all the modern improvements. The magnificent dimensions of the building bore testimony to its flourishing condition. In passing it on the street I often peeped into its spacious windows, and looked down the row of its gentlemanly and elegantly dressed colored clerks, with the pens behind their ears and buttonhole bouquets in their coat-fronts, and felt my very eyes enriched. It was a sight I had never expected to see. I was amazed with the facility with which they counted the money. They threw off the thousands with the dexterity, if not the accuracy, of old and experienced clerks. The whole thing was beautiful.[H14]

As he peers in through the windows of the bank, Douglass is sold a vision of the freedmen's promise beyond what even he had speculated. It is what Douglass has longed for but "never expected to see": "I felt my very eyes enriched." Douglass's subjective response to the bank, in contrast to the bank's actual insolvency, points to perhaps the most vulnerable chink in his program of material progress: real estate is always speculative and in that sense, it can never be "real." As one critic of the bank put it: "A man having property in a town like this or any other is very apt to believe that it is worth more than anybody else supposes it is, and he is imagining constantly that he is getting rich by the increase of the value of his property."[H15]

In 1876 the trustees of the bank bought a ten-acre property from the bankrupt, and segregationist, developer of Uniontown, a neighborhood in Washington. One year later, they sold the property to Frederick Douglass.[H16] Douglass turned the estate into an ironic challenge to the racism inherent in the demise of the Freedman's Bank, and, more largely, of radical Reconstruction. Douglass's estate serves as a summation of his materialist campaign and his own speculation in the future of an interracial American domestic space.

๑ ๑ ๑

In point of residential rights and privileges in the city of Washington, all Americans are created equal . . . the rights and immunities of the National Capital are no longer limited by reason of race, color or previous condition of servitude. . . . No American is now too black to call Washington his home, and no American is so mean as to deny him that right. —FREDERICK DOUGLASS, 1875[1]

Frederick Douglass's glowing portrait of Washington, following its passage of a local civil rights bill in 1875, does not reflect the city's social reality so much as it tries to create it. Despite the passage of several far-reaching civil rights bills, Washington's upper classes maintained a strict social and physical distance between themselves and the city's growing black population.[2] In his editorial, which appeared on the front page of the city's liberal newspaper, Douglass attempts to clinch the new bill's promised gains. He equalizes the city's population by referring to all of its citizens, black and white, as simply "Americans," while he shames any "mean"-spirited citizens into abiding by the new law. But Douglass does not rely only upon his rhetoric to redefine Washington as the place where, at last, all Americans are created equal; he indirectly encourages African Americans to make Washington their home.

During Reconstruction, Washington led the nation in local civil rights legislation, making it, for Douglass, "the most luminous point of American territory."[3] Thousands moved to the city—abolitionists, rebels, and, above all, freedmen—to have a hand in the nation's reconstruction. The city's associations with Lincoln and Emancipation suggested that in Washington the nation's republican values would at last be fulfilled. While the new place that freedmen might hold in the nation's social and political landscape was debated, Douglass himself speculated heavily in Washington real estate. His numerous properties included a large home on Capitol Hill (occupied by his children) and the impressive estate where he lived the last fifteen years of his life, located on a high hill overlooking the Capitol.[4] Douglass bought these properties, I shall argue here, not simply because real estate was the most feasible form of investment for African Americans.[5] Rather, as Douglass's speculative portrait of Washington suggests, each civil rights law opened up a space to African Americans that, if it were not physically seized, might be lost. Through his properties, Douglass puts forth a new social landscape, one that fully integrates public and private, law and custom, whites and blacks.

During the early years of Reconstruction, Republicans yoked demands for land reform to those for black suffrage. Both measures were held to be indispensable for securing political power. According to Senator Thaddeus Stevens, only if the physical landscape of the nation were altered—if southern plantations were confiscated and broken up into homesteads for landless ex-slaves—would the nation at last become, "as it has never been, a true republic." Black suffrage was won in 1870. As controversial as that measure was, land confiscation plans proved to be beyond the pale of legislation altogether, and no significant land reform measure ever succeeded.[6] The lack of enforcement and eventual defeat of most of Washington's integration laws would seem to bear out the insufficient force of words alone against racist customs and beliefs.

The disappointments of Reconstruction help account for a dominant theme of Douglass's late career: "Accumulate property," he preached to his listeners. At his death in 1895, Douglass's own estate was worth $100,000, the equivalent of roughly $1.5 million today.[7] This foundation to Douglass's lofty rhetoric has been overlooked. One critic specifically lauds Douglass for being a "spiritual prophet" and not a materialist:

Observing that Douglass (unlike Booker T. Washington) "built no institutions and laid no material foundations . . . no showy tabernacles of clay," [Kelley] Miller argued that "the greatest things of this world are not made with hands, but reside in truth and righteousness and love." The true lesson of Douglass's life lay in his love of liberty, his courage, and what Miller rightly judges to be the transcendent dimension of his life: "Douglass was the moral leader and spiritual prophet of his race."[8]

Yet other critics cite the self-promotion and bootstrap rhetoric of Douglass's Washington years as evidence of the degree to which he had lost touch with his people and betrayed the radicalism of his abolitionist career. As George Fredrickson contends, "the last twenty years . . . of Douglass's life was a relatively ineffectual and uncreative period" offering "no new strategy or insight."[9] Yet what might appear as the best proof of Douglass's co-optation—his amassing of property—uncovers new information that makes possible a reassessment of his entire career. Douglass's eloquent properties show that his materialism was certainly highly creative, if only partly effective.

Trailblazing

For Douglass, racial equality boiled down to the very concrete problem of access. He accordingly fashioned himself as a trailblazer: "I have been the thin edge of the wedge to open for my people a way in many directions and places never before occupied by them."[10] His autobiographies (he wrote three) recount numerous incidents of transgression by which he tested the extent to which the social landscape could be reformed. Was color prejudice, as Lincoln had warned, an irreversible fact? Through his stories of conquest, Douglass seems out to prove that there is no hotel and no restaurant that can withstand the almost physical force of his rhetoric and wit. In his second autobiography, *My Bondage and My Freedom,* he writes: "Some people will have it that there is a natural, an inherent, an invincible repugnance in the breast of the white race toward dark-colored people; and some very intelligent colored men think that their proscription is owing solely to the color which nature has given them . . . my experience, both serious and mirthful, combats this conclusion."[11] Separate cars on trains for "colored travelers" were adopted in New England in 1843, while Douglass was living in Lynn, Massachusetts. "Regarding this custom as fostering the spirit of caste," Douglass "made it a rule to seat myself in the cars for the accommodation of passengers generally," and for this he was often beaten and dragged off trains. Douglass tells of one such "incident," which occurred while he was "attempting" to travel from Lynn to Newburyport:

I went, as my custom was, into one of the best railroad carriages on the road. The seats were very luxuriant and beautiful. I was soon waited upon by the conductor, and ordered out; whereupon I demanded the reason for my invidious removal. After a good deal of parleying, I was told that it was because I was black. This I denied, and appealed to the company to sustain my denial; but they were evidently unwilling to commit themselves, on a point so delicate, and requiring such nice powers of discrimination, for they remained as dumb as death. I was soon waited on by half a dozen fellows of the baser sort, (just such as would volunteer to take a bulldog out of a meeting-house in time of public worship), and told that I must move out of that seat, and if I did not, they would drag me out. I refused to move, and they clutched me, head, neck and shoulders. But in anticipation of the stretching to which I was about to be subjected, I had interwoven myself among the seats. In dragging me out, on this occasion, it must have cost the company twenty-five or thirty dollars, for I tore up seats and all. So great was the excitement in Lynn, on the subject, that the superintendent . . . ordered the trains to run through Lynn without stopping, while I remained in that town.

Douglass adds as a postscript, "After many battles with the railroad conductors, and being roughly handled in not a few instances, proscription was at last abandoned." The pressure of the "people" and the bill introduced by Charles Francis Adams, Henry Adams's father, in the Massachusetts State Legislature eventually finished the work Douglass had begun.[12]

Douglass's account interweaves material and rhetorical gains. Possession is the first step to defeating color prejudice: "The only way you can make yourself respected is to get something somebody else wants," Douglass would later insist.[13] By taking a prohibited seat in the white car, Douglass creates a chance to prove his racial equality; riding in the Jim Crow car offers no such chance, since it already establishes his inferior status. Instead of being thus silenced, Douglass silences the conductor, through his disarming claim that he is not black. The conductor resorts to force, but here, too, the Samson-like Douglass wins. Legislation follows to secure the social territory first gained by Douglass's necessary trespass.

The artful presentation of this tale stresses the importance of the actual seat itself. Douglass sets us up for the conclusion of the story by focusing on the seats at the start, which were "very luxuriant and beautiful." Douglass paid for his seat. If the train master will deprive him of one, he will deprive the train of one as well. The "cost" of denying Douglass a seat is measured triumphantly in "real" terms: it "must have cost them upwards of thirty dollars," a significant sum in 1843. By physically "interweaving" himself with the actual seat, Douglass proves that even it, and the social hierarchy it represents, can be unfixed.

The incident reveals on Douglass's part a seemingly unbeatable strategy, whereby he physically forces racial prejudice out into the open and then, through his gentlemanly diction and conquering wit, dismantles it beyond repair. By sitting in the sacred space of the white railroad car (likened to a "meeting house" of worship), Douglass hits a nerve and produces the desired response in the conductor. The conductor must defend the irrational position that a man with money enough should be deprived of a seat because he is black—something that the conductor's "parleying" shows he is reluctant to do. Douglass even rejects the authority of the conductor to decide that Douglass is black. The entire passage gains force from the contrast between the elevated diction and the disconcertingly brutal scene it blithely depicts. So, too, Douglass's power is enhanced by the incongruous combination of his gentlemanly bearing and his amazing strength, an attribute that, ironically, points to his days as a slave. It was under the hated overseer Covey, Douglass tells us, that he grew strong.

Gaining access to white society's sacred sites became one of Douglass's first occupations, and he did not stop at the "most luxurious" train cars. During his extensive travels on behalf of the abolitionist cause, Douglass noted that while his white colleagues were ready to associate with him in public spaces, some were uneasy about having him in their homes; they could not bring themselves to offer Douglass a much-needed bed for the night. Douglass attributed his colleagues' reluctance to their being only "half-cured" of color prejudice; such a person indeed "is sometimes driven to awkward straits, especially if he happens to get a genuine specimen of the race into his house." In his autobiography, Douglass tells how he rid one "half-cured" abolitionist of his disease.[14]

He was traveling and lecturing in 1843 in Indiana with a friend, William White (who was, in fact, white). A family of abolitionists had "in the enthusiasm of the moment" offered Douglass and White a bed for the night, seeming, Douglass says, "to have forgotten they had but one spare bed," and that it was in the one bedroom of the house, where all of the family slept. That fact and the "idea of putting us [Douglass and White] in the same bed was hardly to be tolerated." Douglass lets the embarrassed confusion continue for a while, whereupon he takes matters into his own hands, by "playfully saying, 'Friend White, having got entirely rid of my prejudice against color, I think, as a proof of it, I must allow you to sleep with me tonight.'" According to Douglass, "White kept up the joke, by seeming to esteem himself the favored party, and thus the difficulty was removed."[15]

In his writings and speeches, Douglass portrays the home as a space of activism rather than retreat, a place to surface and challenge prejudice rather than hide and nurture it. As in the incident on the train, Douglass wins his way into the bedroom of the Indiana family by bringing the cause of the difficulty right out in the open and meeting it head on. Douglass disarms color prejudice by reversing its assumptions. It is not Douglass's black skin but his friend's white skin that is the problem, and hence it is Douglass who must overcome his color prejudice and permit his white friend to share a bed with him. By turning the problem on its head, Douglass shows how arbitrary and illogical color prejudice is, thereby taking control of the situation and of the bed. He has something White wants and thus acquires the power to bestow it: "After witnessing the confusion as long as I liked," Douglass decides to "relieve" his hosts. Douglass's status no longer depends upon his acceptance by his hosts; he is their equal, their superior even, because of his rhetorical brilliance and ingenious sense of humor.

Imbedded in this incident is Douglass's suggestion that it is only when different races can share without qualms the most intimate spaces that "colorphobia" is fully cured. When we think of civil rights movements, we think of gaining access to public spaces—to railway cars, buses, lunch counters, schools—but for Douglass the center of the struggle for racial equality was the home.

During Reconstruction, Douglass continued to keep the integration of private space at the center of his fight for racial equality. Douglass moved to Washington in 1872, in part to edit the *New National Era*. He reinforced this work with his properties. His Anacostia estate, for example, which he called "Cedar Hill," does not offer a black version of the sentimental middle-class home but a domesticity that is open, public, politically engaged, and racially integrated. After the death of his first wife in 1882, Douglass married a white woman. Through his estate, Douglass projects a prominent and irreproachable example of an integrated home.

"Open" Houses

Owning nothing was, Douglass suggests in his *Narrative* (1845), the very condition of slavery. Separated from their mothers at birth, subjected to the overexposure of plantation life—the lack of clothing, even in winter, the lack of privacy in the quarters—African Americans had lost the "natural" human connection to a secure and permanent home.[16] This loss only confirmed their social inferiority as less civilized people. Property offered a second skin, the very means by which Douglass's race could challenge any meaning ascribed to their first skin. But religion and the sins of slavery had taught his people to "despise wealth" and to instead look forward to a better home in the sky.[17] Douglass instead insisted, "We want natural things before we want the spiritual. When the child first comes into the world it don't cry for metaphysics or theology, but for a little milk. When I go to my bedroom I don't want to find a pane of glass out of the window and an old hat stuck in. What I want is a comfortable place to sleep. Take care of the body is what we need to be taught."[18] The old hat stuck in the window reflects the mindset of slavery; the tenant, used to exposure, makes due with a makeshift solution. As Gillian Brown has argued, "blackness was associated with an unstable domesticity."[19] Douglass exhorts his audience to think instead like owners. The window is a particularly sensitive site, for it not only lets in the weather but the view of the outside world as well. Fix the window, Douglass admonishes—what will the neighbors think? "Neither we, nor any other people, will ever be respected till we respect ourselves, and we will never respect ourselves till we have the means to live respectably."[20]

Owning property enables one to control how one is seen, as Douglass makes clear in a startling self-portrait in his *Narrative*. He reflects that had he not been sent to Baltimore as a boy, "I should have to-day, instead of being here seated by my own table, in the enjoyment of freedom and the happiness of home, writing this Narrative, been confined in the galling chains of slavery."[21] In the midst of his compelling tale, Douglass all of a sudden turns the camera on himself at work—"here" at *his* table. In doing so, he radically integrates the familiar image and voice of the gentleman of letters, the sentimental author extolling "the happiness of home," with that of a fugitive slave whose secret whereabouts now feel as if they have been exposed. In this way, Douglass exploits his exotic position while making himself seem terribly familiar—he is much like the reader, and it is only, hence, an accident of birth—of color prejudice—that deprived him of his natural position.

For Douglass, property is inseparable from authorship. It is not, then, enough to own property; one must use it to advertise oneself as literate. Douglass argues:

When I go into a colored man's house now when they used not to allow you to have books, I begin to want to see books lying around, I want to see papers there. I do not want it to be said if the whole negro race were blotted out there would be nothing left in two hundred years to tell they ever had any existence; that they never read any, never labored any, they never published any books or periodicals. . . . They used to say that of us, but this must not be said of us two hundred years hence.[22]

Douglass replaces the overexposure of slavery with a new kind of exposure, as he draws his socially marginalized audience into the circle of conspicuous consumption. But the only leisure Douglass cares to advertise is the leisure with which to write. Douglass's emphasis upon a literate decor argues that it is possessions that define social standing, and in this way he negates the importance of race. It is not that black skin was seen as inferior but that people with black skin were not associated with literacy.

In the passage above Douglass seems to position himself as an imperious voyeur, peering into black homes. The "old hat in the window" suggests that he knows how they live and expects better. He "want[s] to see books." But this opening up of private space to social scrutiny is essential to Douglass's radical domesticity. Slavery had shown the danger of homes protected from the enlightened gaze of public opinion. Indeed, one of the key strategies of the abolitionist movement had been to expose the hidden crimes of the slave plantations through slave narratives and books such as *Uncle Tom's Cabin*. As Douglass notes in *My Bondage and My Freedom*, "Public opinion is . . . an unfailing restraint upon the cruelty and barbarity of masters, overseers, and slave-drivers, whenever and wherever it can reach them; but there are certain secluded and out-of-the-way places, even in the state of Maryland . . . where slavery, wrapt in its own congenial, midnight darkness, can, and does, develop all its malign and shocking characteristics . . . without . . . fear of exposure." Hidden from the superego posed by the law, the id reigns supreme at the slave plantation, forming "a little nation of its own, having its own language, its own rules, regulations and customs. The laws and institutions of the state, apparently touch it nowhere. . . . The overseer is generally accuser, judge, jury, advocate and executioner."[23] Through the public gaze, Douglass plans to bring all citizens, white and black, into the national fold.

For Douglass, the material counterpart to these rhetorical exposés is the window, and windows are indeed crucial in his use of property. His homes suggest how he subjected his own family to public scrutiny in order to contradict preconceptions about race. In his house on Capitol Hill, for instance, Douglass added a large bay window within easy view of the street. He added two bay windows to the East Parlor at his Anacostia home, Cedar Hill; his irregularly shaped study there, open to the parlor and with no intervening door, is itself dominated by a large bay window. Douglass's predilection for this architectural feature deserves some attention.

Bay windows are exaggerated openings; they let in more light and more

of the outside world as they create a "bay," or reservoir of space and repose, right at the point where inside meets outside. The bays in the parlor
of Douglass's Anacostia home had window seats with cushions—they were
spaces for reading, writing, and intimate conversation. It is possible that he
gave his Capitol Hill bay window the same treatment. Bay windows thus
invite speculation in every sense of the word: one can look out, one can
think and dream, and one can promote a vision that will tempt passersby.
As shops use their large windows to display their best merchandise, Douglass put the intellectual and refined activities of his family out front.

A remark by Anna Murray Douglass, Douglass's first wife, who was far
more private than her husband, suggests that she perhaps thought her
house had become too public. Her daughter tells of a visit paid her mother
by some young women, who

> commenting on her spacious parlors and the approaching holiday season, thought
> it a favorable opportunity to suggest the keeping of an open house. Mother replied:
> "I have been keeping open house for several weeks. I have closed it now and I ex-
> pect to keep it closed." The young women, thinking mother's understanding was
> at fault, endeavored to explain. They were assured however that they were fully un-
> derstood. Father, who was present, laughingly pointed to the new bay window,
> which had been completed only a few days previous to their call.[24]

Could an "open house" be a home? Douglass's house on Capitol Hill and
his estate in Anacostia suggest that, even for Douglass, the answer was yes
and no.

Before considering Douglass's own experience with his strategy, however, we shall look at how it played out in Washington as a whole. As more
social spaces, such as restaurants and theaters, became opened up to African Americans, segregationists sought to close them and create instead a
separate space of unchallenged white supremacy. In some sense, the private, undemocratic "little nations" of slavery, condemned before the war,
became the model for the nation after the war.

Closed "Houses"

The work of turning Washington into an integrated home where all men
were created equal underwent gains and setbacks as segregationists sought
to redefine public space as private space. In 1872 Douglass's son Lewis, who
sat on the Washington City Council, successfully introduced a ground-

breaking local civil rights bill that prevented restaurants, bars, and hotels from denying service due to a person's "race, color, or previous condition of servitude." The law was tested by African Americans, who pressed charges against those establishments that refused to serve them. The first rulings upheld the law. But upon appeal, a judge ruled in the proprietors' favor, reasoning, "The proprietor of a hotel or a restaurant was the proper judge of who should have either refreshments or lodgings in his house, and no one could dispute his authority in that matter." The government could force a white person to share a trolley with a black person, but it could not force a white person to permit a black person into his home. Segregationists found a loophole by which to curtail civil rights laws—any distinction between public and private space was arbitrary and could be contested. What proponents of civil rights termed public spaces, because they were "theoretically open to the public," opponents termed privately owned "houses" that were hence closed to legislative intervention.[25] This judge's ruling proved Frederick Douglass right: a civil rights bill could not survive among a racist population. Social change had to begin in the home.

In 1883 the Supreme Court declared the national Civil Rights Act unconstitutional. Douglass portrayed the decision as an act of personal betrayal: "We have been, as a class, grievously wounded, wounded in the house of our friends, and this wound is too deep and too painful for ordinary and measured speech." The decision showed that it was indeed impossible to separate the private from the public. If the failed Civil Rights Act served, in Douglass's words, as "advance legislation," a vulnerable "banner on the outer wall of American liberty," Douglass's Washington properties offered a new set of strategies by which to change Americans, both inside and out.[26]

A Convention of Houses

[W]hite men are . . . in convention against us in various ways. . . . The practical construction of American life is a convention against us. Human law may know no distinction among men in respect of rights, but human practice may.[27] —FREDERICK DOUGLASS

Douglass began purchasing property while living in Rochester, New York. His pattern, which was not unusual, was to buy near or adjoining lots with the intention of consolidating the properties. A typical purchase was the three adjoining lots at the corner of Seventeenth and U Streets, N.W., in Washington, purchased by Douglass in 1876, upon which he built a row of three townhouses. In 1871, shortly after his move to Washington, Douglass bought a lot on Capitol Hill (316 A Street, N.E.) just three blocks from the Capitol, where he had his first Washington home. Two years later he bought the neighboring lot (318 A Street). At that time, Douglass also considered buying another set of three adjoining lots on East Capitol Street and Eighth Street, N.E., but the title proved to be defective. At his Anacostia residence, Douglass purchased the lot adjoining his (adding five acres to his original ten-acre lot) and held the mortgage on the other neighboring lot of eight acres.[28] Three of his properties in Washington suggest that Douglass, still acting as trailblazer, might be making the first or most impressive example of black domesticity in the blocks where he bought. Although Washington was not as segregated then as it would eventually become, there is evidence that Douglass encountered opposition to his purchasing both the Capitol Hill and Seventeenth and U Street properties, in the form of higher prices.[29] By owning several adjoining properties, a real estate speculator gains greater flexibility in developing the lots and makes the property that much more attractive to potential buyers.

But Douglass's strategy of consolidation and expansion had an activist component as well, as a photograph of the Douglass family taken in front of their A Street house suggests (fig. 3.1). The house was two separate houses until Douglass joined them into one double house. Douglass bought the house on the left (number 316) in 1871. He bought the adjoining lot on the right (318) in 1873. Douglass's treatment of the two lots shows that he did not simply add lots together but truly consolidated them, fusing much of their differences into a unified whole.[30] Interestingly, 318 was far less valuable than 316. By the time the photograph was taken, the gap in value between 316 and 318 had been greatly diminished, most likely due to Douglass's improvements to the second house.[31] The more prominent side is still 316; the bay window insures its dominance, along with the fact that the facade of 318 is slightly recessed. But the two properties share a fence, appear to be of the same color, and share the same treatment of windows on the second and third floors. Also, note that the photo is taken from across the street. A passerby standing on the sidewalk in front of the house would have a clear view into the bay window.

FIG. 3.1. Frederick Douglass (standing in front of right side of house) with his daughter Rosetta Sprague and her daughter, 316–318 A St., N.E. The other people cannot be identified. *FDRO 11001. W. W. Core, Photographer, c. 1876. Frederick Douglass National Historic Site.*

The most striking thing about the photograph is that the family "group" is spread across the entire space of their property. The women stand at the main entrance; their position leads the eye into the house itself and identifies them more closely with its interior. The men are placed across the front of the house. The first gentleman stands in front of the bay window, then Douglass, and then a third man, just barely in view, on the porch of 318. (The two other men are presumably Douglass's sons.)[32] The man on the porch of 318 brackets the family group, defining it according to the dimensions of their property. After all, the purpose of the photo is to show the house with its family, since we do not get a very good picture of the family itself. It is a picture, first and foremost, of their affluence. Douglass and the other male figure out on the right flank suggest further progress.

Douglass's curious position, alone in the center of 318 but turned slightly toward 316, identifies him with the main family group to the left but also as the "annexer," the one who is extending the money and property of the family while the women are home, minding the fort.

Just one month before purchasing 318 in October 1873, Douglass spoke on behalf of "Union and Improvement," an apt phrase by which to describe his treatment of his properties. In his speech, Douglass says African Americans must give "proof to the world" that, given a chance, they can improve their condition—that African Americans are not inherently slaves. For Douglass, the question boils down to "Whether the black man will prove a better master to himself than his white master was to him."[33] His properties give precisely such "proof"; the photograph of his family with their house is the picture of self-mastery.

Douglass, his properties confirm, is a most conservative speculator. He did not simply exhort his audience to acquire property but to "accumulate" it. Through consolidation, one builds upon the old, as 318 adds a second "story" to 316, to accommodate the next generation of Douglasses. We see this in his series of three autobiographies, where his second subsumes and recontextualizes the first, as his third again adds on to, and recontextualizes, the first two. This double urge toward the past and the future, toward home and expansionism, is conveyed by Douglass's position in the photograph: poised in the field of the added house, Douglass depicts his restlessness (as the trailblazer) and what he would call his "staying qualities." Black separatism, colonization—these were all cases of radical invention, ill-fated attempts to escape the past:

We should get married, rear children, love them, and secure a home. Let us have more staying qualities. Why, the negro spends nearly all his money buying railroad tickets. He won't stay in Chicago because it's too cold; he won't stay in Detroit because he can't get work. . . .There is too much moving about. . . .This is our home. Let us stay here. We won't go to Hayti, we won't go to Liberia, we won't go to Mexico. This country cannot get rid of us in that way. This country had our services when we were slaves, and now that we are free we will compel the government to make good citizens of us. . . . I have been insulted here on account of my color, but I mean to stay here to the end. I advise all my race to stay here also.[34]

Eschewing dramatic new beginnings in Haiti or Mexico, Douglass embraces a more conventional route: through the woman he has married, the money he has saved, and the property he has accumulated, he has increased the amount of space his family takes up—their numbers and their house proclaim that this African American family is here to stay. So, too, Douglass tells his life story again and again, increasing the amount of space it takes up on his reader's shelf, until what once might have seemed mainly exotic—the rise of a man from slavery to freedom and national eminence by his genius and his luck—becomes its own convention.

Cedar Hill

It is said that a house in some measure reflects the character of its occupants; [John Brown's house] certainly did. In it there were no disguises, no illusions, no make-believes. Everything implied stern truth, solid purpose, and rigid economy. —FREDERICK DOUGLASS, *Life and Times*, 272

In the West Parlor of Frederick Douglass's Anacostia home hung an engraving from *Othello* (fig. 3.2). When the Washington correspondent to the *Cincinnati Enquirer* visited the Douglass home in 1886, he called the engraving "the most suggestive thing in the room."[35] What are we to make of such an engraving there? Obviously, Douglass can be likened to Othello in many ways, including his experience of slavery and great professional success, as well as his marriage to a white woman.[36] More suggestive still, I think, is the insight that the engraving gives into Douglass's rhetorical use of physical space.

The picture shows Othello confidently and comfortably telling his life's story in the drawing room of Brabantio's home. Father and daughter sit, entranced. This scene does not actually occur on stage but is described by Othello. It was the effect of his life's story, not "some conjurations," that led Desdemona to fall in love with him:

> My story being done,
> She gave me for my pains a world of sighs.
> She swore, i' faith, 'twas strange, 'twas passing strange;
> 'Twas pitiful, 'Twas wondrous pitiful.
> She wished she had not heard it; yet she wished
> That heaven had made her such a man. She thanked me;
> And bade me, if I had a friend that loved her,
> I should but teach him how to tell my story
> And that would woo her . . .
>
> (I, iii, 158–66)[37]

FIG. 3.2. C. Becker, Othello engraving, c. 1880, Cedar Hill. *Frederick Douglass National Historic Site. Photograph by Bill Clark.*

The "strangeness" of Othello's tale, its juxtaposition of slavery and nobility, woos Desdemona. So, too, as we have seen, it is largely through Douglass's use of irony, of strange juxtapositions, that he conquers space. Elizabeth Cady Stanton similarly noted that Douglass's abolitionist speeches had "completely carried away his audience." By alternating "wit, satire, and indignation," Douglass made his listeners "laugh and [weep] by turns."[38]

Douglass bought his estate from a segregationist developer who had gone bankrupt. When the developer built the house, it was a testimony to white supremacy and racial difference: at the feet of his property spread the whites-only neighborhood—ironically called "Uniontown"—that he had developed.[39] Douglass uses the estate to make the opposite point. Throughout the property he argues that the distinctions "black" and "white" are not real or material but arbitrary. The estate makes what might seem strange—an ex-slave in a fine large house on a commanding prospect—look conventional.

At first glance, Douglass's house seems to be a rather straightforward bourgeois home in the country gothic style (fig. 3.3). That fact and its elevated site might simply suggest Douglass's rise from rags to riches and his

FIG. 3.3. Cedar Hill, Anacostia, Washington, D.C. *Frederick Douglass National Historic Site. Photograph by Bill Clark.*

assimilation into white bourgeois society. The house was, certainly, a conspicuous tribute to Douglass's own social ascent. But considered against Douglass's conquests of segregated spaces, as chronicled in his autobiographies, the home offers a direct challenge to segregationists who would divide the national landscape to solidify a racial hierarchy. The challenge that Douglass poses to the nation is underscored by the view from his front verandah. The city of Washington, with the Capitol in the foreground, spreads itself out at Douglass's feet. His position as the nation's overseer materializes the somewhat equivocal stance Douglass took toward the federal government: he wanted both to be rewarded by it (he was given three minor posts) and to judge it from on high. That an ex-slave would enjoy this prospect is doubly ironic, since perhaps the only other person to have possessed such a rare view of the capital from his front porch was Robert E. Lee.[40]

On his site, Douglass established the family home that slavery and racism had denied him. His sense of irony must also have been drawn to the house's resemblance in situation and architecture to a plantation home. The white columns, the verandah that extends the whole width of the house, and the commanding prospect recall essential features of Douglass's original plantation home, Colonel Lloyd's Wye House in nearby eastern Maryland: "The great house itself was a large, white, wooden building, with wings on three sides of it. In front, a large portico, extending the entire length of the building, and supported by a long range of columns, gave to the whole establishment an air of solemn grandeur."[41] Douglass developed Cedar Hill into a small plantation. The original property included the house and ten acres of land. Douglass doubled the size of the house and added five acres more to its property. He created extensive gardens and a woodland park—two features of Colonel Lloyd's estate that Douglass particularly admired. He built or remodeled at least seven outbuildings, including a carriage house, stables, servant quarters, and a strange structure that recalls a slave cabin.[42] But Douglass then reverses this familiar, color-coded landscape: he turns the "big house" into the rightful home of his black, maternal ancestry rather than that of his white, paternal ancestry. (Douglass didn't know who his father was but believed he was white; at one point he speculated that it was his master, Aaron Anthony.)[43] Similarly, Douglass turns the "slave" cabin into a gentleman's private study. Through his estate, Douglass reclaimed his original plantation home, altering its landscape, however, to accommodate himself as its master.

Through his name for the estate, Douglass redefines his black family's history from that of slaves to that of nobility. In his autobiographies, Douglass describes his mother as tall and dignified, and at one point he finds her likeness in a picture of an Egyptian pharaoh.[44] Similarly, his grandmother was "held in high esteem" and was privileged to live apart from the other slaves in a cabin that the young Douglass considered a "noble structure." The name Cedar Hill substantiates Douglass's claim to nobility. He named the estate not only for the cedars that surrounded his house but for his self-designated birthplace. In 1878, shortly after his purchase of Cedar Hill, Douglass revisited the site of his grandmother's cabin, where he had spent the first six years of his life, believing it to be the place where he was born.

The cabin had been destroyed by time but Douglass remembered, and found, a tall cedar that stood nearby, and this, Douglass ceremoniously proclaimed (he had brought witnesses), was his birthplace. As Douglass once remarked, "Genealogical trees do not flourish among slaves."[45] He makes up for this lack by inventing his own family tree, the cedar, a symbol for majesty. In the Bible, "cedars of Lebanon" attest to the majesty and omnipotence of God. In the nineteenth century, the term was used to describe someone as a pillar of the community, such as Douglass and his grandmother were.

Douglass gave material representation to this genealogy as well. When he visited the site of his grandmother's cabin, Douglass brought back some of the soil from the base of the cedar tree to Cedar Hill.[46] This gesture confirms that the name Cedar Hill is not a kind of personally coded oxymoron, ironically contrasting what Douglass called the "depths" from which he originated to the "heights" that he attained. Rather, through the name, the situation, and the soil of his estate, Douglass elevates his maternal ancestry to its proper social position, joining the two seemingly irreconcilable ends of his life—the cedar and the hill—into a structural whole. This presents Cedar Hill as an inherited family estate, rather than (as in a more conventional interpretation of it) the new acquisition of a self-made man. While the extremely long flight of steps leading from the street to Douglass's front door emphasizes his ascent from slavery to success, it may also be seen to heighten the ceremony with which Douglass restores his maternal heritage to its proper place (fig. 3.4).

The strange cabin that Douglass had built behind the big house suggests the impossibility of making meaningful distinctions based upon race (figs. 3.5 and 3.6). Like many slave cabins, the structure (a reproduction of which still stands today) is composed of one small room, roughly ten by twelve feet; it has no windows and only one low doorway and a fireplace for light. In this unlikely space Douglass put a desk, chair, bookshelf, and lounge; this was his retreat when he wished to work in peace.[47] Douglass's placement of a lounge and a desk in a space that, when associated with slavery, offered little leisure to a reputedly illiterate people fits with his penchant for radical inversions. Such furniture challenges the assumption that all slaves, and blacks generally, were illiterate. Douglass stresses the fact that his mother taught herself, "against all odds," to read, and that it was, he writes, "not to my admitted Anglo-Saxon paternity, but to the native

FIG. 3.4. Cedar Hill, street level view. *Frederick Douglass National Historic Site. Photograph by Bill Clark.*

genius of my sable . . . uncultivated mother" that credit went for his love of letters.[48] The cabin symbolizes this bequest.

Of course, if we forget that Douglass was "black" and think of him simply as an American writer, then we can recognize the cabin as a more familiar literary retreat.[49] Made of stone and picturesquely covered with flowering vines, the cabin evokes the rustic cottage of the romantics, while its spare roughness suggests Thoreau's cabin at Walden. Douglass's name for his retreat—"The Growlery"—suggests a lion's den, but the *Oxford English Dictionary* traces the name to Dickens, and it indeed refers to a gentleman's study. In *Bleak House,* a character shows his study to a guest: "this as you must know is my Growlery, when in bad humor I come here to growl." Douglass creates a structure that integrates these seemingly incongruous sources and thus eludes labeling as black or white, African or European.

As such, the Growlery again frustrates what Douglass sees as a peculiarly American obsession with pigeonholing things in terms of race. When Americans hear of an unknown person, Douglass observes, "The first question that arises in the average American mind concerning him and which must be answered is, Of what color is he? and he rises or falls in estimation by

FIG. 3.5. The Growlery, Cedar Hill, c. 1893.

the answer given. . . . Hence I have often been bluntly . . . asked . . . in what proportion does the blood of the various races mingle in my veins? . . . Whether I derived my intelligence from my father, or from my mother, from my white, or from my black blood?"[50]

The interior decor of Douglass's home answers the question Douglass wanted asked about a man: it documents Douglass's principles rather than his genetic make-up. Lacking conventional family heirlooms, Douglass displays pictures and heirlooms of abolitionists, both white and black; these crowd the walls and shelves of his home, constituting a moral, political family for Douglass rather than a genealogical one. To these people, Douglass said, who were "ready to own me as a . . . brother against all the scorn . . . of a slavery-polluted atmosphere, I owe my success in life."[51] Among those on the long list of people represented in this family portrait gallery are Wendell Phillips, William Lloyd Garrison, Blanche K. Bruce (the black U.S. senator), Rev. Henry Highland Garnet (the ex-slave and outspoken reformer and abolitionist), Elizabeth Cady Stanton, and Susan B. Anthony. If Douglass's mix of black and white blood would have seemed strange to some at the time, it certainly becomes more natural in the biracial pantheon of his home.

As the exterior of Cedar Hill integrates the plantation, so its interior in-

FIG. 3.6. The Growlery, modern-day restoration. *Frederick Douglass National Historic Site. Photograph by Bill Clark.*

tegrates the bourgeois American family home. Abolitionist souvenirs take their place beside more conventional bourgeois objects. Figure 3.7 shows one end of the East Parlor. The table in the foreground belonged to civil rights advocate and U.S. senator Charles Sumner, and it was purchased by Douglass at an auction following Sumner's death. The bust to the right is of abolitionist Wendell Phillips, one of three representations of Phillips in the house. The bust exemplifies the decor's conflation of visionary politics and gentility. Phillips is given a conventional classical treatment, despite his very radical views against capitalism and its "enslavement" of the laboring class. Across from Phillips is a large portrait of Douglass. Giving these politically loaded furnishings a more conventional look is the wallpaper and border, the Brussels lace curtains, the statue of Venus, the small bust on

FIG. 3.7. East Parlor, front, Cedar Hill. *Frederick Douglass National Historic Site. Photograph by Bill Clark.*

the mantle, and the various landscape paintings (fig. 3.8). The rocker is from Haiti, a gift to Douglass while he served as the U.S. minister to that country. Its back and seat are of tooled leather, and the wooden sides are carved with medallions depicting figures of black men, while the lace anti-macassar helps to conventionalize this conversation piece. If one looks directly into the mirror above the fireplace, one sees a reflection of the portrait of Lincoln hanging directly across in the West Parlor.

The West Parlor continues the eclectic decor (fig. 3.9). Here is the piano, the essential feature of a middle-class home. On top of it is Hiram Powers's symbolically complex statue of a Greek slave. This neoclassical statue reminds us that blacks were not the only ones to have been enslaved, but it also serves as an allegory of democracy: the chains of slavery, modestly placed across the woman's genitals, are also chains of chastity and symbolize the self-restraint necessary to self-government. The statue, thus, is another of Douglass's unexpected rhetorical inversions. Because of their history of enslavement, African Americans were thought by some to be incapable of self-government and hence should be denied the vote. Powers's statue instead suggests that ex-slaves might be better prepared to meet the demands of an ideal democratic government, having learned to sacrifice their own immediate desires for a higher goal (such as freedom) and the

FIG. 3.8. East Parlor, rear. Cedar Hill. *Frederick Douglass National Historic Site. Photograph by Bill Clark.*

common good. To the right of the statue, on the easel, is another portrait of Phillips, and behind him on the wall hangs a portrait of General Dumas, father of the writer Alexandre Dumas (who was part black), and a picture of President Hippolyte of Haiti, out of view directly beneath. Figure 3.9 gives a view into the dining room, with its solid oak dining table, butler's table, sideboard, and good china displayed there.

The eclectic decor redefines the American family to accord with Douglass's vision of what he termed a "composite [American] nationality."[52] It is a family of both races, joined not only by principles and ideals but by marriage—joined, in other words, not simply in the public sphere but in the home. To the many who criticized Douglass's marriage to a white woman, these virtuous and refined surroundings defend his act as perfectly natural—a fulfillment of the belief in racial equality.

The idealism of Douglass's estate contrasts with the innumerable obstacles the new class of freedmen encountered in their efforts to save money and acquire property during Reconstruction. Perhaps the most sensational tragedy was the collapse of the Freedman's Savings and Trust Company, to which many African Americans had been lured into entrusting their savings. As its temporary director, Douglass himself oversaw the dismantling

FIG. 3.9. West Parlor, Cedar Hill. *Frederick Douglass National Historic Site. Photograph by Bill Clark.*

of the bank. Even those African Americans who achieved bourgeois life-styles still found themselves excluded from the social and political life of the nation, and Douglass himself probably chafed at never being offered an important government post. Anyone who entered into the system of conspicuous consumption made themselves vulnerable to the volatile fluc-tuations of public opinion and the real estate market; African Americans made themselves doubly so.[53]

Douglass's own life even conflicted with the political vision he projects at Cedar Hill. By the time he honored his abolitionist friends through de-pictions in his home, Douglass had, in fact, fallen out to some degree with almost all of them.[54] And despite his reported fondness for the estate, Douglass himself suggested that it did not quite succeed. At the end of his life, he wrote to an old friend, "For these past fifteen years I have had no constant abiding place—been 'a stranger and sojourner as all my fathers were.'"[55] Douglass's children certainly did not embrace his domestic plan—they deeply resented his second wife, both for her youth and her race. Douglass willed the estate to Helen rather than to them, whereupon they sued her for its possession. Helen purchased the house from Doug-lass's children to preserve it as a monument to her husband and racial equal-

FIG. 3.10 Frederick Douglass in his study at Cedar Hill, c. 1890. *FRDO 3886. Frederick Douglass National Historic Site.*

ity, or in her words, as the "Mt. Vernon of the colored race." Cedar Hill is now owned by the National Park Service.[56] Its surrounding neighborhood is almost entirely black and is isolated from Washington's federal core.

I have attributed Douglass's reconstruction of his house to his rhetorical skill, marked by his signature ironic wit. I conclude with an image of the literary genius that animates the house: it is another portrait of Douglass at work, this time in his library at Cedar Hill (fig. 3.10). Like the house, the image is a conscious, posed autobiographical statement. (Notice, for instance, the contrived inclusion of Douglass's violin, which is exhibited to his right on his desk.) Douglass pretends not to see the photographer, who seems to have caught him "unawares." He is busy with his writing, surrounded by books and intellectual clutter; the doors of the bookcase are open, signifying that its contents are in use. Douglass, the cultured man of letters, turns his back on racial definition. Rather than his face, and the color of his skin, we see only his white head of hair. Douglass does not hide behind his white hair; rather the image eludes the question of race altogether. It defines Douglass by his books, his prosperity, his occupation, his hat, his home.

Chapter 4

DEMOCRACY'S CHURCH

The Hay-Adams Houses during the Gilded Age

HEADNOTE: *Speculation in the Gilded Age*

Early in his career, Henry Adams became a historian of what in 1862 was claimed to be "the greatest era of speculation the world has ever seen."[H1] In his essay "The New York Gold Conspiracy" (1870), a discussion of the rise and fall of Jay Gould, Adams suggests that no one was immune to speculation fever: "Not only in Broad Street, the center of New York speculation, but far and wide throughout the Northern States, almost every man who had money at all employed a part of his capital in the purchase of stocks or of gold, of copper, of petroleum, or of domestic produce, in the hope of a raise in prices, or staked money on the expectation of a fall."[H2] Adams himself succumbed and invested in copper.[H3]

In the world of speculation, value was volatile, and Adams warned that it rested more on fiction than on substance: "Stock was almost exclusively held for speculation, not for investment; and in the morals of Wall Street speculation means, or had almost come to mean, disregard of intrinsic value. In this case society at large was the injured party, and society knew its risks."[H4] Jay Gould made no effort to deny the source of his railroad's "actual value": "There is no intrinsic value to it probably; it is speculated in here and in London and it has that value."[H5]

In *The Gilded Age* (1876), which includes a biting portrait of post–Civil War Washington, Mark Twain and Charles Dudley Warner show how Wall Street's fictitiousness spread to the capital. In their Washington, the city is overrun by greedy speculators promoting schemes that come to little more than a chance to make, or lose, money. An appropriations bill for internal improvements to launch a new town gets spent on buying votes for support of the bill and promotion for the new town. There is no money left to pay for the new roads and improve the river.[H6] Edward Chancellor notes the truth in Twain and Warner's attack: "The corruption of speculation was not limited to company promoters and stock operators; it infected the entire political class in the 1860s (even three decades later, the "reforming" President Grover Cleveland was implicated in a stock market pool ...)."[H7]

The novel's most famous character, Colonel Beriah Sellers, is a grand schemer, and in Washington, Sellers feels right at home:

He was now at the centre of the manufacture of gigantic schemes, of speculation of all sorts, of political and social gossip. The atmosphere was full of little and big rumors and of vast, undefined expectations. Everybody was in haste, too, to push on his private plan, and feverish in his haste, as if in constant apprehension that to-morrow would be Judgment day ...

The Colonel enjoyed this bustle and confusion amazingly; he thrived in the air of indefinite expectation. All his own schemes took larger shape and more misty and majestic proportions; and in this congenial air, the Colonel seemed even to himself to expand into something large and mysterious.[H8]

The *Gilded Age* uses its dark humor to claim that the city of Washington has given up on good home values and sold itself in the unrestrained pursuit of greed. The fact that what was to be a model city has been turned around by the very sorts of speculators George Washington feared, those who put self-interests before national ones, is dramatized by the Capitol building itself. The novel raises one of the city's most obvious mysteries—why is the back of the Capitol so often treated as its front? (We now even hold the presidential inauguration at the back of the Capitol, facing the Mall, rather than on its front, eastern steps, as was done in Twain's day.) As Twain and Warner put it, "the front [of the Capitol] looks out over this noble situation for a city—but it doesn't see it." They charge that once the need for land to make a fine neighborhood in front of the Capitol was known

the property owners at once advanced their prices to such inhuman figures that the people went down and built the city in the muddy low marsh *behind* the temple of liberty, so now the lordly front of the building, with its imposing colonnades, its projecting, graceful wings, its picturesque groups of statuary, and its long terraced ranges of steps, flowing down in white marble waves to the ground, merely looks out upon a sorrowful little desert of cheap boarding houses.[H9]

Adams's satire *Democracy* (1880) presents only a slightly less scathing view of the capital, and the novel can be read as the political sequel to "The New

York Gold Conspiracy." Adams's Washington is beyond hope of reform. His idealist heroine, Madeleine Lee, at the end turns her back on the capital and retreats to Virginia. Just prior to publishing the novel, Adams suggested that he too would no longer make a concerted effort for political reform. He had tried to influence the presidential election of 1876 and had lost. He would retreat to the quieter life of history writing and house building. After 1876, Adams embarked on two building projects, a vacation home and a house in Washington on Lafayette Square. In fact, Adams built his house on the spot where Madeleine Lee had lived. *Democracy,* and other texts by Adams as well, speculates upon a new political ground, one that in fact he would not abandon. When Madeleine Lee moved out, Adams moved in.

For George Washington it was of crucial importance to the capital's success that its investors would not only buy and trade its lots but develop them and ideally live on them. The city was not about making capital but building a capital. At the end of the nineteenth century, Adams embraces that project. He buys his lot and develops it, both financially and politically. For all of his New England pedigree, Adams becomes a Washingtonian.

o o o

Inside 1603 H Street between the years 1885 and 1918, one might well have found Henry Adams sitting in his study at his enormous desk playing with magnets. The desk had been specially designed for this obsession: it measured five by seven feet and had wide drawers to hold the large pieces of paper that he covered with iron filings.[1] In *The Education of Henry Adams* (1918), Adams describes himself, the amateur philosopher of science, at work:

> He knew not in what new direction to turn, and sat at his desk, idly pulling threads out of the tangled skein of science, to see whether or why they allied themselves. The commonest and oldest toy he knew was the child's magnet, with which he had played since babyhood, the most familiar of puzzles. He covered his desk with magnets, and mapped out their lines of force by compass. Then he read all the books he could find, and tried in vain to make his lines of force agree with theirs.

From all his "maps" of magnetism, Adams fails to arrive at one definitive image of how and why magnetism—"literally the most concrete fact in nature, next to gravitation"—works. On the same desk, Adams pursues his "scientific history," whereby he tries to chart the sequence of "natural forces" that drove the political events of this nation's past. This experiment also fails: the "old roads" of history "ran about in every direction, over-running, dividing, subdividing, stopping abruptly, vanishing slowly, with side-paths that led nowhere, and sequences that could not be proved."[2] Discovering that he cannot determine the source of magnetism or historic events leads Adams to the appreciation of another magnetic force—mystery. Adams's work suggests that mystery is a force he *does* understand, because he uses it to help turn himself, a self-described "failure," into a success.

At the heart of Adams's manipulation of mystery is his appreciation for and creation of paradoxes. For instance, in his self-portrait of himself at work, Adams uses his failure to enhance his authority: by putting himself down (he is only "playing" with a "child's toy"; he is befuddled), he raises himself up (he admits the truth, while others distort it). Adams is a man of leisure who has the time and freedom to consider events more fully, and he alone, we might conclude, is the person who can arrive at a form of history roomy enough to be able to acknowledge and trace the wild swings of human experience. Such a form would preserve the mysteries and paradoxes of human behavior; like the mysterious magnet, such a history would have great intellectual force. In this chapter I will trace how Adams experimented with such a form, and how he gave it material expression as well. In his self-portrait lie the principles behind the blueprint for the house in which this portrait takes place, the house Adams built in Washington, D.C.

Adams makes a fitting conclusion to this study because he offers an end-of-the century critique of where we began—with the idealistic attempt by Washington and L'Enfant to build a new national political landscape. Both Adams's drawing and L'Enfant's plan for a new capital are, in their way, maps of "lines of force." At the center of Adams's map is the secret, impenetrable mystery of nature and human actions; at the center of L'Enfant's map is a rational plan of balanced government to be realized by the energy of an expanded marketplace. Adams's design asserts the powerlessness of human reason over natural force. L'Enfant's design asserts that reason's design, when circulated through the marketplace, could itself become a powerful force. Thus the new capital's dazzling national vision would attract citizens and overwhelm their ties to their hometowns. One hundred years later Adams saw how that "commercial republic" had failed. Monied interests—what was just beginning to be called "business"—had overwhelmed national politics and republican idealism. In response, Adams devises a more practical and far less ambitious design.

On Lafayette Square, directly across from the White House, Adams designed his own political landscape as the antidote to Washington's ills. While the capital favored the gigantic and the extensive, Adams's house is built on both a massive and a diminutive scale. While Washington's buildings and roads stressed access, openness, and empowerment, Adams's house stresses exclusivity, privacy, passivity, and mystery. While Washington was to be magnetized by the force of the speculative marketplace, Adams instead turns to the mysterious force of religion.

Adams thus fits into the tradition outlined in this study of a speculative national domesticity, in that he, most concretely of all, builds a model of his political vision to advance his program for reform. As with the other cases studied here, Adams's physical model augments the power of his written works, which to his mind would never be adequately understood. The work of building offered a way to redress what William Decker has described as "Adams's increasingly fragile enterprise as an author . . . to publish . . . the text of a redeemable America . . . or to find a readership willing to espouse it."[3] Adams's house would transcend the limits of reformist prose and make the power of his paradoxical views concrete. H. H. Richardson, Adams's architect, reassured Adams of his house that "people will not know it, but they will *feel* it."[4]

Adams's building project is further inspired by its intensely personal nature. Through it he restores his family home at the center of Washington. In the *Education,* Adams relates that the political ascendancy of his family had been thwarted by the "machine politics" of the party system—because of it, they had lost their lease to the White House. "As for the White House, all the boy's family had lived there, and barring the eight years of Andrew Jackson's reign, had been more or less at home there ever since it was built. The boy half thought he owned it, and took for granted that he should some day live in it."[5] Henry's father, Charles Francis Adams, was frustrated in his two attempts to regain the presidency occupied by his father and grandfather. Statesmanship—an almost genetic disposition toward reasoned leadership—was, it seemed, no longer valued. Power was bought, traded, and sold, brokered by speculators and party bosses whose own volatile political fortunes mirrored the unpredictable surge and crash of the marketplace.

Characteristically, Adams turns his family's political failure into the occasion for his own successful career, as he builds another place of influence for himself on Lafayette Square. By his own account, the presidency holds no interest for him; he opts for what he deems the more strategic post of political critic. Recounting his idea to write "a permanent series of annual political reviews," he explains:

he hoped to make [them], in time, a political authority. With his sources of information, and his social intimacies at Washington, he could not help saying something that would command attention. He had the field to himself, and he meant to give himself a free hand, as he went on. Whether the newspapers liked it or not, they would have to reckon with him; for such a power, once established, was more effective than all the speeches in Congress or reports to the President that could be crammed into the government presses.

Henry Adams never held any position in the national government. But his house supplied the superior position he had already carved out for himself as a critical outsider in the heart of Washington, D.C. As Adams reports in the *Education:* "To the house on Lafayette Square Adams must return. He had no other status, no position in the world."[6] From this strategic vantage point, Adams mounts an offensive against the executive across the way.

Washington at the end of the nineteenth century might have inspired an observer less cynical than Adams to argue that L'Enfant's plan for a magnificent capital city had succeeded. After the Civil War, the population of the city rose 75 percent to 131,720, reflecting the influx of freed African Americans to the city as well as the tremendous expansion of government during the war. By 1890 the city's population had increased to 230,392, and the number of federal jobs had gone from 13,000 to 20,000.[7] Such growth spurred a period of immense development in Washington. Industrialists built homes there in order to have closer access to political power, and Washington became "a sort of winter Newport" whose "social season was equaled in splendor only by that of New York." Large mansions were built along the city's wide avenues and statue-studded circles. It was a "golden age . . . of improvement," when many talented architects lived in the capital city, enjoying a steady flow of work.[8]

In his portrait of Washington in *Democracy* (1880), his satire of Washington politics, Adams, however, derides the city's "incoherent ugliness."[9] Its failed monumentalism is summed up by the stump of the Washington Monument, begun in 1848 and still less than half finished in 1880, stalled by political controversy and lack of funds.[10] (The monument was finally completed in 1885.) From the start, Adams complains that the capital had lacked the faith to fulfill itself: The "Capitol threatened to crumble in pieces and crush Senate and House under the ruins, long before the building was complete," the result of a "government capable of sketching a magnificent plan, and willing to give only a half-hearted pledge for its fulfillment."[11]

Adams's study of Chartres cathedral would lead him to suggest that only the superhuman force of religious devotion could build something truly great. He quotes an account that tells how princes as well as commoners joined together to haul huge loads of stone. Sometimes "a thousand persons and more are attached to the chariots,—so great is the difficulty," and yet their work is made light by their religious fervor. "When they halt on the road, nothing is heard but the confession of sins, and pure and suppliant prayer to God," and this uplifts them so that their "march is made with such ease that no obstacle can retard it." The French citizens bowed themselves in devotion to Mary and were empowered by it, Adams claims: "At Chartres, one sees everywhere the Virgin, and nowhere any rival authority; one sees her give orders and architects obey them."[12]

Adams's fascination with Chartres carries a wistful note of achievements beyond the possibility of American ideas. Bound by their belief in rational self-government, Americans were ignorant of the greater power unleashed by the mysteries of religious devotion. Instead of a National Church, Americans had built the Patent Office, a shrine to technological invention and progress. This seemed to be the nation's most animating force, but Adams argues that while friends such as Augustus Saint-Gaudens "felt a railway-train as power; yet they and all other artists constantly complained that the power embodied in a railway-train could never be embodied in art. All the steam in the world could not, like the Virgin, build Chartres."[13]

In the following I analyze the alternative site of power that Henry Adams constructed amidst the corruption of Washington, D.C., and the house that he built there. Between that house and his writings there exists a relationship, I shall argue, not unlike the one that Adams draws between the *Chanson de Roland* and the abbey at Mont Saint Michel: "The Poem and the Church are akin; they go together, and explain each other," and later, "Verse by verse, the song was a literal mirror of the Mount."[14] In *Democracy* Adams arrives at the precise site for his political challenge; in his second novel, *Esther* (1884), he names the architect and style. Through these two novels, Adams draws the plans for a church of democracy. There he

could make the attraction of mystery and paradox—the success of his failure, the activism of his repose—felt.

An Interior Politics

In 1883 Adams and his wife, Marian ("Clover"), worked closely with the architect H. H. Richardson on the design of a double house to be built on
Lafayette Square, directly across from the White House (fig. 4.1). The
smaller of the two houses was for the Adamses, and the larger and much
grander house next door was for their best friend, the statesman-poet-
historian John Hay, and his family. Together, the houses were for Adams
"a vast pile, glaring into the White House windows."[15] (Hay's house, in
fact, faced the room he had occupied in the White House while serving
as private secretary to Abraham Lincoln.) The Hay-Adams houses modeled a union of politics and reflection. In his house, John Hay completed
his ten-volume *Abraham Lincoln: A History* and served as secretary of state
under Presidents McKinley and Roosevelt. In his house, Adams finished
his nine-volume *History of the United States,* wrote *Mont Saint Michel and
Chartres* and *The Education of Henry Adams,* and carried on his active career
as a "companion to statesmen" through his literary salon and legendary
breakfasts, which formed one of the "important nerve centers of the diplo-
matic corps."[16] Together, the houses describe what I will call an "interior
politics"—a politics of deep, reflective discussion in the informal privacy of
one's home among an intimate circle drawn together by shared aesthetic
and moral values. This circle did not organize itself into a political party;
instead, transcending party lines, it was a kind of anti-party—an exclusive
literary salon quite in contrast to the "exterior" politics modeled by the
party-dominated White House.

I derive my term "interior politics" from Henry James's characteriza-
tion of Henry and Clover Adams as the "Bonneycastles" in the story "Pandora." Mr. Bonneycastle was, in James's words, "not in politics, though
politics were much in him." At the time the story was written, the Adamses
were holding court over their literary salon in a house dubbed the "little
White House" on Lafayette Square, next door to the empty lot on which
they would soon build the double house with Hay (fig. 4.2). The Adamses'
"bonny" little "castle" did attract the interest and envy often felt toward
aristocracy, and it was quite celebrated in Washington society. As James ob-

FIG. 4.1. The Hay-Adams Houses, 1603 H St.–800 16th St., N.W., c. 1900 (Hay House foreground, Adams house with double arches at left). *Photograph by Frances B. Johnston. This item is reproduced by permisson of The Huntington Library, San Marino, California.*

serves in "Pandora," "the house . . . left out, on the whole, more people than it took in."[17] Biographer Patricia O'Toole comments, "The exclusivity of their H Street salon had the perverse if predictable effect of attracting swarms of unwanted guests. . . . Faced with sheaves of invitations from newcomers longing to penetrate the innermost sanctum of social Washington, the Adamses adopted a policy of saying no to everyone."[18] Through his home, Adams created a place for repose and reflection within Washington, where he would not foolishly attempt to reform political forces by designs of his own thinking but instead would simply try to chart them. Such an exclusive and withdrawn site, at the very center of the nation, might acquire the aura of an inner sanctum, a holiest of holies, and hence possess its own magnetic force.

To assess the effectiveness of Adams's strategy, one need only look at a much better known site whose design he also oversaw—his grave (fig. 4.3). Adams commissioned the sculpture that marks it from his friend Augustus

FIG. 4.2. "The Little White House" [Slidell House], 1607 H St., N.W., c. 1907. *Library of Congress, Prints and Photographs Division, Wilhemus J. Bryan Collection.*

Saint-Gaudens after Clover committed suicide in 1885. Adams was buried beside her at his death in 1918. The grave is shrouded in mystery. It is located in a remote cemetery in Washington, quite far from the beaten path. High holly bushes surround the site, which must be entered through a narrow break in the hedge. No names or dates mark the grave, only the enigmatic sculpture. And yet, according to one commentator in 1926, "nothing in Washington attracts greater interest than this statue."[19] Eleanor Roosevelt used to visit it to get away from her life as first lady.[20] It remains today one of the city's most visited "undiscovered" attractions. Through it Henry Adams continues to exhibit the power of self-effacement, privacy, and mystery that emanates from his habitual retiring stance, and to offer this contrasting aesthetic as an antidote to the large, self-evident, and monumental city of Washington. The site and its statue confirm the power of the intimate and the enigmatic to attract national recognition.

In the *Education* Adams eerily describes himself watching the reactions

FIG. 4.3. Augustus Saint-Gaudens, Adams Memorial, Washington, D.C. *Photograph by Jerry L. Thompson.*

of visitors to his future grave: "the figure seemed to have become a tourist fashion, and all wanted to know its meaning." For Adams the power of the sculpture lay not in its meaning, which he suggests is obvious, yet refuses to name. Its power was instead in the reflection it offered of Americans by their responses to it: "Like all great artists St. Gaudens held up the mirror and no more." The statue showed that Americans had "lost sight of ideals" and of "faith." The inability of Americans to understand the simple idealism of the statue leaves Adams feeling "forgotten in the center of this vast plain of self-content."[21] But this, we shall now see, was just the position Adams wanted. He withdraws to the center, as he did with his house on Lafayette Square.

◦◦◦

From the time of his first residency in Washington, Adams sought to alter the political discourse of Washington by changing its physical space. While working in the capital as a lobbyist in 1869, Adams wrote that the trouble with Washington is that it has no space where cultivated gentlemen and governing officials can meet. This lack of "an established center of intelligence and social activity," Adams implies, directly influences the quality of political debate in the nation's capital. Instead of quiet spaces that might encourage well-reasoned and focused debate, politicking happens anywhere, on the fly, in the lobby. A person wishing to meet with "congressmen and senators . . . must hunt them to their separate retreats . . . cornering one in a lobby, or running another to earth in his office, or his bed-chamber, or at his favorite bar-room."[22] Washington's political scene draws no boundary between public and private space.

Adams insists that space affects the nature of the debate, a charge borne out by the very fact that his profession takes its name from the lobbies of the deliberative chambers in which it occurs. The lobby, Adams acknowledges, is a "disgrace": "the reason is to be partly found in this same disintegration of society which shuts the door of influence to what is sound and respectable at the capital, and leaves it open to what is low and blackguard. There is no room for social influences to act, but low agencies can act anywhere." The politics of lobbies, of quick and blunt exchanges, crude threats, and deals, lends itself to "low agencies," whereas gentlemen require "room," not just in the abstract sense but as a physical place where the "fragments" of cultivated society can be reunited so as to act as a moral force upon the government. Adams advises Washington's "respectable and well-to-do citizens" to form a "cosmopolitan club" where "society and politics can meet on equal terms . . . where lawyers, editors, the more respectable reporters, . . . clergy and laymen can . . . learn to know each other." In this way, "one may perhaps decide the question whether what is respectable may not after all prove strong enough to make itself respected and put blackguards under a ban."[23]

This unsigned manifesto anticipated a prolonged effort on Adams's part. In 1879, he helped found the Cosmos Club "to bind the scientific men of Washington by a social tie and thus promote that solidarity which is important to their proper work and influence."[24] The club was located in Dolley Madison's house on Lafayette Square. Adams was a member of the Metropolitan Club, whose members included men of letters and scientists as well as those in government.[25] In 1883, he helped found the Washington Casino, planned as a cultural center much like today's Kennedy Center, with an opera house, restaurant, and club rooms. H. H. Richardson submitted a design for the building, which was to be located two blocks off Lafayette Square. The casino was, however, never built.[26]

Adams can be said to have inherited his interior politics from his family. For the Adamses, politics was a domestic affair. Outside of and opposed to the dominant political scene in Boston, the Adamses had clung to the family homestead in the nearby town of Quincy, where they stuck to their principles while Boston powerhouses such as Daniel Webster compromised on slavery. As Adams says, his family "was anti-slavery by birth, as their name was Adams and their home was Quincy." Politics was bred into their very being. In his Beacon Hill home, Charles Francis Adams fought both Whigs and Democrats alike and started a party of his own—the Free Soil Party, "whose social centre was the house in Mount Vernon Street," and whose members "numbered . . . only three:—Dr. John G. Palfrey, Richard H. Dana, and Charles Sumner." The meetings of these men in the senior Adams's library "became a chief influence in the education of the boy Henry," who was given a desk in the corner and listened "to these four gentlemen discussing the course of anti-slavery politics." Adams, however, dismissed the value of any education he got from these "statesmen"—all "types of the past" whose lack of "dogmatism and self-assertion" had little relevance to the "politicians" of Henry's day.[27] But the image of a small-scale politics whose objective was not to win elections but rather to exert influence must have made an impression on Adams, because he tried to do very much the same thing himself.

Democracy

Adams's *Democracy* records his shift from political reform to political reflection, and from party organizing to house building. In 1877, Adams left his professorship at Harvard and moved to Washington, D.C., in order to write a biography of Jefferson's secretary of the treasury, Albert Gallatin. The move to Washington signaled his shift from "making presidents" to unmaking them through his political histories.[28] Through a clubby politics that involved secrecy and code names, Adams had organized an independent party to influence the presidential election of 1876. As he writes his friend Charles Gaskell in 1875, "I have been carrying on no end of political intrigues. . . . I am engaged single-handedly in the slight task of organising a new party to contest the next Presidential election in '76."[29] Alongside this organizing in 1874, he and Clover also began to draw plans for a summer home in Beverly, Massachusetts. However coincidental, these two activities soon became parallel.

House building emerges in Adams's correspondence as an antidote to ineffectual political reform. After the defeat of his political schemes, Adams retreated to his new summer home: "I was only too happy to escape from town and . . . to bury myself in our woods. Our new house is more than all we ever hoped . . . I am perfectly happy here, and potter about, trimming trees, eradicating roots and rocks, opening paths and training vines, all day, with rapture unknown to poets. I could write a sonnet on the pleasures of picking stones out of one's lawn."[30] Adams paints gardening as a more rewarding form of world-making activity. Adams's own independent candidate for president, Carl Schurz, had jumped the fence at the last minute and supported the Republican nominee in the hope of gaining a cabinet post.[31] Unable to exert much control over the political landscape, Adams sets about "trimming," "eradicating," "opening," and "training" the natural one.

In another letter, Adams describes house building itself in more political terms. The house at Beverly has been a chance to prove his own independence and self-determination:

My cottage, the plans of which I drew up . . . is now built. I have had no architect and consulted no learned men. My wife and I have designed and superintended every detail, or the builder has done so under our eyes. We think the end result very satisfactory and are quite confident that no architect would have done it so well. I do not mean however to start as an architect yet for other people, nor to build a church. Nor do I mean to say that my cottage might not have been prettier or has no mistakes in it. All I mean is that for the use intended, at the cost fixed, it meets the requirements better than any other model I know.[32]

If he had consulted the authorities, Adams implies, his house would have necessarily been grander. Only by keeping personal control of the process from design to finish is the citizen able to build a house that exactly suits his needs: it is simple, economic, self-designed, and for those reasons beau-

tiful: "We are delighted with it and all about it."[33] Embracing the principles of Thoreau at Walden, Adams asserts that only self-representation
can produce the best house—an architect could not "have done it so
well," nor would Adams want to be an "architect for other people." The
house promotes a harmonious organicism as it takes its shape from its
owners' inner needs and the natural site.

Clover Adams's photograph of the house gives her own visual account
of the house's suitability to both its owners and its site (fig. 4.4).[34] The
house takes advantage of the top of the hill while identifying itself with the
trees that surround it, as its name, "Pitch Pine Hill," suggests. Clover takes
the photo from below the house, and this draws a connection between the
house's gambrel roof and the crest of the hill. The angle from which we
view the house also makes a connection between the line of thin trees on
the left and the line's continuation in the house itself through its porch
columns of trees with their branches left on. Seen from Clover's point of
view, the house establishes a conversation between a softened rational
geometric order and a more natural and whimsical design.

The Adams's residences in Washington from 1877 to 1884 marked the gid-
dily successful organizing of Henry's anti-party of interior politics. His first
home, located one block off Lafayette Square, became the meeting place
for his new inner circle of friends. With Henry and Clover this small group
included John and Clara Hay and the geologist Clarence King. Together
they called themselves "the Five of Hearts." Members of their extended
club included the sculptor Augustus Saint-Gaudens, the artist John La
Farge, H. H. Richardson, and many other intellectuals whose names Adams
recites again and again in the *Education*. During this period, Adams also
wrote two secret books: *Democracy*, which was published anonymously; and
Esther, which was published under a pseudonym. Both novels historicize
the collaborative efforts of Adams's salon to offer a counteraesthetic to the
nation, a collaboration that would produce numerous works of literature,
art, and architecture, including the Hay-Adams houses and Saint-Gaudens's
memorial for Clover.[35] *Democracy* uses and promotes the witty political cri-
tiques that the "Hearts" enjoyed over five o'clock tea. *Esther* documents the
building of Trinity Church (1874–76), designed by Richardson with mu-
rals and windows by La Farge and architectural sculptures by Saint-Gaudens.
All of these artistic forms sought to establish a deeper sense of repose and
interiority in the midst of an increasingly crowded and busy urban space.

FIG. 4.4. Pitch Pine Hill. The Adams house at Beverly Farms, Massachusetts. Photograph by Marian Hooper Adams. *Courtesy of the Massachusetts Historical Society.*

Through its secrecy, Adams united his salon into an effective cultural force that commanded attention and established the superiority of his set. *Democracy* offered an exclusive inside view of Washington, and many of its characters were assumed to be only thinly disguised "portraits" of prominent politicians. The mystery surrounding the novel insured its success. To guess the true identities of characters and author became a popular Washington parlor game. King, Clover, Hay, and Adams himself were all named as possible authors. The 1880 edition went through nine printings, and it was reprinted in France and in England, where the novel "was nothing short of a sensation."[36]

Democracy tells the story of Madeleine Lee, who comes to Washington to "[get] to the heart of the great American mystery of democracy and government." She rents a house on Lafayette Square, where "the stage was before her, the curtain was rising, the actors were ready to enter; she had only to go quietly on among the supernumeraries and see how the play was acted and the stage effects were produced; how the great tragedians mouthed, and the stage-manager swore." In addition to her front-row seats, Madeleine enjoys the tutelage of several seasoned, but cultivated, political men. Charmed by the novelty of Madeleine's "civilized house" in the generally barbaric city, these men immediately form a salon about her.[37] Into this circle comes the most powerful senator in town, Silas Ratcliffe from Illinois. It is Ratcliffe's politics that will eventually decide the question posed by the salon as to the presence or absence of democracy in Washington.

Ratcliffe has his sights set on the presidency and, being single, decides Madeleine would nicely fill his need for a wife. Madeleine is sorely tempted; although she knows Ratcliffe has engaged in shady political dealings and disapproves of his bullying nature, she believes she can reform him, and in marrying him reform American democracy as well. Madeleine, in other words, becomes tempted by "POWER," as Adams writes it, to walk across Lafayette Square and take up residency in the White House. At the same time, the quiet and unassuming Carrington, a southerner and an "isolated rebel," is also in love with her. It is through his indirect intervention that Madeleine is informed of the extent of Ratcliffe's immoral political maneuverings; she realizes that she could never reform him, and in the end she barely escapes "being dragged under the wheels of the machine" by which her self-respect would have been crushed.[38] She flees Washington and, as we hear in the novel's postscript, will eventually marry Carrington and retreat to his Virginia home instead.

Adams wrote *Democracy* while living one block away from Lafayette Square at 1501 H Street. In 1880, Adams published his novel anonymously and moved to the site that Madeleine had vacated. An astute reader might have considered Adams's new residence as practically a confession of authorship, identifying himself with his heroine.[39] Adams took the risk, perhaps, because the site he had discovered in *Democracy* was the perfect spot for the reflective politics he was practicing as a historian. In her renunciation of her hopes for reform, Madeleine had to withdraw from Washington altogether; Adams, on the other hand, moves to the site as an ex-reformer now in need of a place from which to best observe the subject of his "scientific" history.

In one crucial scene of the novel, we see how Adams opposes key sites in Washington, and this suggests why he himself must live directly across from the White House. Adams describes a visit by Carrington and Madeleine's younger sister Sybil to the former home of Robert E. Lee. As noted previously, the mansion, where Lee lived until the Civil War, is on a hill across the Potomac that directly faces the Washington Mall. At the time *Democracy* was written, the house was already surrounded by Arlington Cemetery—which was crowded with the graves of Union soldiers—and stood in a straight line with the unfinished stump of the Washington Monument and the Capitol beyond. Adams describes the view from this peculiar vantage point: "From the heavy brick porch they looked across the superb river to the raw and incoherent ugliness of the city, idealised into dreamy beauty by the atmosphere, and the soft background of purple hills behind. Opposite them, with its crude 'thus saith the law' stamped on white dome and fortress-like walls, rose the Capitol."[40] The failure of Washington is softened only a bit by nature. The "fortress-like" Capitol shows the Union's vulnerability; the dome, the nation's reliance upon gigantism and intimidation to enforce its laws.

Adams's iconoclastic view melds with that of Carrington, who acts as a historian, opening Sybil's uneducated eyes to the southern view of the war. Carrington, a close friend of the Lee family, tells how in 1861 they sat on the same porch overlooking the city: "We never thought there would be war, and as for coercion, it was nonsense. Coercion, indeed! The idea was ridiculous. I thought so, too, though I was a Union man and did not want the State to go out." Carrington's loyalty to the Union cannot override his first loyalty to his home state. The nation's violation of private rights and domesticity persists in the continued violation of Lee's home, its rooms now "bare and gaunt," its dignified and isolated repose disturbed by numerous tourists, such as "Eli M. Grow and lady, Thermopyle Centre," whose name Sybil reads in the guest book. Surely Mr. "Grow" and his new town of "Thermopyle Centre" demonstrate how speculators have overwhelmed the old "heavy brick" venerable home. For Sybil, "not even the graves outside had brought the horrors of war so near. What a scourge it was! This respectable family turned out of such a lovely house, and all the pretty old furniture swept away before a horde of coarse invaders 'with ladies.'" Viewed from the perspective of the historian, the entire scene becomes reversed. Carrington the traitor becomes "dignified in his rebel isolation." The "incoherent" city with its "crude" dome betrays a usurped domesticity, a violation of independence and political rights. Even the tombstones look "as though Cadmus had reversed his myth, and had sown living men, to come up dragons' teeth." The superior power of this historical view is confirmed by Sybil's reaction. "Overcome" by Carrington's story, "she saw neither the view nor even the carriages of tourists who drove up, looked about and departed."[41]

Adams has now established two axes in his novel whereby he directly opposes a moral, refined domestic politics to the brutish politics of a national edifice. Madeleine Lee's house faces down the White House as Lee's mansion faces down the Capitol. Both domestic sites, which are further identified by sharing the name of Lee, serve as spaces of reflection that produce, like a mirror, an inverse image of what they face. The northern senator Ratcliffe (from Lincoln's state) is the villain, the southern rebel the hero.

Both Henry and Clover Adams were very interested in photography; Clover Adams also did her own darkroom work. In a letter to her father, Clover mentions that she photographed Lee's home and the cemetery on an excursion there.[42] From the vantage point of Lee's Arlington House, we get an image of the Capitol as if in negative, as Sybil now sees the dark, coercive side of the Union. Through the reflection enabled by his opposite site, Adams is able to unmake the revered national object. So, too, when Madeleine "walked across the Square" one evening to attend the president's reception, she encountered "two seemingly mechanical figures, which might be wood or wax, for any sign they showed of life. The two figures were the President and his wife; they stood stiff and awkward by the door, both their faces stripped of every sign of intelligence, while the right hands of both extended themselves to the column of visitors with the mechanical action of toy dolls." Madeleine demands to her escort, "'Take me somewhere at once where I can look at it. Here! in the corner. I had no conception how shocking it was.'"[43] Participating in this masquerade of democracy is unthinkable. Watching is the only possible response.

It is through similarly indirect means that the gentle Carrington overcomes Ratcliffe, "the Prairie Giant." Perceiving Carrington as a threat, Ratcliffe sends him to Mexico on government business to get him out of the way. Again acting as a historian, Carrington leaves behind a letter in which he tells Madeleine what he hoped he would not have to tell—that Ratcliffe purchased elections, information Carrington acquired when he was asked to organize the papers of a deceased Washington figure. Armed with this information, Madeleine is able to resist Ratcliffe's bullying proposal of marriage. "I need your aid," he insists, "there is nothing I will not do to obtain it." Madeleine flees Washington, while Ratcliffe is left wondering how Carrington "had baulked his schemes" while out of town, how he "had managed to be present and absent" at the same time.[44] By choosing Carrington over Ratcliffe and then retiring to Carrington's family home, Madeleine puts history to rights again by reuniting the Carringtons and the

Lees. Madeleine was a widow whose first husband was "a descendant of one branch of the Virginia Lees" and a "distant relation" of Carrington himself.[45] Hence democracy ends happily only with a retreat to the higher, uncompromised principles of a quasi-aristocratic domestic realm and, in this case, the welcomed restoration of the House of Carrington and Lee.

Madeleine leaves her rented house on Lafayette Square convinced that democracy could never find a home there. Indeed, the coercive politics of Senator Ratcliffe are directly tied to his failure to achieve any kind of attractive domesticity at all:

His quarters in Washington were in gaunt boarding-house rooms, furnished only with public documents and enlivened by western politicians and office-seekers. In the summer he retired to a solitary, white framehouse with green blinds, surrounded by a few feet of uncared-for grass and a white fence; its interior more dreary still, with iron stoves, oil-cloth carpets, cold white walls, and one large engraving of Abraham Lincoln in the parlour; all in Peonia, Illinois!

The sterility of Ratcliffe's "gaunt" rooms shows, like the "gaunt and bare" rooms of the violated Lee mansion, the complete exteriorization of domesticity under a politics of coercion. Lincoln—preserver of the Union— is the only ancestor, government papers the only heirlooms. Unlike Mr. Bonneycastle in "Pandora," Ratcliffe lives "in politics" rather than politics living "in him." Even Ratcliffe feels the lack: "He would have given his Senatorship for a civilized house like Mrs. Lee's, with a woman like Mrs. Lee at its head, and twenty thousand a year for life."[46] It is Adams's one concession to Ratcliffe, that the beauty of Madeleine's life, and perhaps democracy itself, requires the leisure and repose made possible by an inherited income.

The failure of Ratcliffe's domesticity is fatal, the novel suggests, because it is only through the home that democracy can attain its necessary religious force. This missing magnetism of democracy is recovered in the reflection enabled by Madeleine's salon. Asked to define democracy, one character balks at having to expose his "political creed." Democracy and universal suffrage, he protests, "are matters about which I rarely talk in society; they are like the doctrine of a personal God . . . subjects which one naturally reserves for private reflection."[47] When properly arranged, the home itself could offer just such a church to democracy.

Madeleine's salon came close. One reason for its success is that it stands apart in Washington for its comfort and beauty. Upon taking possession of her rented house, Madeleine "cover[s]" over the "curious barbarism" of the house's decor: "the wealth of Syria and Persia was poured out over the melancholy Wilton carpets; embroidered comets and woven gold from Japan and Teheran depended from and covered over every sad stuff-curtain." Over her parlour fireplace, Madeleine hangs her "domestic altar-piece," a "mystical Corot landscape." With that, her make-over is finished. She has created a safe space where the "catechism" of democracy can be rehearsed.[48]

Like Madeleine, Henry and Clover descend upon Washington and rent a house with only their things to establish themselves and personalize their surroundings. Shortly after their arrival in 1877, Henry wrote a friend: "We have taken a large house in which we seem lost. Our water-colors and drawings go with us wherever we go, and here are our great evidence of individuality, and our title to authority."[49] One reason for their home's magnetism and its good talk, Clover suggests, is that it possesses a real fireplace instead of a gas heater. She and Henry understand "the coziness of a fire" and so it seems do their friends: "People usually stay here til eleven and after . . . but I fancy it's only because we have an open fire and no chandelier."[50] While Madeleine's residence is temporary, like her décor, the Adamses decide to remain in Washington and effect its landscape in more lasting ways by building a massive double house on the vacant lot next to the little White House on Lafayette Square. Clover writes her father enthusiastically that their money will no longer be frittered away on "bric a brac" but invested more seriously in "bricks a bat [for building]"; "No more jewelry or bric a brac—our minds are set on drains, plumbing and bricks."[51] The question now was, what would the new house look like, and who should be the architect?

Esther

In *Democracy*, Adams shows how Washington has failed aesthetically and degraded democracy from a religion to demagoguery. *Esther* continues Adams's search for a powerful political aesthetic that achieves the force of religious architecture, a force he will study more closely in his *Mont Saint Michel and Chartres*.

Critics have grounded *Esther* in many details of Adams's own life. The novel, set in New York, opens with a critical appraisal by Esther and her

friend George of the new Fifth Avenue Church of St. John and its minister, Reverend Hazard. Critics tie the discussion of the church's construction to the fact that Adams watched Richardson's Trinity Church being
built (1874–76) in Boston's Back Bay while Adams was still living in that
neighborhood. Not only are Clover and her father present in the novel but
several other intimates of Adams may have been models for characters.[52]

Yet by focusing on Adams's private salon and the personal nature of the
novel, critics have overlooked its political thrust. William Decker sees the
setting of the novel in New York as perhaps due to Adams's desire to hide
his authorship by not setting it in Boston, where he had lived. (Adams published *Esther* under the pseudonym Frances Snow Compton). But, Decker
adds, "the nature of [Adams's] inquiry itself makes Washington or Boston
an unthinkable alternative. In keeping with what had increasingly become
Adams's preoccupation with his country's cultural as opposed to its nar-
rowly political development, he appropriately set *Esther* in that city which
above all others represented material success as yet unennobled by ideals."[53]
Adams's interest in culture is opposed to his interest in politics, and yet
both Boston and Washington are implicated in Adams's critique. Boston's
Puritanism is invoked by the austere Stephen Hazard, as is the city's new
and much commented upon Trinity Church. Most quietly of all, perhaps,
Adams alludes to Washington through the name of his Fifth Avenue church.
Across Sixteenth Street from the little White House stood the "president's
church"—St. John's—designed in 1815 by the nation's leading neoclassical
architect, Benjamin Latrobe. At the time Adams wrote *Esther* nothing
stood between his house and St. John's but the empty lot on which he
would soon build. When *Esther* was issued, Adams was already overseeing
the design of the massive front of Hay's house, which would face St. John's
church directly across the street. Adams's "increasing preoccupation" with
this country's "cultural development" was always political, and it was precisely through architectural form that he sought to bring the two together.

Esther poses in part the question of whether modern-day America can
arrive at a religious architecture that will inspire belief, loyalty, and sub-
mission. The novel opens with the failure of the new Church of St. John,
led by the austere Reverend Hazard, to improve its congregation. The novel
ends by pointing to the kind of building that might succeed. At Niagara
Falls in winter, where Esther flees in order to escape Hazard, who is in love
with her, she finally finds the "huge church" she has yearned for.

Hazard's new church is declared an aesthetic failure from the start. Its images of gaunt, ascetic saints, "the sternest strongest types," which reflect the stern, scholastic tradition that Hazard represents, are out of sync with its very modern congregation members, who decorate themselves like proud peacocks, the ladies wearing their beautiful, and soul-diverting, bonnets into church.[54] Yet the red walls of the church in their way are as guilty of a "display of vanities" as its congregants. The stained-glass "figure of St. John in his crimson and green garments of glass . . . scattered more color where colors already rivaled the flowers of a prize show."[55] Both minister and audience share the idea of religion as theater. In a "grotesque" way, Esther notes, the dramatic Hazard presides over his "opera-house horribly like Meyerbeer's Prophet," ordering his flock about in "a fine tenor voice."[56] Her friend complains that this theatricality is "'what ails our religion. . . . I would like now, even as it is, to go back to the age of beauty, and put Madonna in the heart of their church. The place has no heart.'"[57] The church is instead built upon a hollow faith in (male) human supremacy. Hazard preaches that "behind all thought and matter" exists "only one central idea . . . I AM!"[58] Esther complains that his church is "all personal and selfish": "I despise and loathe myself, and yet you thrust self at me from every corner of the church as though I loved and admired it. All religion does nothing but pursue me with self even into the next world."[59] Instead of an awed wonder at the mysteries of the universe, there is only self-promotion, hubris, and show.

At Niagara Falls Esther delights in the religious power of the falls in winter. While Hazard's church is all energy and no repose, these two forces are seamlessly reconciled by the frozen cataract: the falls are at once "boiling" and "frozen," "furious" and full of "peace." Niagara ricochets incessantly between these now merged states of stasis and movement: "The river boiled at their feet; the sun melted the enormous icicles which hung from the precipice behind them; a mass of frozen spray was banked up against the American fall opposite them, making it look like an iceberg, and snow covered every thing except the perpendicular river banks and the dark water. The rainbow hung over the cataract, and the mist rose from the furious waters into the peace of the quiet air."[60] The frozen falls suggests the perfect paradoxical forms of nature. Covered with a "mass of frozen spray," the American falls look like an iceberg. Beneath, behind, across from, and above the observers are spaces representing the full spectrum of chaos and quiet, beautiful and sublime. A miracle of unity and difference, the same element—water—boils, melts, hangs, freezes, covers, flows, and mists. Here at last is a place of exhilaration and contemplation such as Esther has longed for. The fascination of its paradoxical liquid ice inspires where St. John's cannot.

Adams's description of Niagara does not simply record nature. It promotes the work of his scientist friends, notably Louis Agassiz and Clarence King, who had helped to reveal nature's paradoxes. Agassiz, the "father of glacial theory" and Adams's mentor at Harvard, had discovered that glaciers were not inert masses, as had been believed, but "behaved somewhat like a viscous fluid."[61] King had attempted to apply the Second Law of Thermodynamics to his geological studies. That law states that matter reaches equilibrium at its point of greatest instability. Hence, chaos is the state of repose. At Niagara, Adams highlights the attraction of that paradox by giving us a powerful image of liquid ice.

Far from being an anti-architectural ending, Adams's description of the falls suggests what James O'Gorman terms the then "common" "theme of nature's architecture" suggested by the "popular coverage of the opening of the West."[62] Adams celebrates the form within the fall's chaos. The banks are perpendicular, the frozen spray is massed into the banks, the rainbow is an arch that spans the cataract, the icicles hang from a precipice. Sensitive and awed, Esther fully engages with the power of the falls' contradictions. She enters into a kind of intimate relationship with "this tremendous, rushing, roaring companion." Looking at the falls from the window of her bedroom at the inn, Esther feels "as though she had tamed a tornado to play in her court-yard." And she reflects on the "ludicrous contrast . . . between the decoration of St. John's, with its parterre of nineteenth-century bonnets, and the huge church which was thundering its gospel under her eyes."[63] Niagara gives the blueprints for a sublime architecture that could inspire even skeptics to faith.

The Adamses saw in the work of H. H. Richardson a similar fascination with the power of natural form, and they were drawn to the "geological imagery" of some of Richardson's domestic architecture. O'Gorman notes that "Richardson . . . might indeed be taken with the idea of turning the architectural image in nature into the geological image in architecture."[64] When Clover's father proposed building an annex to his house that would be designed by Richardson, she wrote, "I wish you'd have it of cobble-

FIG. 4.5. H. H. Richardson, Ephraim W. Gurney house, 1884–86. *Boston Athenaeum.*

stones, like Mr. Fred Ames's lodge that is fascinating."[65] The Ames's Gate House in North Easton, Massachusetts, designed by Richardson (1880–81), seemed to be a massing of boulders straight out of the earth. While the Adamses were still working with Richardson on their own house, the architect was designing a summer home for Clover's sister, Ellen Gurney, that was similarly organic (fig. 4.5). The house was described by the newspapers as "'built of rough stones with their moss on, and present[ing] a most picturesque and unique appearance.'"[66] Because it was located near the Adams's summer home, Henry Adams wrote that one of their "innocent interests is to go up there and watch [the] progress" of its construction during the summer of 1885, when Adams's own Washington house was also being built. "It is built of granite boulders and blocks, and looks like the cave of Polyphemus or any other fellow. I wonder whether my Washington house has the same air."[67] While the red brick of the Hay-Adams houses makes them seemingly less organic, nevertheless Adams and Hay both referred to their houses as "caves"; Hay's house was also known as "troglodyte hall."[68] Both houses are shaped by their owners' and archi-

FIG. 4.6 St. John's Church, Lafayette Square. *Photograph by E. David Luria.*

tect's shared interest in the tension between nature and geometry, energy and repose, serenity and force.

We have seen how Adams indirectly promotes his friends through his own writings; so too *Esther* contrasts the admirable aesthetics of Richardson's Trinity Church to the failed Church of St. John in New York. For example, the use of color backfired at St. John's, but Trinity Church, which Richardson dubbed his "color church," enjoyed a huge critical success and was quickly considered to be one of the ten most important buildings in America.[69] In a similar way, the houses Richardson designed for Hay and Adams serve as a corrective to Washington's St. John's Church. We can suppose that for Adams this church too has "no heart" (figs. 4.6 and 4.7). The neoclassical "president's church" bases its aesthetic on geometrical rational form and the power of the mind to create symmetry and balance.

The Adamses did not attend St. John's (as Henry's grandfather John Quincy Adams had). Instead, Clover watched the churchgoers as they passed under her window with Esther's same critical eye. Clover described the scene in a letter to her father: "I'm sitting by an open window behind

FIG. 4.7. From Lafayette Square looking toward St. Johns Church. The Hay house stood directly opposite the church. *Photograph by E. David Luria.*

a screen of roses and heliotrope, partly writing to you and keeping my left eye on the 'miserable sinners' who are going by to church in very good clothes. I fancy no prayer-book repentance would bring them to confess that their Sunday clothes are bad—those are no matter of heredity, but so very personal." Finally, the president himself walked by: "There goes our chuckle-headed sovereign on his way from church! He doesn't look as if he fed only on spiritual food."[70] Clearly Clover believes that her Sundays offer much more sustenance as she writes to her father from the sanctuary of her home.

Lafayette Square

If there was one site in Washington where a domestic union of elite aesthetics might successfully gain ground, it was on the square in front of the White House.[71] Capitol Hill, dominated by senate caucuses and lobbies, had no "room" for civilizing forces, but the "circle of houses round La Fayette

Square" still kept faith with the Enlightenment and mingled politics and culture in an everyday, informal manner. For Adams, it was a neighborhood of "antiquities": Dolley Madison, Henry Clay, Daniel Webster, and Charles Sumner had all lived there.[72] During the 1880s, the square was home to an impressive number of intellectuals devoted to what Henry's brother Charles called "literary politics."[73] In addition to John Hay, there were historian George Bancroft, banker and art collector William Corcoran, Senator Don Cameron and his wife, Elizabeth (one of the city's most admired hostesses and Adams's personal confidant), and newspaper publisher John R. McClean. But the politics of the square was hardly unified, and this probably added to its attraction for Adams. Next door to the Camerons lived Senator James G. Blaine, whom Adams considered to be detestably corrupt. Blaine was believed by some to be the model for Silas Ratcliffe.[74] (Hay, on the other hand, supported Blaine's bid for the presidency.) Most provocatively, in the center of the square stood a large monument to Andrew Jackson by the American sculptor Clark Mills (1853); Jackson was the man who had overthrown the Adams dynasty, banishing them to Quincy "to eat out their hearts in disappointment and disgust" (fig. 4.8).[75] Standing literally between Adams and the White House, the Jackson statue must have continually baited Adams to settle old scores.

In *Democracy,* Adams obliquely suggests that Madeleine Lee's move to Lafayette Square signals its reclamation for the forces of civilized taste and morality. He compares her to Jackson as she reforms the "barbaric" decor of her rented house: "not a chair, not a mirror, not a carpet was left untouched, and in the midst of the worst confusion the new mistress sat, calm as the statue of Andrew Jackson in the square under her eyes, and issued her orders with as much decision as that he had ever shown. A new era, a nobler conception of duty and existence, had dawned upon that benighted and heathen residence."[76]

Knowing Adams's opinion of Jackson, whom he likens to Napoleon in *Education,* we may suppose that it is Jackson who initiated the "curious barbarism" that had invaded President's Square.[77] Jackson's wild inauguration party overflowed onto the square, where free liquor was handed out in order to lure the too-large crowd out of the White House.[78] President Grant, Adams's second most detested populist, had turned the square into a zoo, where he kept his "pet deer and prairie dogs." The smell caused so many complaints the animals were removed.[79] Lafayette Square was known as the

FIG. 4.8. Andrew Jackson Statue, Lafayette Square, with White House in background. *Photograph by E. David Luria.*

"lobby of the White House."[80] Adams's behavior suggests that he meant to turn that lobby into an exclusive political salon that would not have any president for a member. In James's story "Pandora," Mr. Bonneycastle plans a party: "Let us be vulgar and have some fun—let us invite the President."[81]

Surrounded by an attractive paling fence, with its great gates surmounted by gold eagles, Lafayette Square was in Adams's day as close as it would come to a residential square such as London's Russell or St. James Squares. (The gates and part of the fence were removed in 1889.)[82] Its park had been landscaped by Andrew Jackson Downing with winding picturesque paths touring an impressive collection of trees. For urban planner Elbert Peets, Lafayette Square stood in stark contrast to the other dispersed circles formed by Washington's intersections of streets: "Lafayette is in quite another class . . . an area loses half the value of being open if wide avenues lead out from every side. It is [Lafayette's] bounding wall which aesthetically creates the space."[83] It was here that Adams and Hay took their afternoon stroll together to discuss the political decisions of the day.

Adams, who worked and socialized at home, portrays the solid domesticity and political breadth he enjoyed with his friends around the square, as if the square's enclosure protected it from the less stimulating social life of official Washington. His friends Mrs. (Henry Cabot) Lodge and Mrs. Cameron

had been kind to Adams, and a dozen years of this intimacy had made him one of their habitual household, as he was of Hay's. In a small society, such ties between houses become a political and social force. Without intention or consciousness, they fix one's status in the world. Whatever one's preferences in politics might be, one's house was bound to the republican interest when sandwiched between Senator Cameron, John Hay and Cabot Lodge, with Theodore Roosevelt equally at home in them all, and Cecil Spring Rice to unite them by impartial variety. The relation was daily, and the alliance undisturbed by power or patronage, since [President] Harrison, in those respects, showed little more taste than Mr. Cleveland for the society and interests of this particular band of followers, whose relations with the White House were sometimes comic but never intimate.[84]

Here we see how, by Adams's logic, small is beautiful and must inevitably become "a social and political force." Adams enjoyed an "almost common household" with Hay. If Clarence King had been able to join their building project, as had been hoped, their domestic alliance would have been even more impressive—three homes bound together in an edifice that, far from having "no heart," would have instead had five of them.[85]

The pleasure Henry and Clover took in house building was closely tied to their attempt to outdo the prosperous status quo. As a new winter watering place, the half-developed neighborhoods of Washington were being filled in with the new palaces of the rich. These homes were almost anti-homes, built primarily for entertainment and show. Cavernous ballrooms and galleries edged out the cozy den, as families established their status through conspicuous consumption. The Adams's new house would be a corrective to Washington's corrupted aesthetics—a "spartan box" and yet "unutterably ultra," "ultimate," and "original." In short, it would "rouse a riot." When the house was finished, Adams felt Richardson had achieved a "new kind of domestic architecture," one that "required public taste be educated up to it."[86]

At a time when double parlors were the fashion, the Adamses design a house without any parlor at all. As Clover announces to Elizabeth Cameron: "We're going to build . . . Have drawn our own plans *inside*—for a squalid shanty, no stained glass, no carving—no nothing. A library size of this one [little White House's] on the South . . . no parlor because I can sit all day in the library—a study next to it, a dining room behind opening onto a balcony with steps into the garden."[87] "No stained glass, no carving—no nothing"—it is a house defined in opposition to convention and expectations. Library, study, and dining room—the needs of the house's inmates will entirely fill these spaces. Rather than designing their home to cater to and impress the outside world, they will ignore it; indeed, the house will have no clear place for outsiders to be received.

"A company parlor I hate," Clover writes her father.[88] She describes the radical domestic manners of the little White House at the time of their planning of the new house: "The winter watering place part of this life is getting intolerable & the pushing people who almost force their way into your house have to be adroitly met—no one is admitted now by my majestic [servant] if they ask if I 'receive'—& so only those who walk in without asking come at all."[89] The lack of parlor in the new house underscores the difficulty for outsiders to see how to even gain an entrance. The practices here are unknown, unless one is already an initiate. The inner sanctum quality of the new house will be reinforced by the fact that Clover can immerse herself in concentration in the comfortable library rather than squander the hours in a formal parlor. The higher degree of intimacy suits the barging in of intimate friends, just as it suggests the rejection of formal requests altogether.

In looking for an architect for his house, Henry Adams characteristically turned to one of his friends. He and Richardson had met while they were undergraduates at Harvard. But considering the pride that Henry and Clover took in designing their Beverly summer home all by themselves, there was bound to be tension, for Richardson was known for exceeding his budget and overwhelming his clients, talking them into expensive carvings, woodwork, and furniture. Like Esther, who wished to "tame the tornado to play in her own courtyard," part of the fun for Henry and Clover, it seems, was to see if they could rein Richardson in. Their modest furniture, Clover assures her father, would "pitch the key note beforehand" to which Richardson would have to answer and prohibit such luxuries as mahogany paneling or carvings.[90] Their confidence was short-lived. During the planning process, Adams complains to Hay that he has lost ground: Richardson is "an ogre. He devours men crude"; later he vows, "What I paid for this house no soul shall ever know." The Adamses were in the end unable to resist adding numerous carvings both on the interior and the exterior, "as the devout work on their churches," Clover said. The dining room mantelpiece was elaborately carved with wild roses, while outside, above the meeting point of the two arches, Clover added (much to Henry's dismay) the carving of a cross.[91] For all that, the Adamses still succeeded in exerting their wills beyond Richardson's other, more pliable clients. James O'Gorman notes that "both Hay and Adams should be given partial credit for the design of their houses," yet this may be exactly why the Hay-Adams houses are not counted among Richardson's most important works.[92] The Adamses prevailed in their insistence upon large windows to let in lots of light as well as a brick rather than stone façade, both features running counter to Richardson's developed style.[93]

The houses got underway in tandem with the presidential election of 1884, and once again Adams sandwiches his architectural interests with his political interests: house building seems the right antidote to political ineffectuality and disappointment. He writes to a friend, "My immediate interest is in a house which I am about to build. . . . My second interest is politics."[94] Adams watches the process of each with the close attention of a scientific historian. For Adams, house building is a chance to see his design played out against natural forces—the weather, labor strikes, the lack of materials—all of which plagued his house. Would his venture be a success? With its crude manipulation of power, politics was worth watching only to see how it would fail. He writes a friend after Democrat Grover Cleveland won the election: "As things look now, the democratic party will spare us the trouble of opposition, by going to pieces. . . . So ignorant and stupid a body of men never took charge of a great country before, and already corruption has begun." Then, turning his attention back to his side of the square, he continues: "My roof is on. My house and the new [Grover Cleveland] administration got under shelter at the same time. I hope my house may be more solid than the democratic party seems to be."[95]

Adams was hard at work on his *History of the United States of America During the Administrations of Jefferson and Madison* in the fall of 1884, when the construction of the houses had really begun to progress. For Adams his own writing is also sandwiched by the building of the houses. During construction, Henry and Clover were still living in the little White House next door: "Ten times a day I drop my work and rush out to see the men lay bricks or stone in your house," he writes to Hay. Watching the workers gives him "infinite amusement."[96] Friends were all taken next door to see the progress of the Hay-Adams domestic experiment. Detailed, almost daily, accounts were sent to Hay in Ohio, charting the houses' progress and recording the events that set the plans awry. These reports were at times matched by the photographic record Clover and Henry made of the particular stages of the houses' development. In one letter Adams writes to Hay, "I photographed your house for you last Monday, to show you your big arch hanging in the air . . . meanwhile the arch is no longer in mid-air, but solid in a complete front up to the flooring above."[97]

Such photographs and written reports amount to a dissection of the houses. Each recorded moment of the houses' construction comprises a history of their making while at the same time unmaking them. In no time these two construction sites would be solid edifices whose massive appearance would cover up the framework upon which they depended and the wobbly way in which their many parts took their places. Hay's arch in particular would look particularly "serious," as if it had the entire house to support, and would never admit to the fact that it itself once hung rather ridiculously up in midair. Adams's photograph would help to set the record straight. It would remind the viewer of the fact that architecture, although seemingly "solid," is always moving, always changing. Once complete, a house begins to settle and decay under its own weight, the victim of weather, human events, and time. Adams's photo would correct the narrow point of view that sees a building as permanent with a historical point of view of the building over time and its reflection of the impermanence of any solid thing.

Another remarkable photograph taken by Clover Adams plays with history as well (fig. 4.9). The image is defined by the tension between watching and doing. There is the gentleman, contrasted with the craftsmen; the gentleman is also a stand-in for Clover herself, who is observing and recording the progress of the house. That chain of watchers and doers comes full circle with the craftsman who looks at the woman who is taking his photo. All combine to form a moment of repose in this narrative of progress in the house's construction.

The photograph frames the connection between time and space. The sweep of the sidewalk contrasts and echoes the rising-up of the house that is promised by the scaffolding already in place. Both house and sidewalk are narratives of the time inherent in physical space. The view of St. John's church, whose cupola can still be seen here, will be blocked once the house is complete, just as the passerby will lose sight of the church once she has walked on. As if to turn any confident narrative of progress on its head, we

FIG. 4.9. Adams house under construction. *Photograph by Marian Hooper Adams. Courtesy of the Massachusetts Historical Society.*

cannot be sure whether the building being worked on is old or new. The left corner is beautifully lit and highlights Richardson's sculpted treatment of stone and use of the Romanesque revival style. That finished corner of the building, and even the barrel in front of it, give a feeling of almost medieval craftsmanship, so that a non-initiate might wonder if she is looking at the restoration of an old building or the construction of a new.

This photograph might be seen as a high point in Clover's artistic life, a moment when the sporadic activity and unpredictable contingencies of building became poised in an exceptional composition. The photograph exhibits Clover's mastery of her art, both in her technical skill (with the lighting and processing of film) and her skill at composition. Clover photographs the Washington house not dead-on but from a similar angle to that which she used to photograph Pitch Pine Hill (see fig. 4.4), and she dramatically captures both the side and the front of the houses. Poised among its various contrasts, the photograph creates an in-between space such as Laura Saltz argues Clover fashioned for herself in her photography: "A life both inside and outside domestic boundaries."[98] We are outside, on the street, but we are still focused on domestic space. We are in Washington, but Clover confines her context; we have no sense of the White House being across the way, although someone familiar with Lafayette Square might recognize St. John's cupola. This photograph is a studied arrangement of space just as its subject is house building, itself the arranging of domestic space.

This moment of pleasure in the dynamics of building would soon come undone. Clover's father became ill and then died, and Clover sank into depression. In December 1885, just over one year after having taken this photograph, Clover swallowed potassium cyanide, a chemical she used in her darkroom for fixing images. She died in the little White House, just as her house next door was being completed. If building gave Henry the pleasure of modeling the forces of human life and nature, Clover's death put him back at the mercy of chaos again.

The finished houses were by all reports impressive. A reporter in Hay's hometown paper, *The Cleveland Leader*, praised the "massive impression conveyed by" Hay's house due to its "sculpt[ed]" quality and the "thickness of the walls and the many windows looking out as though cut deeply into them.[99] The wide expanse of the adjoining houses, which Richardson treated as a single mass, argues for a union between the intellectual and the official life, the public and the private (see fig. 4.1). Fortresslike, the houses make a highly visible display of their private alliance; they figure the personal relationship between Hay the statesman and Adams the historian and advisor. Hay's house on the corner is larger and more showy, with its turrets, gables, and grand Syrian arched entrance, as befitted his social life and prominence as secretary of sate. In contrast, Adams's house, itself not small, looks tucked in and intimate, a literary retreat. Richardson balances the two different scales and makes them equal. On one hand, the Adams house appears to be a dependency—a servants' quarters for the Hay house; but on the other hand, standing guard on the corner, the Hay house appears to protect the Adams house, much as the body protects the heart. The net effect is that each house improves the status of the other: the diplomat saves his soul and his intellect by maintaining contact with the cultured elite, while the historian has a window of influence through which he can put his erudition to direct political use. Indeed, during Hay's tenure as secretary of state under McKinley and Theodore Roosevelt, Adams served as "Hay's shadow," walking with him every afternoon in Lafayette Square to review the day's events.[100] Adams's comments about the houses under construction suggest he feels both competitive with and allied to Hay. Adams wrote Clover, then looking after her sick father in Boston: "[Hay and I] inspected the houses, and I think Hay was a good deal impressed by them. Ours is certainly going to be handsomer than his . . . but the double result will make a sensation."[101]

In a huge country of tall statesmen and capitalist "giants," the unconventional entranceway of the Adams house exhibits the power of the small, the intimate, the mysterious (fig. 4.10). The low, elongated Renaissance arches, unusual for Richardson, disarm the viewer, and the house has no clear single focus—the arches themselves lack the single structural center of a round arch but are instead termed "three centered." Furthermore, the arches offer contradictory messages: their width opens up the first floor to view, while their low height protects the small, informal front door. Here, then, is an intense juxtaposition of scale by which one is brought, within a few steps, and without a staircase or other bold separating device, from the broad national scene onto which the house faces into the withdrawn, private life of its interior. This tunneling effect resembles that of the entrance to Adams's gravesite. One leaves monumental Washington and enters a small and intriguing world, the cave of Adams. At five foot four, Adams was himself rather small. The intimate interior of the Adams house is built to this scale: the low risers of the main stairs made climbing effortless, and the comfortable furniture was built noticeably close to the ground. Like the little door that Alice found to Wonderland, Adams's entrance creates desire, stimulates the imagination, and narrows one's chances of getting in.

Adams watched the theater of politics directly in front of center stage. The opera box opening on the third floor of his facade figures the withdrawn, but also stagy, position that he devised from which to view the show. Indeed, it suggests the coup by which Adams turned himself into a show of comparable interest. Framed in their withdrawn superiority, the audience in the boxes draw attention to themselves; one looks at the stage and one looks at the boxes. Adams's prominent reclusiveness likewise made him more interesting.

Richardson's guarded exteriors go hand-in-hand with a greater degree of openness within. The flow of space from Adams's entrance hall to the principal rooms above recalls the unity of the medieval hall. Sitting at his desk in the study, Adams looked across the entire width of the front of the house, through sliding doors "that were never closed" to the library fireplace.[102] The house was praised, too, for its sunny warmth and informal comfort. The library, where Adams generally entertained his friends, was

FIG. 4.10. Adams House. *Photograph by Frances B. Johnston. Library of Congress, Prints and Photographs Division, Frances Benjamin Johnston Collection.*

cluttered with books, "choice bibelots, Chinese bronzes," and his best watercolors. One friend describes the effect: "The chairs and sofa had been built to his measure and were extremely low, covered with a dark maroon leather and, I need hardly add, superlatively comfortable, so that once folded into their depths, one had no wish to move. The whole room had a mellow patina left by the much good talk it had harbored."[103] Adams's interior fused dynamism and repose, openness and privacy, the home and the gentleman's club: "In all these rooms there was a sense of color and light, but a definitely masculine atmosphere."[104] In addition, the six large windows across the front of his house gave his elevated library and study a wide panorama on the political scene. Through his collaboration with Richardson, Adams claims to have achieved the kind of organic fit he enjoyed in his Beverly home. He wrote one cold winter: "Washington is arctic. I never leave my house, which is the best place in the city, and the only one where I feel comfortable."[105]

A watercolor of Adams in his study done by his niece Mabel Hooper La Farge in 1894 portrays the interior politics of the house by demonstrating the magnetic power of reflection (fig. 4.11). Comfortably seated in his low armchair, Adams does not write or read but simply reflects. Books are there, surrounding his head, but they are in the background, as if he has absorbed them all and now turns them over in his mind. He gazes toward the fireplace, the center of warmth and light and force and magnetism; the beauty of the flowers is balanced by the masculinity of his cigar. It is a "thinker" portrait: he has enough thoughts to occupy him during the length of his cigar. Despite his relaxed and lounging pose, the perspective of the painting places Adams slightly above us in his superior detachment. The attractive privacy of the picture is heightened by its oblique point of view, letting us spy on Adams unawares as he sits all alone with his thoughts. *Henry Adams in His Study* might have been a rather aggressive portrait—Adams looking us dead in the eye, surrounded by carefully documented possessions as a testimony to his cultivated taste and collecting—an oil painting meant to give his persona immortality. Instead we have a more fragile watercolor, that unconventional medium Henry and Clover collected so successfully. The portrait shows the power of passivity, indirection, smallness, and interiority. At the same time it shows how the "naturalness" of Adams's seclusion remains a studied pose to increase his effect.

Adams lived this life at 1603 H Street for more than thirty years. It was a period of quiet, and of restlessness. He wintered in Washington, dividing his time between history, politics, and his active social life. He politicked, but on his turf and from the comfort of his home: "Think of it!" he writes his niece in 1893, "I had four Senators to eat Terrapin last week: Cameron of Penn.; Butler of S.C.; Gray of Del.; and H. Cabot Lodge of Mass.!!!"[106] In the summer he went to Beverly Farms or occasionally to Europe, but he also embarked on extensive and arduous travels. He saw Russia, Scandinavia, Cuba, the South Seas, and Japan. His house was the antidote to his travels: it was his fixed star—the "place to which he must always return"—and his inseparable shell. As he told his niece, "he wore it on his back wherever he went."[107] In his house, Adams achieved the equilibrium of dynamism and repose, the mysterious magnetism that in his eyes had eluded the rest of the city in which he lived.

FIG. 4.11. Mabel (Hooper) La Farge, *Henry Adams in his Study*. *By permission of the Houghton Library, Harvard University (pfMS Am 1837 (2))*.

Coda

Chicago asked in 1893 for the first time the question whether the American people knew where they were driving. Adams answered, for one, that he did not know, but would try to find out. On reflecting sufficiently deeply, under the shadow of Richard Hunt's architecture, he decided that the American people probably knew no more than he did; but that they might still be driving or drifting unconsciously to some point in thought, as their solar system was said to be drifting towards some point in space; and that, possibly, if relations enough could be observed, this point might be fixed. Chicago was the first expression of American thought as a unity. . . . Washington was the second.
— HENRY ADAMS[108]

One hundred years after the planning of the Federal City, the White City, the jewel of Chicago's Columbian Exposition, modeled the vision of a grand city created all at once. As Alan Trachtenberg has argued, the White City, with its colossal scale and classical style, modeled how aesthetics could "incorporate" the various branches of culture into an imposing whole.[109] In an article entitled "White City, Capital City" that was published in *Century Magazine,* the architect Daniel Burnham made bold claims for the achievements of the White City in words that echo the Federalist rhetoric of L'Enfant. The White City, Burnham claimed, showed "what the matter was with our public improvements": "[We] had built great public works in piecemeal, unrelated, and without the unity of a comprehensive general plan." The colossal vision presented by the White City has revealed to Americans their unrecognized longing for unity: "No ancient traditions bind [the American] to the outworn. The new has come, and he will possess it. So works out the ambition of the New World's pioneer ancestry in the children of the new day."[110] The White City promises that reason can overcome chaos, that expansion can occur without limit. The White City became a prototype for cities across the country, the most prominent of which would be Washington, D.C. In 1902, five years after the Columbian Exposition, the Senate Park Commission, which counted among its members several White City architects including Burnham and Saint-Gaudens, submitted a plan for the aesthetic unification of the capital: "The one thing lacking in the development of the capital has been that unity for which L'Enfant strove," Charles Moore argued in an essay appended to Burnham's.[111]

Adams wanted to believe in the White City but ends up concluding that it is an impressive sham, "a sort of industrial, speculative growth and product of the Beaux Arts" that only showed how little had been learned. "Since Noah's Ark, no such Babel of loose and ill-joined, such vague and ill-defined and unrelated thoughts and half-thoughts and experimental outcries as the Exposition, had ever ruffled the surface of the lakes." For Adams the "only unity was natural force," and the only way to create unity was to submit to such limitations.[112]

In contrast to the model presented by the White City and Washington, Adams offers the "ocean steamer" as the "nearest of man's products to a unity." Such an invention was bounded strictly by the limits of natural force. At the White City, Adams calculates "exactly when, according to the given increase of power, tonnage and speed, the growth of the ocean steamer would reach its limits. His figures brought him, he thought, to the year 1927; another generation to spare before force, space and time should meet."[113] Submitting to the exigencies of nature, the ocean steamer pushes toward the maximum size, weight, and speed it can achieve while maintaining those forces in equilibrium. Adams's ominous targeting of the year 1927 warns that the steamer cannot exceed the natural limit to its growth. The point of its maximum force is the point at which it will have to rest. The ocean steamer represents for Adams a technological trinity of natural forces—size, weight, and speed—that recalls the mysterious unity of the Holy Trinity itself.

The rival unities of Adams and Burnham came face to face at the turn of the century on Lafayette Square. The Senate Park Commission's McMillan Plan of 1902 proposed tearing down all of the buildings on the square, including St. John's Church, and building an "unbroken line of 'Roman' facades" as a means of unifying the departments of government directly related to the White House (fig. 4.12).[114] The transformation of the square would exemplify the federal government's coercive exteriorization of domesticity. "Lafayette Square may come to be occupied by buildings for the Departments of State and of Justice, and by such other monumental structures as the growing needs of the republic may demand."[115] In place of the local, historic character of the square and its individual residences, the square would be an extended "home" for the executive branch, a model of systematic incorporation to inspire the nation's other capitals and locales. Hay, at least, was not opposed. He reportedly "expressed his unqualified approval of the Commission's Plans": "[Hay] stated that his feelings were so strong on the subject that 'even my house can go to carry out the scheme of having Executive Department buildings around Lafayette Square,'" adding "with a smile, 'probably my house will not be needed during my lifetime.'"[116]

In 1922 William Corcoran's house and the little White House were razed to make room for the new, neoclassical United States Chamber of Commerce. In the same year, Elbert Peets protested the changes to the square:

The bounding walls of the old square have begun a radical transformation. . . . The new Lafayette Square will be crowded with automobiles and trucks, the lawns will be clotted at noon with clerks and typists, streetcar tracks may even by laid in Sixteenth Street and the usual tatterdemalion lunchrooms and little shops will cling to the skirts of the office buildings and spread back into the resident streets to the north, producing another one of those anemic business districts of which Washington already has so many.[117]

Echoing the violation of Lee's estate in *Democracy,* Lafayette Square appears destined to become a Thermopyle Center. Peets's dire prediction did not entirely come true. As it turned out, the speculative plan for a unified executive center was defeated by the square's physical limits. As the plans were being adopted, the executive offices were already growing too numerous to fit comfortably around the square. A few more new buildings were built before congressional support and funding for the plan dried up

FIG. 4.12. Cass Gilbert, rendering of Senate Park Commission's 1902 plan for rebuilding Lafayette Square, c. 1917. *U.S. Commission of Fine Arts.*

and prevented any more "monument building."[118] The commission's plans remained, as L'Enfant's had for so many years, largely a plan.

The development of Lafayette Square was haphazard and even neglected up until the 1960s, but it did retain its reputation, promoted by Adams, as a focus for political reflection. The Brookings Institution occupied a large office building there, built in 1931.[119] A private institute, it sponsored research in government and economics and contained residences and a club for its fellows. While Adams was still alive, philanthropist Bernard Baruch made daily visits to his "'park bench office'" in the park's square in order to indulge in the "'detached contemplation'" he considered essential in "'this hectic Age of Distraction.'" In 1962, President John F. Kennedy successfully won funding for the preservation of the historic buildings on the square and its general improvement. Since then it has maintained its eclectic composition of federal offices, historic houses, the Renwick Museum of American Arts and Crafts, and nonprofit think tanks.[120]

In 1927, the year in which Adams predicted the ocean steamer would reach its limit and attain its ultimate unity—when "force, space and time should meet"—the Hay-Adams houses were razed. Adams died in 1918; Hay had died in 1905. For a time the Hay children sought to preserve both

FIG. 4.13. The Hay-Adams Hotel. *Photograph by E. David Luria.*

houses, buying the Adams house in 1918.[121] All of the thought and planning reflected in the men's correspondence, all of the money, labor, materials, and design, had lasted less than fifty years. Like Robert Morris's
house, where L'Enfant had built his short-lived vision of national domesticity, the Hay-Adams houses were a speculation. But as with Adams's self-
proclaimed "failure" to acquire "education," he may well have considered
the destruction of his house, in his perverse way, as a sign of his success.
The house was not replaced by some "anemic" federal department but
rather an elite hotel reminiscent of old Washington and called, in tribute,
the Hay-Adams Hotel (fig. 4.13). It is an obscure reference and few perhaps know the source of the hotel's name. But there Adams's name is, still
tied to Hay's, a ghostly and mysterious presence that seems most fitting,
because it preserves Adams as he figured himself, "forgotten in the center
of this vast plain of self-content."[122]

As a failure Adams made an indelible impression. The success of *Democracy* (anonymous), the attraction of his anonymous grave, the "irresistible literary style" of the *Education,* the envy and interest created by his
very private house and salon—it would seem that the man who could not
understand magnetism could not have found a more calculated way to im-

itate its allure and capture its paradoxical force.[123] His self-effacement left the stage open for others to lionize him. Adams would have rather died than publish his *Education* himself, but he wrote it nevertheless and might have predicted that others would publish and promote it for him. They did, and it has done a great deal to establish the prominence of his quiet publications in American letters. And so one reviewer of the *Education,* when it was finally released to the public after Adams's death, could be seen to be acting right on cue when he complained: "it is unfortunate that the general public in his own country has given so little of its attention to the American historian who was Charles Francis Adams's son."[124] Adams, one suspects, could not have said it better himself.

EPILOGUE

I conclude this selective tour of Washington spaces at the city's most speculative ground, the National Mall. It is not the monuments, which of course contribute immensely to the connection the Mall makes between political vision and physical actuality, that interest me here. Instead it is all of the grass in between, the enormous green space of the Mall, because in one sense it has been the most controversial feature of it. The greensward of the Mall alters L'Enfant's original plan for the city in a crucial way. L'Enfant's plan of 1791 called for a Grand Avenue, which would be flanked by open space, and beyond that gardens and fine residences. The McMillan Plan of 1902, which most influenced the Mall of today, calls for a lawn flanked by roads and monumental public buildings. This may not sound like a very big difference: both plans feature open space and roads; they simply differ on how these are arranged and what is in the center, an avenue or a "green carpet" of turf.[1] But urban planning historian Norma Evenson notes, "One of the most conspicuous, and perhaps controversial, departures from the L'Enfant plan by the Senate Park Commission in 1901 was the rejection of L'Enfant's concept of a major street extending westward from the Capitol, in favor of a swath of grass."[2] Depending upon one's point of view, the open space of the Mall is where the capital's monumentality is most keenly felt, or where the connection between monumental space and the actual city falls apart. Depending upon how one looks at it, the Mall makes or breaks Washington, D.C.

The greensward of the National Mall exemplifies the qualities of the speculative spaces we have seen so far. The space is anomalous; for many, its enormous scale is extremely problematic. Contemplating the McMillan Plan's vision for the Mall and its buildings, urban planner Elbert Peets asks, "Was there ever such a group? Can [the Mall] possibly be felt as a whole?"[3] The Mall does not fit into the standard vocabulary of urban design, and critics are hard put to define just what today's Mall is: not an avenue and not exactly an urban park such as Central Park, the Mall is instead a "new kind of park," a "long, wide swath of open space—something between a park and a boulevard."[4] The Mall is an in-between space in the fullest sense of the term. It hovers between national and civic space; it is both a "national front lawn" and a popular place to play soccer.[5] If, as we have seen, Washington was conceived as a political romance, hovering, as Hawthorne describes that literary genre, between the "Actual and the Imaginary," then the Mall is its central stage.[6] It is this very speculative nature of the Mall that supporters praise, because it offers a space like no other, and critics fault—one steps down from its elevated plane into the uneven and troubled city beyond.

This step down is the point where L'Enfant's vision becomes derailed. L'Enfant's avenues were to be the lifelines of the city, and the Mall was the premier avenue of L'Enfant's plan. The avenues would fuse monumental, national, and domestic spaces because the Mall would connect the Capitol, George Washington's statue (L'Enfant's planned precursor to today's Washington Monument), and private residences and gardens. Most importantly, L'Enfant's avenues were the very picture of the energetic marketplace that would help to tie the nation together. L'Enfant imagined that the avenues would show off the city to its visitors by "necessitating a constant going in every direction" that "would to the ey[es] of all visitors best have depicted the grand feature of the city plan" and thereby lure them to invest: "the ride over accidentally to have discovered a variety of Situations more pleasing and convenient for houses than are describable."[7] As people circulated down the avenues, the city would rise up. Like a flat hose filling slowly with water, what began as a line on paper would end up as a three-dimensional monumental city. The plan would have been fulfilled.

During the first century of the capital's existence, the Mall remained unevenly developed. Andrew Jackson Downing had created ornamental gardens in front of the Smithsonian building, but the rest of the Mall was far from glorious: the Washington Monument remained half-built for much of the century, and the Baltimore and Potomac Railroad Company found it convenient to locate their Washington terminal right on the Mall, beneath the Capitol.

The Senate Park Commission, which authored the McMillan Plan, saw itself as fulfilling L'Enfant's plan at last, but instead of a central avenue for the Mall the commission proposed a broad green lawn modeled after the aristocratic *tapis verts* of European country estates. The commission was made up of four of the nation's most prominent architects and artists: Daniel Burnham, Charles McKim, Frederick Law Olmsted Jr., and Augustus Saint-Gaudens. All four men saw Washington as a place to fulfill the theories of the City Beautiful movement, which they had modeled so successfully in their previous collaboration, the White City of Chicago's World Columbian Exposition.[8] Critics of the plan argue that, like the White City, the greensward of the Mall forms another court of honor ringed by large public buildings to "seal off" rather than connect the monumental space from the rest of the city.[9] By substituting a green lawn for a paved avenue, the Mall substitutes a stagy, symbolic connection for an instrumental, authentic, working one.

The huge scale of the Mall exacerbates its separation from the rest of the city of Washington. As a paved "Grand Avenue," the Mall might have functioned much as Paris's Champs-Elysées does, only more so. Today's Mall is 1,000 feet wide; L'Enfant's Grand Avenue was to be 400 feet wide; by contrast, the Champs-Elysées is approximately 230 feet wide.[10] Norma Evenson describes the exhilaration she felt from Paris's premier avenue, whose more modest scale integrated monumental space with everyday life:

In the course of extended stays in Paris, I found the Arch of Triumph forming part of my daily experience of the city. I never intentionally visited the arch; it was simply there. It suddenly loomed up with almost hallucinatory splendor when I emerged from the Metro on my way to have root canal work. I passed it in taxis, glimpsed it while crossing streets. No matter what the circumstances, I was momentarily moved by its solemnity. Surrounded by urban distractions, it embodied an enduring island of memory, and provoked a disquieting layering of sensations. Involuntarily, I found myself pondering such things as madness and nobility, heroism and savagery, life and death, and all while waiting for a traffic light to change in front of Le Drugstore.

The Champs-Elysées is the unseen connector here, as it brings together metro station, traffic light, monument, and stores. Traveling through such space in the course of her day, Evenson is "involuntarily" moved by this crucial juxtaposition of the prosaic actions of everyday life with the monumental arch. Evenson herself grew up in Washington, D.C., on Capitol Hill, and the fact that the Capitol was in her neighborhood led her to form a personal connection to it: "I went to the Capitol for solitude and escape"; and again, "I owned it. It was where I lived."[11] By embedding monuments with the everyday features of city life—its stores, residences, and streets—such spaces foster the personal link to the national landscape that was the central objective of L'Enfant's Hamiltonian plan.

Stirred by such evocations of integrated monumental civic space, it is easy to long for the capital that might have been had only L'Enfant's plan been followed more closely. Elbert Peets cites the space in front of the Capitol as a key example. L'Enfant's memorandum on his plan calls for a square to be built in front of the Capitol: "Around this square, and all along the avenue from the two bridges to the Federal house, the pavement on each side will pass under an arched way, under whose cover shops will be most conveniently and agreeably situated."[12] Peets imagines that this space would have been something akin to the Piazza San Marco in Venice— an exciting mix of the commercial and daily life of Washington city with the tourist and official life of the nation's capital. There one could enjoy "such a feeling of life, and such a full and pleasant perception of the three dimensions of space."[13] Henry James called the Piazza San Marco the "drawing-room of Europe," and considered in this light the Capitol Square might have been the fulfillment of a national domesticity par excellence.[14] Tourists and Washingtonians could shop and sit in cafes and go about their days while members of Congress and their aides passed by. But the McMillan Plan and subsequent development's concentration upon the Mall has made the western side of the Capitol, its back, the side we relate to most. This is where presidential inaugurations now occur. The Capitol has done an about-face, so that its quiet western aspect is more visible than the working entrance through which lawmakers come and go. In 1929 an ambitious plan to develop East Capitol Street into an "Avenue of the States" was proposed to address the neglected eastern half of the Capitol area and create a ceremonial connection to the Anacostia River.[15] This would have placed the Capitol at the center of a grand axis that would connect the city's two rivers, the Anacostia and the Potomac, which had inspired the capital's location in the first place. Instead, the Capitol has become an end point of the Mall, and the Washington Monument has become the "symbol[ic] . . . axis around which the city revolves."[16] The Capitol's pivotal reorientation underscores the Mall's substitution of a more exceptional symbolic encounter with national space for a more accessible everyday one.

Both the Champs-Elysées and the Piazza San Marco model the importance of centrality, the chance for frequent everyday contact with their spaces, and also of a commercial element to the integration of monumental space with everyday life. Evenson passed the Arch of Triumph frequently just in the course of getting around town. Shopping or sitting in a cafe is another way of extending one's stay in monumental space, of investing in it, connecting with it, owning it. In 1901, however, Frederick Law Olmsted Jr. argued that the Mall should be a space set apart as higher than ordinary civic space, as a national ground. Olmsted rejected the idea that "a straight road should be slashed down the middle of [the Mall]"; "[the Mall] should not be marked by a mere commonplace boulevard." Such spaces would represent the loss of an opportunity to create a far more extraordinary and hierarchical space. While Olmsted saw the Champs-Elysées as one possible model for what L'Enfant may have had in mind, Olmsted argued that in calling for an avenue "400 feet wide" "no one will suppose that [L'Enfant] meant a roadway 400 feet wide," but rather "an impressively broad and simple space of turf," "something recalling the Tapis Vert at Versailles, but on a grander scale." The Mall was a space that should not grow out of the surrounding city but instead out of the Capitol itself. The Mall must "extend the effect of the Capitol, the dominant feature of the city and the most important building in the whole United States, to strike a chord in the magnificent chorus of which the keynote is the great white dome." The Mall was the natural extension of the Capitol, like the park that a country estate would need for its setting. "Looking from the terrace of the Capitol, what does one see beyond the little square of the Capitol grounds to carry its theme to a distance, to echo the note of its magnificence and formality, to mark the extension of its axis in such a way as to proclaim 'All this is but an appanage of the National Capitol.'"[17] Rather than the everyday flow of civic space, the Mall would channel the flow of national space. As we saw in chapter 2, the Capitol dome forms the convergence point in the national political landscape for a fantastic, continent-wide network of railroads, roads, and canals, the energy of all that circulation there rising in one climactic point. The Mall converts this national, industrial, commercial energy of the dome, rolling it out as a long "green carpet," a highly civilized, pastoral—and again, fantastically long—stretch of aristocratic turf.[18]

Today's Mall may look like a "swath of grass," but Olmsted envisioned it as an ideal avenue that would still be a vital artery for Washington. Olmsted rejected the idea of a four-hundred-foot-wide roadway because, by being an avenue, it would be too common, and its extraordinary width would make it too wide: "As for a broader avenue of the same style [as Pennsylvania Avenue], anyone who has walked across it in summer will admit that Pennsylvania avenue suffices." What was wanted instead was a "sort of compound 'boulevard,' marked by several parallel rows of trees, with several pavements and turf strips."[19] Olmsted's grass was not a mere "swath" but a highly shaped, directional space, a green avenue whose innovation could exceed even the broad extent of L'Enfant's plan. In his description of the McMillan Plan, Charles Moore explains that the Mall would run from Union Square, with its towering statue of Ulysses S. Grant, at the western base of the Capitol to the Washington Monument and the Lincoln Memorial. Its trajectory would then continue across the Potomac River to Virginia by the proposed Memorial Bridge, and on to the National Cemetery at Arlington and the Custis Lee Mansion, the former home of Robert E. Lee. The plan urged the creation of a road from Memorial Bridge to Mount Vernon.[20] The Mall, along which one would be able to walk or drive, would form an avenue that was all about political union as it physically connected the capital to Virginia, the north to the south, and Grant, Lincoln, Washington, and Lee to each other.

This elevated national landscape of circulation would course not only through the Mall area but through the city as a whole. An important part of the McMillan Plan was to include the whole of Washington, and not just the Mall, in its plans. As part of the planning commission, Frederick Law Olmsted Jr. planned a series of "park connectors" to encircle the city, much like Frederick Law Olmsted Sr.'s "Emerald Necklace" in Boston, to link the many key sites of interest around the perimeter of the capital.[21] The Mall, then, was simply the featured jewel in one such necklace. Instead of an all-purpose street with all kinds of traffic—pedestrian, commercial, and residential—the Mall would be part of a huge, more ideal circulation system of pleasure drives—boulevards, river drives, and park connectors— that would rise above the fray of ordinary street traffic to elevate the "beauty and dignity" of the capital as a whole.[22] The Mall would thus be connected to the city not by stores, not by cafes, but by its green space. The Mall is part of the "Park System" colored green in the McMillan Plan's appended map: "Public Reservations and Possessions and Areas Recommended As Necessary to be Taken for New Parks and Park Connections."[23]

This infusion of park space into the city's infrastructure would elevate Washington according to the ideas of Frederick Law Olmsted Sr. and his partner, Calvert Vaux. Olmsted Sr. and Vaux had "developed a theory" of the way in which types of streets denoted different degrees of "civilization." At the bottom of the scale were undifferentiated streets where foot traffic, horse traffic, and sewage all flowed together. The addition of elevated sidewalks and gutters represented a step up in civilization. Haussmann's grand boulevards in Paris, divided by a narrow parklike median strip, were another step up. At the top of Olmsted and Vaux's street hierarchy was the parkway, which included "a central roadway reserved for pleasure riding."[24] This represented the highest advancement in "civilized town life." In his "compound 'boulevard,'" with its several parallel rows of trees, pavements, and turf strips, Frederick Law Olmsted Jr. devised his own highly differentiated and hence "civilized" street as the central artery of the United States. All of these park-related connections were ways of interjecting the restorative, civilizing influence of nature throughout a city. Olmsted Sr. and Vaux believed that parks "would refine the tastes of the lower classes and teach them a higher standard of morals."[25] Vaux and Olmsted Sr. saw parkways as crucial to extending the influence of parks into the daily lives of city residents: "People living near the parkways would gain these benefits as they went about their daily routines, even when they weren't traveling to a park."[26] In that ideal sense, as part of the city's parkway system, the Mall's presence might be extended across the city and into its everyday life.[27]

Today's Mall can be said to be as much about the idea of circulation as about actual circulation itself. The twentieth century marked several decisions through which modern, practical, and unsightly transportation features were removed in order to create a much more ideal circulation space. The railway station that used to sit in the center of the Mall to the west of Capitol Hill was removed early in the twentieth century. Later the streets that ran the length of the Mall, which had been lined with cars parked on both sides, were replaced by pedestrian walkways, and a proposed eight-lane freeway across the Mall was blocked.[28] Clearing the land in this way has left an "emblematic" space suggesting "the vast reaches of the country itself."[29] But such a weighty space can be difficult to travel. As architectural critic Paul Goldberger acknowledges, all that green space does make "it hard to stroll from one [monument] to the next."[30] There is little parking near or on the Mall, and this makes it difficult to access the Mall by car. The closest Metro station to the Lincoln Memorial is many long blocks away. One never has the experience that Evenson describes of emerging out of a Metro station to see the Washington Monument looming directly above. It is not quite as hard as it once was to find a restroom or refreshment, but landscape architect Dan Kiley argues that much could still be done to make the Mall more user-friendly.[31] Many visitors choose to tour the area by sightseeing bus, and these vehicles now line the Mall, running their engines and creating a smelly, unpleasant margin to the Mall's carefully planned border of trees, especially on a hot Washington summer day.

If the Mall's greensward epitomizes the limitations of such an excep- tional space, it is this very exceptional quality that other commentators value most. Olmsted argued that "where the scale of the general scheme is large, there should be a corresponding simplicity."[32] It is the simplicity of the Mall's open plain that most contributes to its identity as an anomalous space, a space where anything seems possible, as Richard Longstreth notes: "Space here is ever changing—at one point defined, at the next open and casual—but it is seldom limited to a single or even predominating use." The Mall's openness creates a "neutral" space that "allow[s] people freely to engage themselves in myriad ways," whether for protests or pilgrimages, for playing games or getting married: "The utter simplicity of the parts is an essential contributor to this effect; more detailed treatments might at once distract the eye and erode the coherence. The Mall then would be- come more a collection of things and less a great open forum that allows one to imagine and do so much within its confines."[33] Much like Haw- thorne's "neutral territory" of romance, the Mall takes on that potential of a "space without qualities" from which Mona Ozouf suggests "derived the true happiness" of the first liberating festivals of the French Revolution: "The scenic arrangements required by the Federation [festivals] could be achieved only in the open air: the dramaturgy of national unity required it. In the open, in the healthy neutrality of a free space, all distinction seemed to fall away."[34] Even J. Carter Brown, the longtime chairman of the Fine Arts

Commission who led many of the successful projects to give more definition to the expanse of the Mall to create from its huge "space," as he put it,
more inviting "spaces," saw the value in its open "meadow" and was anxious
to see it preserved.[35] The huge open space of the Mall that remains has provided a much needed central stage for what would perhaps not even fit anywhere else: a million demonstrators, the entire AIDS quilt, Resurrection City.

Looking at the construction of the Mall according to the McMillan Plan,
Elbert Peets decried its grassy center as an appropriation of a space that
should rightly belong to the people. In the Senate Park Commission's mind,
Peets charged, the Mall was not for walking on: "It would spoil the grass!"
David Streatfield concurs that the illustrations provided with the McMillan Plan "were romantic in nature and largely devoid of life."[36] One view
of the Washington Monument included in the McMillan Plan's report went
so far as to show a flock of sheep on the monument's wide and otherwise
empty expanse of grass. Peets was incredulous: "Are multitudes of people
being herded along the sidelines and kept from fully experiencing our
grandest work of outdoor art merely to flatter the idyllic reveries of some
anachronous sect of grass worshipers or to compose a pretty set picture
seen only from an imaginary royal window?" People will naturally want to
be able to walk right down the center of the Mall, not along its side, Peets
insists, because that will give the best view and the most dramatic experience of the monuments and its space: "The beauty of symmetry is not an
abstraction—it is an ocular and muscular phenomenon that occurs with
greatest emotional effect only on the axis line. I expect to see a little boot-
leg path straight down the middle of that green carpet, made there by
hardy souls who like to inhale their beauty with both lungs."[37]

The takeover Peets envisioned has come to pass. While less integral perhaps to everyday circulation (it is hard to imagine someone having to cross
the Mall on the way to the dentist), the Mall suggests perhaps even more
inspiring trajectories in the countless marches and demonstrations that
have moved down its path. Marches on Washington, such as the famous
Civil Rights March in 1963 when Martin Luther King Jr. delivered his "I
have a dream" speech, have made the open space of the Mall "hallowed
ground."[38] The National Capital Planning Commission has argued that
the Mall's greensward has itself become a "monument to democracy." In
the words of one citizens' group, the Mall is the "people's place," where
citizens can palpably feel their own power, a place where political theory

comes alive: "In the twentieth century the Constitution was amended to extend civil rights to all Americans—women and blacks—and so too the Mall has only in our own day come to be the people's place, as the preeminent forum for public celebrations and demonstrations of those rights."[39]

The construction of the World War II Memorial right on the Mall's central axis made the value of that open space increasingly clear. Many people protested the interjection of a memorial on the central axis of the Mall. The memorial would "not only mar a glorious piece of open space, but also break the visual connection between the monuments to Washington and Lincoln memorializing the two events that did the most to shape this Republic," a connection not only visual but physical: "Pedestrians will no longer be able to walk directly through this open space between the Washington Monument and Lincoln Memorial."[40] Paul Goldberger explains the need for all that space on the Mall: "Monuments—especially ones with a high emotional quotient—don't do well cheek by jowl. They aren't stores in a shopping center. The Mall is not a mall. Spacing the monuments out enhances their impact, even if it makes it harder to stroll from one to the next." The gradual approach, by foot, to the Lincoln Memorial and Washington Monument intensifies the personal experience of monumental space that the Mall provides. Goldberger concludes: "It took a long time to get the Mall right. . . . It is a brilliant composition, in which the voids matter as much as the solids."[41]

While it might be tempting to argue for the seemingly integrative realism of L'Enfant's plan when considered next to the divisive idealism of the McMillan Plan, to do so would be to lose sight of their common ground: both plans are fully rooted in the excesses of political and financial speculation. Both plans offered visions that were seemingly as grand as they could be, and both sought to reform American urban design. L'Enfant rejected the "monotony" of America's model gridplan cities, and Burnham sought to reform the haphazard development of cities by uncoordinated private interests. They each challenged the established authority (in L'Enfant's case, the District Commissioners; in the Senate Park Commission's case, the U.S. Army Corps of Engineers), and both sought to generate support for their plans by appealing to the public at large through impressive promotional campaigns. While L'Enfant's attempts to widely distribute his plan suffered many setbacks, the Senate Park Commission was extremely successful as they dazzled the public with models, illustrations, paintings, and a battery of essays explaining the need for their plan. Both plans were inspired by and tried to outdo European precedents and taste. They shared a similar economic aim: their grandeur and style and possibilities for investment were designed to particularly appeal to the rich. If the early Federal City was to make money and generate enthusiasm, L'Enfant and Washington had to hope for well-heeled investors who would build fine residences that would help make the city truly grand. The McMillan Plan's program to buy up the district's parkland was part of a strategy to influence the development of all of those empty lots still within the district's boundaries. Daniel Burnham wrote in a letter, "My own belief is that instead of arranging for less, we should plan for rather more extensive treatment than we are likely to find in any other city. Washington is likely to grow very rapidly from this time on, and be the home of all the wealthy people of the United States."[42] Overall, Burnham's "presumptiousness" and "audacity" seemed quite in keeping with the original planner of Washington, D.C. "It was as if," Jon A. Peterson argues, "L'Enfant himself had won a second chance."[43]

Most significantly, both L'Enfant and Burnham's group believed in the power of the grand plan. Burnham's essay "White City, Capital City," which appeared in *Century Magazine* in concert with the public unveiling of his commission's plan in January 1902, is a manifesto of the City Beautiful movement and its belief in the power of "comprehensive" planning that attended to the city as a whole. "The general plan is the thing," Burnham proclaimed. Only a general plan could override the conventional improvement of cities in a haphazard and small-minded way. "As a people we are beginning to see that in no architectural or landscape composition do many parts of themselves make a whole, unless by plan and design they are primarily laid out to have the reciprocal relations of a whole."[44] As Alan Trachtenberg has shown in his analysis of the White City, Burnham's emphasis upon planning was not simply an aesthetic vision but a social and economic one as well: Chicago's White City sought to "inaugurate a new Chicago, a new urban world."[45] L'Enfant's plan for Washington was in its own way similarly far reaching. The 1822 engraving of the proposed Federal City (see fig. 1.8) is not a vision of seamless integration between a nationalist political marketplace and the surrounding local landscape but an assertion of the power of the rational, bold plan that would eventually redefine America's social, economic, and political landscape.

Both Burnham and L'Enfant follow the logic of speculation, that a plan's strength lies as much in its boldness as its feasibility. The quote most often attributed to Burnham could easily have been applied to L'Enfant: "Make no little plans: they have no magic to stir men's blood and probably themselves will not be realized. Make big Plans. Aim high in hope and work remembering that a noble logical diagram once recorded will be a living thing asserting itself with ever growing insistency."[46] The soundness of Burnham's assessment is suggested by the paradoxical endurance of L'Enfant's plan. Despite the many ways in which the first plan for the capital was refuted and has never been fulfilled, "L'Enfant's vision continues to be invoked as the essence of Washington and as a guide for current policy and practice. Indeed the name of L'Enfant is probably cited more often in these contexts than are those of all the others who may have had greater impact on the city as it now exists."[47] The National Park Service brochure on Washington opens with the L'Enfant plan. It is as if the city can't fully be appreciated without reference to its early plan. If L'Enfant's plan had been fulfilled, would we still need to remind ourselves of it now, or would the city itself be sufficient? It is an *unfulfilled* "big plan," and as such that plan remains, as Burnham charged, "a living thing." The plan's prominence helps to explain why the bicentennial of the capital could not be fixed on one particular year but had to be spread out over nine years, beginning in 1991 with the bicentennial of L'Enfant's plan and continuing until 2000, the bicentennial of the national government's relocation to the new capital.

The speculative nature of Washington, as envisioned by both L'Enfant and the Senate Park Commission, suggests that the disconnect between city and plan, between national and civic space, is inherent in the plan for Washington itself, and this in turn suggests that Washington will always remain a city divided among the city's majority of poor and largely black neighborhoods, the city's affluent neighborhoods, concentrated in its northwest section, and the city's monumental core, or, as a character in one Washington short story put it, "what the white people called the federal enclave."[48]

In his study of the meteoric rise during the 1990s of the dotcom magazine *Wired*, Gary Wolf pinpoints two "engines" that "fuel" the "financial bubbles" created by speculation: "loose credit and enthusiasm for a good story."[49] The Mall's "swath of grass," with its expanded sense of movement and possibility, is like a wide green line that highlights the importance of increased circulation and a "good story" to this nation's own meteoric growth. In previous chapters we have seen how accelerated circulation (L'Enfant's network of avenues; a nation crisscrossed by telegraph and railroad) was fueled by a "good story" (the financial and political profits to be gained in investing in the nation's capital and its infrastructure). The combination was to result in the story's fulfillment: L'Enfant's magnificent capital would be built. The nation would be united. But the Mall's open space also dramatizes how this scenario breaks down.

Speculation has built into it a story that must remain a story if it is to retain its appeal. The L'Enfant plan maintains its aura because its fantastic blend of capital and city, of grand monumentality and everyday life, remains still to be fully experienced. As Wolf explains, the more such stories become accepted, the more plausible they are perceived to be and the less excitement they generate: "A bubble, while dependent upon its story, renders the story's truth irrelevant. This is because, paradoxically, a bubble feeds upon skepticism."[50] The open space of the Mall provides an ideal space of endless speculation; it feeds the desire for a "good story" of national progress and keeps that story center stage. The Mall hovers between the actual and the ideal, between personal experience and political vision. It is a physical model of the monumentality the entire city was to have enjoyed. On the speculative plane of the Mall, the plan does indeed become the thing. Its gigantic green swath seems to promise unrestricted movement toward infinite possibilities, but when one considers the city beyond, the ideal avenue of the Mall suggests that the stories it invites are perhaps as far as we will ever get.

Notes

Numbers containing the letter "H" refer to notes within the introductory texts at the beginnings of chapters 1, 2, 3, and 4.

Introduction

1. Among some of the many important histories of Washington are Catherine Allgor, *Parlor Politics;* Kenneth Bowling, ed., *Washington History: Special Bicentennial Issue,* and *Coming into the City;* Constance McLaughlin Green, *The Secret City;* Richard Longstreth, ed., *The Mall in Washington;* and John W. Reps, *Monumental Washington,* and *Washington on View.*

2. Scott, "'This Vast Empire,'" 37; Young, *Washington Community,* 8.

3. In his *Architecture in the United States,* Dell Upton writes: "Those who have spent time in any western nation are usually able to 'read' its public spaces easily" (59). It is not my wish to disavow such terminology but to suggest an alternate way of describing the relationship between spaces and texts.

4. *Oxford English Dictionary, Compact Edition, vol. 2* (New York: Oxford University Press, 1977), 2952.

5. Chancellor, *Devil Take the Hindmost,* ix–xiv.

6. Qtd. in *Oxford English Dictionary, Compact Edition,* 2952.

7. I suggest that Washington's plan "translates" the Constitution with this distinction, offered by Dell Upton: "It is . . . important to understand that buildings and landscapes are commentaries on political economy, not merely its translation into bricks and mortar. That is, raw economic power is filtered through the economic beliefs of builders and users, giving the landscape a variety that would not exist were it a simple vector of monetary forces" (*Architecture in the United States,* 191). The Federal City offers such commentary by George Washington and Alexander Hamilton on the political economy they saw embedded in the Constitution.

8. Wolin, "The People's Two Bodies," 133–34.

9. Anderson, *Imagined Communities,* 6.

10. Miller, *Empire of the Eye,* 7.

11. For a complete history of real estate speculation in the early years of the capital, see Arnebeck, *Through a Fiery Trial,* passim.

12. This is not to deny that *Walden* remains at the same time a fantasy of independence, built as it is on Emerson's land and hence dependent upon their friendship. This "detail," not mentioned by Thoreau, potentially undermines the political and economic autonomy argued for by *Walden* and its building. Other details, such as the fact that Thoreau took many of his meals in Concord while living out by the pond, do not detract from his experiment, since he never claimed to be attempting to live in complete self-sufficiency. Indeed, that could be said to make *Walden* more inspiring. It doesn't suggest a radical break with human society and modern conveniences but instead argues for a very conscious interaction with town life and the cash nexus. I'm grateful to Augusta Rohrbach for discussions on this point.

13. See D. W. Meinig, *The Shaping of America.* I am hugely indebted to John W. Reps's documentation of Washington's development, upon which I have drawn extensively. See *Monumental Washington* and *Washington on View.* See also John Seelye, *Beautiful Machine.*

14. See Gillian Brown, *Domestic Individualism;* Amy Kaplan, "Manifest Domesticity," and *The Social Construction of American Realism;* Lora Romero, *Home Fronts;* and Dell Upton, *Architecture in the United States.* For my discussion in chapter 1 of national domesticity in Washington during the early national period, I am indebted to the work of Catherine Allgor, Barbara Carson, and Cynthia Earman. See Catherine Allgor, *Parlor Politics;* Barbara Carson, *Ambitious Appetites;* and Cynthia Earman, "Remembering the Ladies: Women, Etiquette, and Diversions in Washington City, 1800–1814."

15. Dell Upton's analysis of the power issues involving movement through domestic space was particularly helpful in the early phase of this project. See Dell Upton, "White and Black Landscapes in Eighteenth-Century Virginia," in *Material Life in America, 1600–1860,* ed. Robert Blair St. George (Boston: Northeastern University Press, 1988), 357–69.

16. See Rasmussen and Tilton, *George Washington: The Man Behind the Myths,* 103–5.

17. See Wayne Franklin and Michael Steiner's important collection of essays, *Mapping American Culture,* 8, and Harvey, *Consciousness and the Urban Experience,* xiii. One exceptional study that explores the relationship between literature and land settlement is Alan Taylor's *William Cooper's Town* (New York: Vintage, 1996).

18. "Reground" is Franklin and Steiner's term. See *Mapping American Culture,* 3. Katherine Kinney grounds Walt Whitman's response to the "uncanny" space of Washington during the Civil War in her essay "Making Capital: War, Labor, and Whitman in Washington, D.C." Kinney's insightful essay was extremely helpful to my analysis of Civil War Washington in chapter 2. Lauren Berlant pinpoints a key factor in Washington's instability when she describes the capital as "a jumble of historical modalities, a transitional space between local and national cultures," "a

place of national *mediation,*" "a borderland central to the nation." See Berlant, *The Queen of America Goes to Washington City,* 25.

19. Gillian Brown has shown the benefit of considering Harriet Beecher Stowe's *Uncle Tom's Cabin* in light of the design ideas included in *The American Woman's Home.* See Brown, *Domestic Individualism,* 13–28. For a discussion of the realist aesthetic promoted by Wharton in her *Decoration of Houses* see Sarah Luria, "The Architecture of Manners: Henry James, Edith Wharton, and the Mount," *American Quarterly* (June 1997), 298–327.

20. Twain and Warner, *The Gilded Age,* 249.

Chapter 1. George Washington's Romance

H1. Quoted in Chancellor, *Devil Take the Hindmost,* 156.

H2. Quoted in Reps, *Washington on View,* 44.

H3. See Reps, *Washington on View,* and Arnebeck, *Through a Fiery Trial* and "Tracking the Speculators." His quote here is from that essay (see p. 113).

H4. Chancellor, *Devil Take the Hindmost,* 155. For an account of Patrick Henry's real estate investments, including his "several ambitious ventures" in amassing lands in the Ohio Valley, see Henry Mayer, *A Son of Thunder* (New York: Franklin Watts, 1986), 117–28. On Washington's involvement in and promotion of the Potomac River through the "Patowmack Company," see Joel Achenbach, *The Grand Idea: George Washington's Potomac and the Race to the West;* and Bowling, *Peter Charles L'Enfant,* 26. For an account of Ben Franklin's speculation in land in Nova Scotia and his frustrated attempts to invest in western lands through the Illinois Company, see Brands, *The First American,* 382–84.

H5. Atack and Passell, *A New Economic View of American History,* 266.

H6. Arnebeck, "Tracking the Speculators," 113n, 114.

H7. Quoted in Arnebeck, *Through a Fiery Trial,* 261.

H8. Quoted in Reps, *Washington on View,* 31 (emphasis mine). The quote is from a letter by Washington to the Commissioners of the Federal City, Aug. 20, 1793.

H9. Quoted in Arnebeck, "Tracking the Speculators," 113n.

H10. Quoted in ibid., 115.

H11. Quoted in Reps, *Washington on View,* 32.

H12. Upton, *Architecture in the United States,* 20–55.

H13. Arnebeck, "Tracking the Speculators," 121n.

1. Wood, "The Would-Be Gentleman," 37.

2. Until this time the national government had convened in different cities; this gave a wide variety of citizens contact with it and kept it the guest of the host city, with the curtailed power that status implies.

3. L'Enfant's plan for Washington, D.C., was inspired by the great baroque European capitals, including Versailles, as many historians have already shown (see Reps, *Monumental Washington,* 21, and Elkins and McKitrick, *The Age of Federalism,*

180). Yet L'Enfant took these models and adapted them to the peculiar needs of the new federalist design, as I will explain below.

4. Pierre L'Enfant anglicized his first name to Peter and added an apostrophe to his last name after he arrived in this country. I am grateful to Kenneth Bowling for pointing out to me that the reversion to "Pierre" was "a late-nineteenth-century, early-twentieth-century construction used by architects and the French minister for purposes of public policy" (Bowling, letter to the author). See also Bowling, *Peter Charles L'Enfant*, 1–5. L'Enfant was raised in Versailles, and his plan clearly engages French innovations in urban design that date from its first theoretical conceptions in 1670 to its climactic fulfillment in the mid-nineteenth century under Haussmann (see Van Zanten, *Building Paris*, 11, 79, 115). While such plans combined grids with boulevards and the monumental treatment of axial centers, urban planner Elbert Peets concludes that L'Enfant's plan is "unique" and "unlike the plan of any other city in the world" (see Peets, *On the Art of Designing Cities*, 19).

5. From the "References" listed by L'Enfant on his "Plan of the City, Intended for the Permanent Seat of the Government of the United States," 1791 (Kite, *L'Enfant and Washington*, 65).

6. The research for this chapter occurred before the appearance of C. M. Harris's important essay on the founding of Washington, D.C. My essay, like that of Harris, considers "the design history" of the capital "within [its] political context." While Harris seeks to further clarify and interpret the history behind Washington's support of L'Enfant's design, I explore the political ideas associated with the plan's various components, such as its scale and avenues, and describe the dialectical way they can be said to interact with Washington and L'Enfant's vision. See C. M. Harris, "Washington's Gamble, L'Enfant's Dream."

7. Quoted in Bowling, *Peter Charles L'Enfant*, 18, 23.

8. Harris, "Washington's Gamble, L'Enfant's Dream" 564, 562.

9. Quoted in Carter, "Benjamin H. Latrobe and the Growth and Development of Washington," 138.

10. Schuyler, *The New Urban Landscape*, 15.

11. Elkins and McKitrick, *The Age of Federalism*, 182.

12. See Catherine Allgor, *Parlor Politics*, 102–146, whose argument I paraphrase below.

13. Peets, *On the Art of Designing Cities*, 27; Longstreth, "Introduction," 11.

14. Quoted in Skowronek, *Building a New American State*, 7.

15. Bowring, *Works of Jeremy Bentham*, 39; italics original.

16. J. Hector St. John de. Crèvecoeur, *Letters from an American Farmer*, 71, 83.

17. Irving, *Letters of Jonathan Oldstyle*, 186.

18. Ozouf, *Festivals and the French Revolution*, 126. It is important to note, however, that C. M. Harris has shown that, unlike revolutionary France, revolutionary America did not originally concern itself much with the physical trappings of political power. It was slow to generate its own iconography; it remained "at core textual and iconoclastic" and "did not concern itself with questions of architectural

form." But Harris's and my own research into George Washington's enthusiasm for L'Enfant's design suggests that as Washington's political vision became bolder and grander, so did the measures used to further it. I explore here the numerous ways the built environment became instrumental to implementing both Washington's and L'Enfant's designs. See Harris, "Washington's Gamble, L'Enfant's Dream" 530–31.

19. Alexander Hamilton, James Madison, and John Jay [Publius], *The Federalist Papers* (New York: Mentor—New American Library, 1961), 47.301. All citations are from this edition. I list the Federalist Paper number before the period and the page number after; i.e., this citation is from Federalist No. 47, p. 301.

20. On the city plans L'Enfant may have drawn from in his design for Washington, D.C., see, for example, John W. Reps, *Washington on View*, 18. In an earlier study, Reps argues: "It was a supreme irony that the forms originally conceived to magnify the glories of despotic kings and emperors came to be applied as a national symbol of a country whose philosophical basis was so firmly rooted in democratic equality" (See Reps, *Monumental Washington*, 21).

21. See Scott, "'This Vast Empire,'" 43–45. Here, as well as below, I draw from Michael Kramer's argument in *Imagining Language in America* (1992) for how the "ambiguity" of the Constitution's discourse helped to secure its ratification. Kramer demonstrates how the authors of *The Federalist* readily acknowledged that the Constitution was ambiguous. Given the constraints of political discourse, the framers argued, the Constitution must necessarily be a flawed document, but at the same time its very existence showed the "moral victory" of the convention at being able to "knit themselves together as one man" and produce such a document. Kramer writes: "Language matters to Publius because it is ambiguous, because it forces readers to look beyond the letter to the spirit, in this case, beyond the language of the Constitution to the virtuous intentions of the delegates" (134; see also 122–136). The Federal City was perhaps then also envisioned by the Constitution's proponents as a site where the "spirit" of the government could be felt, so as to physically overwhelm any misgivings about the letter of its law.

22. Quoted in Carter, "Benjamin H. Latrobe and the Growth and Development of Washington," 138.

23. Hawthorne, "Custom House Sketch," 1325.

24. Harvey, *Consciousness and the Urban Experience*, 163, 103.

25. These "Handkerchief Maps" are believed to have been printed in Boston around 1792 in conjunction with "the sale of lots in the 'new Federal Town.'" See Works Progress Administration, *Washington: City and Capital*, xiv and endpapers.

26. Reps, *Washington on View*, 66.

27. Both the philosophical and the economic meanings of speculation were in use at the end of the eighteenth century. The use of the term to mean the "deep contemplation upon some subject" dates back to the fourteenth century. The use of the term to mean the "buying and selling of commodities solely to profit from their rise or fall in market value," interestingly, coincided closely with the Ameri-

can Revolution. The *Oxford English Dictionary* records the first usage of speculation in this economic sense as 1774. Adam Smith referred to the practice several times in his *Wealth of Nations* (1776).

28. Quoted in Bowling, *Peter Charles L'Enfant,* 28.

29. Carter, "Benjamin H. Latrobe and the Growth and Development of Washington," 138.

30. Bailey and Kennedy, *The American Pageant,* 143–45.

31. Reps, *Washington on View,* 60.

32. Most historians attribute the grandeur of the plan to L'Enfant's monarchic aesthetic, derived in part from his hometown of Versailles. John W. Reps refers to L'Enfant's famously "expansive nature and imagination" and his old-world taste for grand, imperial spaces (*Washington on View,* 3). The recognition of L'Enfant's importance, however, should not occlude the key role that George Washington played in choosing L'Enfant, approving and modifying his design, and supervising its construction long after L'Enfant had been dismissed due to insubordination. Recent revisionist arguments further suggest the degree to which George Washington was himself prone to romantic speculation and also deeply interested in architecture.

For example, two years prior to his approval of L'Enfant's design, George Washington had himself described such a space in a rejected draft of his first inaugural address: "The New World is becoming a stage for wonderful exhibitions. The discovery of another continent, in some unknown seas, could alone afford a theatre for political action, which could extend in their influence to so large a portion of the earth, or affect so great a multitude of its inhabitants."

The discovery (under a couch in Surrey, England) of this lost page from Washington's draft has been hailed as the discovery of Washington's forgotten identity as a "romantic" visionary (White, "'Lost' Speech," 7). Similarly, Allan Greenberg's *George Washington: Architect,* and William M. S. Rasmussen and Robert S. Tilton's *George Washington: The Man Behind the Myths* rediscover the fact that Washington, no less than Jefferson, was intensely involved in the designing of his house. In "Washington's Gamble, L'Enfant's Dream," C. M. Harris argues, as I do here, that the design of Washington, D.C., was a joint venture between L'Enfant, Washington, and, more largely, a federalist aesthetics and political economy.

33. Quoted in Fasel, "'The Soul that Animated,'" 35–36.

34. Quoted in Chandler, *Wordsworth's Second Nature,* 38–39.

35. Ibid., 37.

36. Paine, *The Rights of Man,* 309.

37. Ibid., 305.

38. Ozouf, *Festivals and the French Revolution,* 126, 132.

39. The creation of straight avenues to promote political access was of course already a staple of imperial design dating back to the baroque period and even earlier. Monica Ozouf's study of the French Revolution's use of space, however, lets us consider such trajectories not from the state's but the citizen's point of view. The

revolutionary rhetoric shows us the liberating and clarifying force also to be found in straight routes to political seats of power. See *Festivals and the French Revolution,* chapter 6.

40. Burke claimed that such a direct relationship to authority could have existed only at man's creation; since then the line between God, country, and man has become quite complex, or bent: "In the gross and complicated mass of human passions and concerns, the primitive rights of man undergo such a variety of refractions and reflections, that it becomes absurd to talk of them as if they continued in the simplicity of their original direction" (quoted in Chandler, *Wordsworth's Second Nature,* 34).

41. Breitweiser, "Jefferson's Prospect," 326.

42. Young, *Washington Community,* 8.

43. For a full account of the many ways in which L'Enfant's plan symbolized the federalist structure of the nation, see Pamela Scott, "'This Vast Empire,'" 37–58.

44. Hamilton, *Papers,* 255.

45. Kite, *L'Enfant and Washington,* 65.

46. Washington, *Diaries,* 154.

47. For George Washington's efforts to develop the Potomac River as a western trade route (which would in turn increase the value of Mount Vernon), see p. 4 and n. H4, above.

48. Quoted in the *Oxford English Dictionary, Compact Edition,* 2952.

49. When L'Enfant was dismissed from the project, the original proprietors were incensed, because they had viewed L'Enfant's "'extravagant plans, added to his great confidence, and mad zeal' as the map to their future wealth" (Bowling, *Peter Charles L'Enfant,* 33).

50. Quoted in Wolin, "The People's Two Bodies," 134.

51. Bailey and Kennedy, *The American Pageant,* 131.

52. Montesquieu, *The Spirit of Laws,* 120.

53. Hamilton et al., *Federalist Papers,* 9.73, 1.33.

54. Ibid., 10.83.

55. Quoted in Duke and Jordan, *A Richmond Reader,* 22.

56. Quoted in Breitweiser, "Jefferson's Prospect," 343.

57. Quoted in Duke and Jordan, *A Richmond Reader,* 21.

58. Ibid., 21–23; see also McLaughlin, *Jefferson and Monticello,* 363.

59. Imitation is also key for the education of the republican citizen. Left to their own devices, Jefferson famously complains, Virginians would erect "a monument to our barbarism which will be loaded with execrations as long as it shall endure." How else, then, Jefferson asks in defense of his choice of a classical model for the state capitol building, "is a taste in this beautiful [classical] art to be formed in our countrymen, unless we avail ourselves of every occasion when public buildings are to be erected, of presenting to them models for their study and imitation?" (M. Peterson, *Portable Thomas Jefferson,* 390, 389). The degree to which Jefferson's famous inventiveness was linked to imitation can be seen in his own Monticello (a com-

posite of admired buildings and styles) and his polygraph, the device by which he made copies of his own correspondence as he wrote it. For an insightful analysis of originality and imitation in Jefferson, including his polygraph, see Fliegelman, *Declaring Independence,* 166–67.

60. Quoted in Reps, *Washington on View,* 18.

61. Bowling, *Peter Charles L'Enfant,* 24; Hamilton, *Papers,* 254.

62. M. Peterson, *The Portable Thomas Jefferson,* 379.

63. Jefferson wrote: "I suspect that the doctrine that small States alone are fitted to be republics will be exploded by experience with some other brilliant fallacies accredited by Montesquieu and other political writers" (quoted in Breitweiser, "Jefferson's Prospect," 346).

64. Jefferson organized his plan around "squares": "For the President's house, offices and gardens, I should think 2. squares should be consolidated. For the Capitol and offices one square . . . For the Public walks 9. squares consolidated" (Jefferson, *Papers,* 460).

65. Breitweiser, "Jefferson's Prospect," 329.

66. Kite, *L'Enfant and Washington,* 47–48.

67. Washington was repeatedly painted with the Federal City plan well into the mid-nineteenth century; this suggests that he continued to be closely identified with his city's planning (from a talk by Scott E. Casper entitled "Washington at Home: Early Images of America's First First Family," American Antiquarian Society Lecture, Worcester, Mass., Nov. 10, 1998). The way in which such portraits might suggest Washington as "King George" was also noted by Frederika Teute at that event.

68. Quoted in Partridge, "L'Enfant's Methods and Features," 31–32.

69. Mumford, *The City in History,* 404–5.

70. Quoted in Caemmerer, *The Life of Pierre Charles L'Enfant,* 401, 404.

71. M. Peterson, *The Portable Thomas Jefferson,* 432.

72. Kite, *L'Enfant and Washington,* 53; emphasis mine.

73. Steuben, *Regulations,* 57.

74. See Meinig, *The Shaping of America,* 350.

75. Quoted in Banning, "Jeffersonian Ideology and the French Revolution," 26.

76. Habermas, *The Structural Transformation,* 44–46.

77. McCue, *The Octagon,* 26, 41.

78. Ibid., 23.

79. Ridout, *Building the Octagon,* 98, 84; Green, *The Secret City,* 15.

80. Reps, *Washington on View,* 54; Green, *The Secret City,* 33.

81. See Allgor's prizewinning *Parlor Politics,* chapter 3, whose argument I paraphrase here.

82. See, for instance, Cynthia D. Earman, "Remembering the Ladies."

83. Allgor, *Parlor Politics,* 135.

84. Ibid., 136–38.

85. Ibid., 118; Carson, *Ambitious Appetites,* 165–66.

86. Brotherhead, "Robert Morris," 702.
87. Ridout, *Building the Octagon*, 21–22.
88. Quoted in Harrison, *Philadelphia Merchant*, 63.
89. Teitelman, *Birch's Views of Philadelphia*, introduction.
90. Quoted in Harrison, *Philadelphia Merchant*, 37–38.
91. Ridout, *Building the Octagon*, 22.
92. Quoted in Harrison, *Philadelphia Merchant*, 37–38.
93. Brotherhead, "Robert Morris," 711, 719.

Chapter 2. The Poetry of Internal Improvements

H1. Adams, "The New York Gold Conspiracy," 101.
H2. E. Foner, *Reconstruction*, 460–61.
H3. Chancellor, *Devil Take the Hindmost*, 160n.
H4. See Starr, *Lincoln and the Railroads*, chapters 8–10.
H5. See Atack and Passell, *A New Economic View*, 437–38.
H6. Oates, *With Malice Toward None*, 97.
H7. Chancellor, *Devil Take the Hindmost*, 176n, 159, 160n.
H8. Quoted in Bailey, *American Pageant*, 476.
H9. Quoted in Chancellor, *Devil Take the Hindmost*, 156, 183–84.
H10. See Wills, *Lincoln at Gettysburg*, 171.
1. Brooks, "A Muddy City," in *Washington, D.C., in Lincoln's Time*, 294.
2. Adams, *Education of Henry Adams*, 810.
3. Quoted in Burns, *The Civil War*, documentary, episode 2.
4. Quoted in Meinig, *The Shaping of America*, 311.
5. *Annals of Congress*, 1063, 1006.
6. Hamilton et al., *The Federalist*, 14.103.
7. Reps, *Washington on View*, 151; Oates, *With Malice Toward None*, 249.
8. Berlin, "Nationalism," 583.
9. Lincoln details his vision in a speech he made to the Wisconsin State Agricultural Society in 1859. See *Speeches and Writings*, 493–505.
10. Whitman, *Complete Poetry and Collected Prose*, 712–13.
11. Kinney, "Making Capital," 174.
12. Seelye also points to the transcendentalists' criticisms of internal improvement rhetoric. Seelye suggests that at one time proponents of internal improvements did attempt to argue that such measures would lead to the nation's moral improvement, but that this idea died with the Whig Party. See Seelye, *Beautiful Machine*, 382. I suggest here that Whitman and Lincoln, a descendent from the Whigs, carried this connection on. Thoreau's quote is from *Walden*, 116.
13. Whitman, *Memoranda During the War*, 65.
14. Ozouf, *Festivals and the French Revolution*, 126.
15. West, *The American Evasion of Philosophy*, 26.

16. Emerson, *Nature*, 10.

17. Webster, *Speeches*, 1:303.

18. Hamilton et al., *The Federalist*, 14.102–3.

19. Lincoln, *Speeches and Writings*, 54.

20. Meinig, *The Shaping of America*, 4–8.

21. Quoted in Remini, *Henry Clay*, 227.

22. Daniel Webster, letter dated Jan. 17, 1825, in *Papers of Daniel Webster: Correspondence, Vol. 2*, 13 (emphasis in original).

23. Even a roll call in Congress, John Quincy Adams wrote in his diary (Feb. 20, 1831), could offer "'a very striking exemplification of the magnificent grandeur of this nation,'" because the larger scene of which it was a part, "the forms and the proceedings of the House . . . the colossal emblem of the union over the Speaker's chair, the historic Muse at the clock, the echoing pillars of the hall," taken altogether "form[s] the subject for a descriptive poem." Quoted in Gowans, *Styles and Types of North American Architecture*, 86n.

24. Wills, *Lincoln at Gettysburg*, 25; quoted in Kunhardt et al., *Lincoln: An Illustrated Biography*, 72.

25. Lincoln, *Speeches and Writings*, 53–54; Oates, *With Malice Toward None*, 49–50; 97.

26. Wills, *Lincoln at Gettysburg*, 171–74 (emphasis on *"message"* original); 160. For the timing of Webster's speech see Bartlett, *Daniel Webster*, 117.

27. Oates, *With Malice Toward None*, 10.

28. Lincoln, "A House Divided," *Speeches and Writings*, 372.

29. Quoted in Wills, *Lincoln at Gettysburg*, 167.

30. Lincoln, *Speeches and Writings*, 586.

31. Wills, *Lincoln at Gettysburg*, 166–68.

32. Mitgang, *Lincoln: A Press Portrait*, 377.

33. Hay, *At Lincoln's Side*, 48.

34. For an excellent analysis of the complex iconography of Crawford's statue, see Fryd, *Art and Empire*, 190–99.

35. Gallagher, *Robert Mills*, 74.

36. Allen, *The Dome of the United States Capitol*, 24, 19; Scott, *Temple of Liberty*, 99–100.

37. Allen, *The Dome of the United States Capitol*, 22.

38. Quoted in ibid., 24.

39. Lincoln, *Speeches and Writings*, 588.

40. Nicolay and Hay, *Abraham Lincoln*, 3:319–21.

41. Wills, *Lincoln at Gettysburg*, 158–59.

42. Nicolay and Hay, *Abraham Lincoln*, 3:325.

43. Kunhardt et al., *Lincoln*, 176; and Eaton, *Grant, Lincoln, and the Freedman*, 89. Capitol architectural historian William C. Allen suggests that the dome construction would have continued anyway, because the workers decided to take the risk that the government would eventually pay them for their labor, which it did,

rather than let the thousands of dollars of marble already ordered go to waste. Lincoln's comment may then have simply been getting mileage out of what was already underway. See Allen, *The Dome of the United States Capitol,* 57n.142.

44. Gowans, *Styles and Types of North American Architecture,* 88n3.10.

45. Thomas, *Robert E. Lee,* 188, 195–96; Blount Jr., *Robert E. Lee,* 77.

46. Gowans offers this explanation of the politics behind the architecture of Arlington House and its "curiously thick columns": "It was built on George Hadfield's designs for eccentric George Washington Parke Custis, George Washington's grandson by adoption and the self-appointed guardian of the Washington tradition of liberty over equality. In the architecture of early Greek city-states, Custis saw liberty's prime affirmation; hence he subordinated the house proper to its huge portico with great squat columns in what he took to be archaic Greek style (the model being Paestum in southern Italy). The whole was conceived as a rebuke to Roman style promoted by the 'egalitarian' third president, Thomas Jefferson." See Gowans, *Styles and Types of North American Architecture,* 85, 88n3.10.

47. Lincoln, *Speeches and Writings,* 588.

48. I am grateful to David Schuyler for discussions on this point.

49. For the possible sources of the dome's design, see Scott, *Temple of Liberty,* 7.

50. Lincoln, *Speeches and Writings,* 793.

51. "Washington: Symbol and City," permanent exhibition, The National Building Museum, Washington, D.C.

52. Owen, *Hints on Public Architecture,* 7–8, 31–46, 51–52, 75; 38–39. Emphasis original.

53. Greenough, *Form and Function,* 36–37.

54. Wills, *Lincoln at Gettysburg,* 160.

55. Quoted in Fryd, *Art and Empire,* 77–78, emphasis original.

56. Ibid., 66–76, 87, emphasis original.

57. Quoted in Bandy, "An Unknown 'Washington Letter,'" 25.

58. Quoted in Kaplan, *Walt Whitman,* 271.

59. Trachtenberg, "Lesson of the City," 163.

60. Whitman, *Correspondence,* 1:82.

61. Whitman, *Complete Poetry and Collected Prose,* 689–90n.

62. Traubel, *With Walt Whitman in Camden,* 26.

63. Whitman, *Notebooks,* 2:659–60.

64. See Kinney, "Making Capital," 174, 186–87.

65. See Mumford, *The City in History,* 404.

66. Whitman, *Complete Poetry and Collected Prose,* 709.

67. Murray, "Traveling with the Wounded," 65–66; Upton, *Architecture in the United States,* 156.

68. Whitman, *Complete Poetry and Collected Prose,* 737.

69. Ibid., 719.

70. Ibid.

71. Trachtenberg, "Lessons of the City," 170.

72. Kinney, "Making Capital," 177–78; Whitman quoted in Kaplan, *Walt Whitman,* 278.

73. Whitman, *Complete Poetry and Collected Prose,* 689–90n.

74. Betsy Erkkila has examined the notebooks and confirmed that "they do appear to be blood smeared," but she notes too that *Specimen Days* is "not a verbatim recording of them" but instead "a remembrance and reinvention of the war written a decade after its close." See Kinney, "Making Capital," 189n2.

75. Whitman, *Complete Poetry and Collected Prose,* 442–45. See lines 49, 33, 40.

76. Whitman, *Correspondence,* 1:81–82.

77. Bandy, "An Unknown 'Washington Letter,'" 25.

78. Ibid.

79. Whitman, *Complete Poetry and Collected Prose,* 459–60.

80. Quoted in Murray, "Traveling with the Wounded," 73.

81. See Certeau, "Walking in the City," 127–28, and Jacobs, *The Death and Life of Great American Cities,* 50.

Chapter 3. A House United

H1. E. Foner, *Reconstruction,* 460.

H2. See Atack and Passell, *A New Economic View,* 400; E. Foner, *Reconstruction,* 603.

H3. Osthaus, *Freedmen, Philanthropy, and Fraud,* 1.

H4. Douglass, *Life and Times,* 402.

H5. Osthaus, *Freedmen, Philanthropy, and Fraud,* 45.

H6. Douglass, *Life and Times,* 405.

H7. Quoted in McFeely, *Frederick Douglass,* 286.

H8. Osthaus, *Freedmen, Philanthropy, and Fraud,* 1.

H9. Ibid., 145.

H10. Ibid., 20–21, 44, 56–58.

H11. Douglass, *Life and Times,* 400–401.

H12. Douglass, *Papers,* 4:373.

H13. Osthaus, *Freedmen, Philanthropy, and Fraud,* 134.

H14. Douglass, *Life and Times,* 401.

H15. Osthaus, *Freedmen, Philanthropy, and Fraud,* 147.

H16. Douglass, "Deeds," reel 30.

1. Quoted in Johnson, "City on the Hill," 291.

2. Ibid., 151.

3. Douglass, *Speeches,* April 14, 1876, 4:429.

4. Douglass's other Washington properties included two large lots on Pennsylvania Avenue, several lots on Colfax Street, N.W. (near Howard University), and three lots at Seventeenth and U Streets, N.W. He also owned the mortgages on several properties in Baltimore, Fall River, Massachusetts, and Rochester, where he had lived before moving to Washington. According to the Frederick Douglass National Historic Site, the full "extent of [his] network of investment properties is yet

to be determined" (F. Douglass, "Deeds"; National Park Service, "Property Investments," 12–13).

5. E. Foner, *Reconstruction,* 398.

6. Ibid., 235–36.

7. National Park Service, "Property," 10; "The Price of Light," 84.

8. Sundquist, *Frederick Douglass,* 19.

9. Frederickson, review of *Young Frederick Douglass,* 3.

10. Douglass, *Life and Times,* 514.

11. Douglass, *My Bondage and My Freedom,* 246.

12. Ibid., 244.

13. Douglass, *Papers* (April 21, 1873), 4:372–73.

14. Douglass, *My Bondage and My Freedom,* 245.

15. Ibid.

16. Douglass, *Narrative,* 260–61.

17. Douglass, *Papers* (April 21, 1873), 4:372–73.

18. Douglass, *Papers* (September 6, 1891), 5:484.

19. Gillian Brown, *Domestic Individualism,* 57–59.

20. Douglass, *Life and Times,* 505.

21. Douglass, *Narrative,* 44–45.

22. Douglass, *Papers* (April 21, 1873), 4:372.

23. Douglass, *My Bondage and My Freedom,* 44–45.

24. Sprague, "My Mother as I Recall Her," 20.

25. Johnson, "City on the Hill," 219–22.

26. Douglass, *Papers* (October 22, 1883), 5:112; 5:121.

27. Douglass, *Papers* (September 25, 1883), 5:91.

28. National Park Service, "Property Investments," 12.

29. Douglass's son Charles, already living in Washington while his father was still in Rochester, encouraged his father to invest in Capitol Hill, where there were "many fine sites." But, he warned, it was "better to buy through an agent because some of these old rebels would sell cheap to a white man, but not so cheap to a colored man. The agents are glad to sell to anybody they can" (Douglass, Letter, March 15, 1870, "Correspondence"). In the letter in which he made his final offer for the Seventeenth Street properties, Douglass implies that the lawyer in charge of the property had not been dealing fairly with him. Douglass seems to be ironic in his almost suggestion that race might be behind his mistreatment:

I cannot think Mr. Riggs [the owner of the property] intends to take advantage of, or to deal inequitably with me, but the demand of $2000.00 is unjust and conceded so to be by all parties who have knowledge of the amount paid by others in the square. The demand is three times as large as the uniform amount charged others. Taken in connection with the fact that Mr. Riggs has kept me waiting for over a year for a definite answer, and out of the interest of my money during that time, it seems to me extortionate. (Letter to B. H. Warner, Esq., May 1, 1876, "Correspondence")

Once again Douglass exposes racial prejudice and wins: his check of $1,500.00, which he included with the letter, was accepted. "I cannot think Mr. Riggs intends to take advantage of me" of course means that it would be possible to accuse Riggs of doing just that. Douglass's manner demonstrates his power and insures he will not be treated "inequitably."

30. At his three lots at 2000, 2002, 2004 Seventeenth Street, N.W. (at U Street), Douglass had built a row of conjoined Second Empire townhouses (that is still standing), although the corner house is bigger than the other two. They can be identified as a unit (Frederika Douglass Perry, "Recollections of Her Grandfather," 6; Fitzpatrick and Goodwin, *Black Washington,* 225). Of 316 and 318 A Street, Frederika Douglass Perry (granddaughter of Douglass) recalls that doors were cut in both the upper and lower halls, "thus enabling the family to have desired ample space" ("Recollections," 7).

31. In 1864, 316 was one of the finest in the neighborhood, assessed at $2,000.00, while 318 was assessed at only $200.00. By 1875, 318 had risen $600.00 in its assessed value, suggesting perhaps that Douglass had made improvements. He may have added on the mansard roof and matching cornice to the original two-story structure (National Park Service, "Property Investments," 20).

32. All three of Douglass's sons were involved in real estate as well as politics, though his sons Lewis and Frederick were never financially independent or secure. His son Charles went on to develop "Highland Beach," the Chesapeake Bay summer resort for black families, where Douglass built a house shortly before he died (see McFeely, *Frederick Douglass,* 372).

33. Douglass, *Papers* (September 18, 1873), 4:393.

34. Douglass, *Papers* (September 6, 1891), 5:484.

35. P. Foner, *Frederick Douglass,* 341.

36. Douglass compares himself to Othello on at least one occasion. Referring to his discovery of the insolvency of the Freedman's Savings and Trust Company, to which he had just been appointed president, Douglass said, "I found that I had been placed there with the hope that by 'some drugs, some charms, some conjuration, or some mighty magic,' I would bring it back" (*Life and Times,* 405), quoting from *Othello* (I, i, 90–91).

37. This citation is to the Pelican edition (ed. Alfred Harbage).

38. Quoted in McFeely, *Frederick Douglass,* 383.

39. See Hutchinson, *Anacostia Story,* 53, 111.

40. Lee's mansion still stands on the hill across the Potomac River from the Lincoln Memorial.

41. Douglass, *My Bondage and My Freedom,* 42.

42. Ketcham, "Cedar Hill," 7; and National Capital Region, "Historical Structures Report," 3–4.

43. Douglass, *My Bondage and My Freedom,* 38.

44. McFeely, *Frederick Douglass,* 6.

45. Douglass, *My Bondage and My Freedom,* 28–29.

46. McFeely, *Frederick Douglass,* 298.

47. Ketcham, "Cedar Hill," 7; and National Capital Region, "Historical Structures Report," 3–4.

48. Douglass, *My Bondage and My Freedom*, 42.
49. I am grateful to Dell Upton for this observation.
50. Douglass, *Life and Times*, 512–13.
51. Ibid., 467.
52. Douglass, *Papers* (December 7, 1869), 4:240.
53. On the failure of the Freedman's Savings and Trust see Osthaus, *Freedmen, Philanthropy, and Fraud,* chapters 5 and 6. On the social acceptance of bourgeois blacks in Washington, see Johnson, "City on the Hill," 291. On Douglass's career disappointments see McFeely, *Frederick Douglass,* 305–6.
54. For example, Douglass rejected the political vision of his mentor and publisher, William Garrison, when Douglass started his own newspaper.
55. Quoted in McFeely, *Frederick Douglass,* 323.
56. Harley, "A Study," 15.

Chapter 4. Democracy's Church

H1. Quoted in Chancellor, *Devil Take the Hindmost,* 165.
H2. Adams, "The New York Gold Conspiracy," 101.
H3. Adams invested in the Calumet copper mines developed by Louis Agassiz. Adams makes a reference to his investments in a letter dated April 27, 1902. See Adams, *Letters,* 5:380.
H4. Adams, "New York Gold Conspiracy," 109.
H5. Quoted in Chancellor, *Devil Take the Hindmost,* 188.
H6. Twain and Warner, *The Gilded Age,* 199–207.
H7. Chancellor, *Devil Take the Hindmost,* 187.
H8. Twain and Warner, *The Gilded Age,* 274.
H9. Ibid., 176 (emphasis original).
1. Cater, *Henry Adams and His Friends,* lxiv.
2. Adams, *Education,* 1082, 1085.
3. Decker, *The Literary Vocation of Henry Adams,* 208.
4. Quoted in Friedlander, "Henry Hobson Richardson, Henry Adams, and John Hay," 246; emphasis original.
5. Adams, *Education,* 762.
6. Ibid., 956, 1010.
7. Evelyn and Dickson, *On This Spot,* ix–x.
8. Goode, *Capital Losses,* xxx.
9. Adams, *Democracy,* 109.
10. Adams, *Education,* 760.
11. Adams, *History,* 27.
12. Adams, *Mont Saint Michel and Chartres,* 436, 444.
13. Adams, *Education,* 1074.
14. Adams, *Mont Saint Michel and Chartres,* 362–63.
15. Adams, *Letters,* 2:638.

16. Samuels, *Henry Adams,* 326.

17. James, "Pandora,"130, 128.

18. O'Toole, *The Five of Hearts,* 131.

19. Blair, "Lafayette Square," 159.

20. Evelyn and Dickson, *On This Spot,* 236.

21. Adams, *Education,* 1021.

22. Adams, "Men and Things," 455.

23. Ibid.

24. Quoted in Samuels, *Henry Adams,* 136.

25. Adams, *Letters,* 2:578n.

26. Commission of Fine Arts, *Sixteenth Street Architecture,* 158.

27. Adams, *Education,* 742, 746–48.

28. Adams, *Letters,* 2:519; *Education,* 1016.

29. Adams, *Letters,* 2:217.

30. Ibid., 2:276.

31. Samuels, *Henry Adams,* 119.

32. Adams, *Letters,* 2:239.

33. Ibid., 2:276.

34. For an important discussion of Clover Adams's photographic career and its relation to the work of Henry Adams, see Laura Saltz, "Clover Adams's Dark Room."

35. Among other instances of this "collaboration," I would cite John Hay's anonymous novel *The Breadwinners* (1884); John La Farge's windows for Hay's dining room; Saint-Gaudens's design for a quarter commissioned by President Theodore Roosevelt (1907); Stanford White's setting for Saint-Gaudens's memorial to Colonel Robert Gould Shaw (Clover's cousin) in Boston, and White's setting for the Adams memorial.

36. Samuels, *Henry Adams,* 144–45.

37. Adams, *Democracy,* 7, 8, 76.

38. Ibid., 8, 168.

39. Edward Chalfant argues that even Adams's residence at 1501 H street could have been seen as a confession of his authorship; see Chalfant, *Better in Darkness,* 330–31.

40. Adams, *Democracy,* 109–10.

41. Ibid., 110, 109, 111.

42. Friedrich, *Clover,* 291.

43. Adams, *Democracy,* 44.

44. Ibid., 177, 172.

45. Ibid., 4, 12.

46. Ibid., 20, 76.

47. Ibid., 40.

48. Ibid., 9, 41.

49. Adams, *Letters,* 2:326.

50. Marian Hooper Adams, *Correspondence,* December 2, 1883.

51. Ibid., December 26, 1883; December 23, 1883.

52. The connections drawn by Robert E. Spiller and Ernest Samuels are re-viewed by Scheyer, "Henry Adams and Henry Hobson Richardson," 9; Friedlaen-der, "Henry Hobson Richardson, Henry Adams, and John Hay," 236n; and Decker, *The Literary Vocation of Henry Adams,* 207. According to Spiller and Samuels, the character of Stephen Hazard draws upon Henry's cousin, Rev. Phillips Brooks (the minister of Trinity Church); George Strong suggests the immensely winning Clarence King; the brooding artist Wharton suggests John La Farge; and Esther's cousin Catherine Brooke draws upon Adams's neighbor on Lafayette Square, whom he so admired, Elizabeth Cameron. In other words, Adams's salon is once again formally, but secretively, presented in the novel.

53. Decker, *The Literary Vocation of Henry Adams,* 207.

54. Adams, *Esther,* 198, 234.

55. Ibid., 187–88.

56. Ibid., 234, 193.

57. Ibid., 234.

58. Ibid., 190.

59. Ibid., 333.

60. Ibid., 319.

61. *Dict of American Biography,* 1928.

62. O'Gorman, *Architectural Forms,* 94.

63. Adams, *Esther,* 314–15.

64. O'Gorman, *Architectural Forms,* 110, 94.

65. Marian Hooper Adams, *Letters of Mrs. Henry Adams,* 452.

66. Quoted in O'Gorman, *Architectural Forms,* 110.

67. Adams, *Letters,* 2:627.

68. Ibid., 2:587; 636.

69. Friedlaender, "Henry Hobson Richardson, Henry Adams, and John Hay," 238n; O'Gorman, *Architectural Forms,* 40.

70. Marian Hooper Adams, *Letters of Mrs. Henry Adams,* 419, 448.

71. Lafayette Square was originally known as President's Square. It was offi-cially renamed in 1824, in honor of the Marquis de Lafayette's visit to Washington that year.

72. Adams, *Education,* 1045, 1018.

73. Samuels, *Henry Adams,* 67.

74. Aiken, Foreword, *Democracy,* x.

75. Quoted in Samuels, *Henry Adams,* 230.

76. Adams, *Democracy,* 9.

77. See Adams, *Education,* 746.

78. Works Progress Administration, *WPA Guide to Washington, D.C.,* 251.

79. Evelyn and Dickson, *On This Spot,* 133.

80. Works Progress Administration, *WPA Guide to Washington, D.C.,* 251.

81. James, "Pandora," 131.

82. Blair, "Lafayette Square," 139.

83. Peets, *On the Art of Designing Cities,* 55–56.

84. Adams, *Education,* 1024.

85. For the first six months of their house planning, Hay and Adams were very excited over the possibility that King might join them (Friedlaender, "Henry Hobson Richardson, Henry Adams, and John Hay," 235). King eventually declined, probably because he couldn't afford to maintain another household. Unbeknownst to the Five of Hearts, there was a sixth heart—King's black wife, Ada Todd King, whose existence he kept secret. King's finances were tied up in supporting her, their children, his mother, and his wild mining speculations and extravagant tastes (see O'Toole, *Five of Hearts,* 401–3).

86. Quoted in Friedlaender, "Henry Hobson Richardson, Henry Adams, and John Hay," 237.

87. Marian Hooper Adams, "Correspondence," January 11, 1884; emphasis original.

88. Ibid., May 4, 1884.

89. Marian Hooper Adams, "Correspondence," February 3, 1884.

90. Ibid., March 9, 1884.

91. Quoted in Friedlaender, "Henry Hobson Richardson, Henry Adams, and John Hay," 240, 245. Friedlaender states that the initial rough estimate for Adams's house was $30,000 and for Hay's, $50,000: "As construction proceeded, these figures, always allowing for such exaggeration or understatement as the circumstances seemed to call for, advanced to 40 then 50 or $65,000 for the Adams house, to 60 then $80,000 for Hay's" (239).

92. O'Gorman, *Richardson and His Office,* 78.

93. In the estimation of architectural historian Henry Russell Hitchcock, the "plans of [the Hay-Adams] houses are not remarkable" (Hitchcock, *The Architecture of H. H. Richardson,* 271). Several of Richardson's houses have been credited with widely influencing American domestic architecture, but the Hay-Adams houses never appear on such lists. See, for example, Thomas C. Hubka, "H. H. Richardson's Glessner House: A Garden in the Machine," *Winterthur Portfolio* 24 (Winter 1989): 209–29, and Jeffrey Karl Ochsner and Thomas C. Hubka, "H. H. Richardson: The Design of the William Watts Sherman House," *Journal of the Society of Architectural Historians* 51 (June 1992): 121–45.

94. Adams, *Letters,* 2:539.

95. Ibid., 2:577–78.

96. Ibid., 2:553.

97. Ibid., 2:558.

98. Saltz, "Clover Adams's Dark Room," 461.

99. From "Carp's Letter" to *The Cleveland Leader,* November 13, 1885. Hay included the article in a letter to Adams on November 19, 1885. See Marian Hooper Adams, "Correspondence."

100. Samuels, *Henry Adams*, 326.

101. Adams, *Letters*, 2:579.

102. Jordy, *Henry Adams: Scientific Historian*, 45.

103. Chanler, *Roman Spring*, 300–301.

104. Cater, *Henry Adams and His Friends*, lxiii.

105. Adams, *Supplement to the Letters of Henry Adams*, 1893–3.

106. Ibid.

107. Cater, *Henry Adams and His Friends*, lxiv.

108. Adams, *Education*, 1034.

109. See Trachtenberg, *The Incorporation of America*, chapter 7.

110. Burnham, "White City, Capital City," 619.

111. Moore, "The Improvement of Washington City," 623.

112. Adams, *Education*, 1031, 1033.

113. Ibid., 1031.

114. Commission of Fine Arts, *Sixteenth Street Architecture*, 6.

115. Moore, "The Improvement of Washington City," 627.

116. Quoted in Reps, *Monumental Washington*, 143–44; Adams mentions the proposed changes to Lafayette Square in a letter dated April 13, 1902: "A great government building is to fill the side of the square. It is very doubtful whether I can maintain myself here two years longer; and the poor old ladies opposite . . . are trembling at being turned onto the street at once." The proposed changes were defeated shortly after in the Senate. The transformation of Adams's block did not begin until four years after his death in 1918. See Adams, *Letters*, 5:373 and 5:374, n.5.

117. Peets, *On the Art of Designing Cities*, 55–56.

118. Commission of Fine Arts, *Sixteenth Street Architecture*, 6.

119. Works Progress Administration, *WPA Guide to Washington, D.C.*, 258–59.

120. Evelyn and Dickson, *On This Spot*, 133, 145.

121. Commission of Fine Arts, *Sixteenth Street Architecture*, 64.

122. Adams, *Education*, 1021.

123. "The Education of Henry Adams," review.

124. Ibid.

Epilogue

1. Moore, "Park System," 44.

2. Evenson, "Monumental Spaces," 32. The members of the Senate Park Commission, which produced the McMillan Plan, did not feel that their vision was a departure from L'Enfant's plan. L'Enfant's hope for a "Grand Avenue" was sufficiently vague that they had to simply try to interpret the spirit in which it was proposed. They also had to adapt L'Enfant's vision to accommodate the changes that a century had wrought. Taking into account the extent to which L'Enfant was influenced by the French landscape architect LeNôtre, the commission arrived at an interpre-

tation that would "consider the Mall as a park or garden rather than an urban boulevard" (Streatfield, "The Olmsteds and the Landscape of the Mall," 117–23).

3. Peets, *On the Art of Designing Cities,* 47.

4. Gutheim, *The Grand Design,* 5; Stern and Gastil, "A Temenos for Democracy," 263.

5. Stern and Gastil, "A Temenos for Democracy," 263.

6. Hawthorne, "Custom House Sketch," 1325.

7. Caemmerer, *Pierre Charles L'Enfant,* 401, 404.

8. For a comparison of the White City and Washington, D.C., see Daniel H. Burnham, "White City, Capital City"; Thomas Hines, "The Imperial Mall: The City Beautiful Movement and the Washington Plan of 1901–1902"; and Howard Gillette Jr., "White City, Capital City."

9. Hines, "The Imperial Mall," 92.

10. Jacobs et al., *The Boulevard Book,* 87.

11. Evenson, "Monumental Spaces," 32, 31.

12. Quoted in Reps, *Washington on View,* 22.

13. Peets, *On the Art of Designing Cities,* 29–30.

14. James, *Wings of the Dove,* 416.

15. Streatfield, "The Olmsteds and the Landscape of the Mall," 133.

16. Goldberger, "Talk of the Town," 27.

17. Olmsted Jr., "Landscape in Connection with Public Buildings in Washington," 28.

18. Moore, "Park System," 44.

19. Olmsted Jr., "Landscape in Connection with Public Buildings in Washington," 29.

20. Moore, "Park System," 121–22.

21. Thomas Hines notes, "Olmsted [Jr.], in a style and manner worthy of his father, promoted the development of a far-reaching park system of naturalistic design" ("The Imperial Mall," 93). David Streatfield notes Olmsted's work on Boston's Emerald Necklace "would serve as a conceptual model for the Washington park system" ("The Olmsteds and the Landscape of the Mall," 121).

22. Moore, "Park System," 83–89, 31.

23. Moore, "Park System," appendix D-289.

24. Jacobs et al., *The Boulevard Book,* 85–86.

25. Ibid., 86.

26. Ibid., 86.

27. David Streatfield cites "a large number of sources from the Renaissance and baroque traditions" as well in his analysis of the "gradual transition in landscape character from the extreme formality of the area around Capitol Hill to the relatively ordered informality of Potomac Park." See Streatfield, "The Olmsteds and the Landscape of the Mall," 129.

28. J. Carter Brown, "The Mall and the Commission of Fine Arts," 249–50.

29. Longstreth, "Introduction: Change and Continuity on the Mall," 14.

30. Goldberger, "Talk of the Town," 27.

31. Kiley, "A Critical Look at the McMillan Plan," 301–2.

32. Olmsted, "Landscape in Connection with Public Buildings in Washington," 26.

33. Longstreth, "Introduction: Change and Continuity on the Mall," 15, 14.

34. Hawthorne, "Custom House Sketch," 1325; Ozouf, *Festivals and the French Revolution,* 132, 128.

35. Brown, "The Mall and the Commission of Fine Arts," 257.

36. Streatfield, "The Olmsteds and the Landscape of the Mall," 125.

37. Peets, *On the Art of Designing Cities,* 97, 96.

38. "Hallowed Ground in Jeopardy—Keep the Mall as It Is," editorial, *New York Times* (July 4, 1997): A18.

39. "World War II Memorial Defaces a National Treasure," *National Coalition to Save Our Mall,* June 24, 2004, <www.savethemall.org>.

40. "Don't Mar the Mall," editorial, *New York Times* (September 24, 2000); "World War II Memorial Defaces a National Treasure," *National Coalition to Save Our Mall.*

41. Goldberger, "Talk of the Town," 27.

42. Quoted in Hines, "The Imperial Mall," 87.

43. J. Peterson, "The Nation's First," 143, 145. For an account of the "battle" that Senator James McMillan and Glenn Brown, national secretary of the American Institute of Architects, both of whom sought the sort of comprehensive design for Washington that Burnham and his group would provide, waged against the U.S. Army Corps of Engineers, see Peterson's full essay "The Nation's First Comprehensive City Plan"; for the European influences on the McMillan Plan, see Streatfield, "The Olmsteds and the Landscape of the Mall," 117–36.

44. Burnham, "White City, Capital City," 620. J. Peterson shows the importance of the term "comprehensive" to modern urban planning in his essay "The Nation's First Comprehensive City Plan."

45. Trachtenberg, *The Incorporation of America,* 211. Thomas Hines sees Burnham's promotional essay as "linking the [McMillan] plan to the incipient Progressive movement—a reform of the landscape, [Burnham] suggested, to complement the burgeoning reforms in other areas of society" ("The Imperial Mall," 95).

46. Burnham's quote appears on the border of a plan of Washington, c. 1948. See Reps, *Washington on View,* 267.

47. Longstreth, "Introduction: Change and Continuity on the Mall," 11.

48. Jones, *Lost in the City,* 148.

49. Wolf, *Wired,* xii. What Wolf suggests is how literary a topic speculation is, that is, the degree to which investor enthusiasm is fanned through the circulation of the most grandiose fictions. He calls his history of *Wired* a "romance." The novelist David Liss has exploited the literary drama of eighteenth-century British stock-jobbing as well in his marvelous novel *The Conspiracy of Paper* (New York: Random House, 2000).

50. Wolf, *Wired,* xiii.

Works Cited

Adams, George Worthington. *Doctors in Blue: The Medical History of the Union Army in the Civil War.* New York: Henry Schuman, 1952.

Adams, Henry. "The New York Gold Conspiracy." In *Chapters of Erie,* Charles Francis Adams Jr. and Henry Adams. Ithaca: Cornell University Press, 1956.

———. *The Education of Henry Adams.* Privately printed, 1907. In *Novels, Mont Saint Michel, The Education,* ed. Ernest Samuels and Jayne N. Samuels. New York: Library of America, 1983.

———. *The History of the United States of America during the Administrations of Jefferson and Madison.* Ed. Ernest Samuels. Abr. ed. Chicago: University of Chicago Press, 1967.

———. *The Letters of Henry Adams.* 6 vols. Ed. J. C. Levenson, et al. Cambridge, Mass.: Belknap, 1982.

———. *Mont Saint Michel and Chartres.* Privately printed, 1904. In *Novels, Mont Saint Michel, The Education,* ed. Ernest Samuels and Jayne N. Samuels. New York: Library of America, 1983.

———. *The Session, 1869–70.* In *The Great Secession Winter of 1860–61 and Other Essays,* ed. George Hochfield. New York: Sagamore Press, 1958. 191–222.

———. *Supplement to the Letters of Henry Adams: Letters Omitted from the Harvard University Press Edition of the Letters of Henry Adams. Part 1.* Ed. J. C. Levenson, et al. Boston: Massachusetts Historical Society, 1989.

[Adams, Henry]. *Democracy: An American Novel.* 1880. In *Novels, Mont Saint Michel, The Education,* ed. Ernest Samuels and Jayne N. Samuels. New York: Library of America, 1983.

[———]. *Esther.* [Frances Snow Compton, pseud.] 1884. In *Novels, Mont Saint Michel, The Education,* ed. Ernest Samuels and Jayne N. Samuels. New York: Library of America, 1983.

[———]. "Men and Things in Washington." *Nation* 230 (Nov. 25, 1869): 454–56.

Adams, Marian Hooper. "Correspondence." Adams Papers, Massachusetts Historical Society, reel 598.

————. *The Letters of Mrs. Henry Adams, 1865–1883.* Ed. Ward Thoron. Boston: Little, Brown, 1936.

Aiken, Henry D. Foreword. *Democracy.* Henry Adams. New York: Penguin, 1961, v–xii.

Allen, William C. *The Dome of the United States Capitol: An Architectural History.* Washington, D.C.: U.S. Govt. Printing Office, 1992.

Allgor, Catherine. *Parlor Politics: In Which the Ladies of Washington Help Build a City and a Government.* Charlottesville: University of Virginia Press, 2000.

Anderson, Benedict. *Imagined Communities: Reflections on the Origin and Spread of Nationalism.* Rev. ed. London: Verso, 1991.

Annals of Congress. 18th Congress, 1st session: House of Representatives. Dec. 1, 1823–Feb. 27, 1824.

Arnebeck, Bob. *Through a Fiery Trial: Building Washington, 1790–1800.* Lanham, Md.: Madison Books, 1991.

————. "Tracking the Speculators: Greenleaf and Nicholson in the Federal City." *Washington History* 3.1 (spring/summer 1991): 112–25.

Atack, Jeremy, and Peter Passell. *A New Economic View of American History.* 2nd Ed. New York: Norton, 1994.

Bailey, Thomas A., and David M. Kennedy. *The American Pageant.* 7th ed. Lexington, Mass.: D. C. Heath, 1983.

Bandy, W. T. "An Unknown 'Washington Letter,' by Walt Whitman." *Walt Whitman Quarterly Review* 2.3 (winter 1985): 23–26.

Banning, Lance. "Jeffersonian Ideology and the French Revolution: A Question of Liberticide at Home." *Studies in Burke and His Times* 17.1 (1976): 5–26.

Bartlett, Irving H. *Daniel Webster.* New York: W. W. Norton, 1978.

Benjamin, Walter. *The Arcades Project.* Cambridge, Mass.: Belknap/Harvard University Press, 1999.

Berlant, Lauren. *The Queen of America Goes to Washington City: Essays on Sex and Citizenship.* Durham, N.C.: Duke University Press, 1997.

Berlin, Isaiah. "Nationalism." In *The Proper Study of Mankind.* New York: Farrar, Straus & Giroux, 1997. 581–604.

Blair, Gist. "Lafayette Square." *Records of the Columbia Historical Society* 28 (1926): 133–73.

Blount Jr., Roy. *Robert E. Lee.* New York: Viking, 2003.

Bowling, Kenneth R. Letter to the author. July 18, 2003.

————. *Peter Charles L'Enfant: Vision, Honor, and Male Friendship in the Early American Republic.* Washington, D.C.: George Washington University Libraries, 2002.

————, ed. *Washington History: Special Bicentennial Issue* 3:1. (spring/summer 1991).

———. "Coming into the City: Essays on Early Washington, D.C." Special issue, *Washington History* 12.1 (spring/summer 2000).

Bowring, John, ed. *The Works of Jeremy Bentham: vol. 4*. Edinburgh: William Tait, 1843.

Brands, H. W. *The First American: The Life and Times of Benjamin Franklin*. New York: Doubleday, 2000.

Breitweiser, Mitchell. "Jefferson's Prospect." *Prospects* 10 (1985): 315–53.

Brookhiser, Richard. *Founding Father: Rediscovering George Washington*. New York: Free Press, 1996.

Brooks, Noah. *Washington, D.C., in Lincoln's Time*. Ed. Herbert Mitgang. Athens, Ga.: University of Georgia Press, 1989.

Brotherhead, William. "Robert Morris." In *The Lives of Eminent Philadelphians, Now Deceased*, ed. Henry Simpson. Philadelphia: William Brotherhead, 1859. 702–22.

Brown, Gillian. *Domestic Individualism: Imagining Self in Nineteenth-Century America*. Berkeley: University of California Press, 1990.

Brown, Glenn, comp. *Papers Relating to the Improvement of the City of Washington, District of Columbia*. 56th Congress, 2nd session, senate document 94. Washington, D.C.: U.S. Govt. Printing Office, 1901.

Brown, J. Carter. "The Mall and the Commission of Fine Arts." In *The Mall In Washington, 1791–1991*, ed. Richard Longstreth. 2nd ed. New Haven: Yale University Press, 2002. 249–61.

Burnham, Daniel H. "White City, Capital City." *Century Magazine* (Feb. 1902): 619–20.

Burns, Ken. *The Civil War*. Documentary. Public Broadcasting System.

Caemmerer, Paul H. *The Life of Pierre Charles L'Enfant: Planner of the City Beautiful, the City of Washington*. Washington, D.C.: National Republic Publishing Co., 1950.

Carson, Barbara. *Ambitious Appetites: Dining, Behavior, and Patterns of Consumption in Federal Washington*. Washington, D.C.: American Institute of Architects, 1990.

Carter, Edward C., II. "Benjamin H. Latrobe and the Growth and Development of Washington, 1798–1818." *Records of the Columbia Historical Society* 48 (1971–72): 128–49.

Cater, Harold Dean. *Henry Adams and His Friends: A Collection of His Unpublished Letters*. Boston: Houghton Mifflin, 1947.

Certeau, Michel de. "Walking in the City." In *The Cultural Studies Reader*, ed. Simon During. London: Routledge, 1993. 151–60.

Chalfant, Edward. *Better in Darkness: A Biography of Henry Adams: His Second Life, 1862–1891*. Hamden, Conn.: Archon Books, 1994.

Chancellor, Edward. *Devil Take the Hindmost*. New York: Farrar, Straus & Giroux, 1999.

Chandler, James K. *Wordsworth's Second Nature*. Chicago: University of Chicago Press, 1984.

Chanler, Margaret Terry. *Roman Spring*. Boston: Little, Brown, 1934.

Commission of Fine Arts. *Sixteenth Street Architecture: Vol. 1*. Washington, D.C.: U.S. Govt. Printing Office, 1978.

Crèvecoeur, J. Hector St. John de. *Letters from an American Farmer and Sketches of Eighteenth-Century America*. Ed. Albert E. Stone. New York: Penguin, 1986.

Decker, William Merrill. *The Literary Vocation of Henry Adams*. Chapel Hill: University of North Carolina Press, 1990.

Dictionary of American Biography. vol 1. New York: Scribners, 1964.

"Don't Mar the Mall." Editorial. *New York Times* Sept. 24, 2000: section 4:14.

Douglass, Frederick. "Correspondence." Frederick Douglass Collection, Library of Congress, reel 2.

———. "Deeds." Frederick Douglass Collection, Library of Congress, reel 30.

———. *The Frederick Douglass Papers: Series One: Speeches, Debates, and Interviews*. 5 vols. Ed. John W. Blassingame and John R. McKivigan. New Haven: Yale University Press, 1991.

———. *The Life and Times of Frederick Douglass*. 1881; 1892. New York: Collier, 1962.

———. *My Bondage and My Freedom*. 1855. Ed. William L. Andrews. Urbana: University of Illinois Press, 1987.

———. *Narrative of the Life of Frederick Douglass*. 1845. Ed. Michael Meyer. New York: Modern Library, 1984.

Duke, Maurice, and Daniel P. Jordan, eds. *A Richmond Reader, 1733–1983*. Chapel Hill: University of North Carolina Press, 1983.

Earman, Cynthia D. "Remembering the Ladies: Women, Etiquette, and Diversions in Washington City, 1800–1814." *Washington History* (spring/summer 2000): 102–17.

Eaton, John. *Lincoln, Grant, and the Freedman*. New York: Longmans, Green, and Co., 1907.

"The Education of Henry Adams." Review of *The Education of Henry Adams*, Henry Adams. *New York Times*, Oct. 27, 1918.

Elkins, Stanley, and Eric McKitrick. *The Age of Federalism*. New York: Oxford University Press, 1993.

Emerson, Ralph Waldo. *Nature, Addresses, and Lectures*. Ed. Robert E. Spiller and Alfred R. Ferguson. Cambridge, Mass.: Belknap, 1979.

Evans, Robin. "Figures, Doors and Passages." *Architectural Design* 48.4 (1978): 267–78.

Evelyn, Douglas E., and Paul Dickson. *On This Spot: Pinpointing the Past in Washington, D.C.* Washington, D.C.: Farragut, 1992.

Evenson, Norma. "Monumental Spaces." In *The Mall In Washington, 1791–1991*, ed. Richard Longstreth. 2nd ed. New Haven: Yale University Press, 2002. 19–34.

Fasel, George. "'The Soul that Animated': The Role of Property in Burke's Thought." *Studies in Burke and His Times* 17 (winter 1976): 27–41.

Fitzpatrick, Sandra, and Maria R. Goodwin. *The Guide to Black Washington.* New York: Hippocrene, 1990.

Fliegelman, Jay. *Declaring Independence: Jefferson, Natural Language, and the Culture of Performance.* Stanford, Cal.: Stanford University Press, 1993.

Foner, Eric. *Reconstruction: America's Unfinished Revolution, 1863–1877.* New York: Harper & Row, 1988.

Foner, Philip S. *Frederick Douglass: A Biography.* New York: Citadel Press, 1964.

Foote, Shelby. *The Civil War: A Narrative: Red River to Appomattox.* New York: Random House, 1974.

Franklin, Wayne, and Michael Steiner, eds. *Mapping American Culture.* Iowa City: University of Iowa Press, 1992.

Frederickson, George. Review of *Young Frederick Douglass*, Dickson J. Preston, and *The Mind of Frederick Douglass*, Waldo E. Martin Jr. *New York Review of Books* (June 27, 1985): 3–4.

Friedlaender, Marc. "Henry Hobson Richardson, Henry Adams, and John Hay." *Journal of the Society of Architectural Historians* (Oct. 1970): 231–46.

Friedrich, Otto. *Clover.* New York: Simon and Schuster, 1979.

Fryd, Vivien Green. *Art and Empire: The Politics of Ethnicity in the United States Capitol, 1815–1860.* New Haven: Yale University Press, 1992.

Gallagher, H. M. Pierce. *Robert Mills: Architect of the Washington Monument 1781–1855.* New York: Columbia University Press, 1935.

Gillette, Howard, Jr. "White City, Capital City." *Chicago History* 18.4 (winter 1989–90): 26–45.

Goldberger, Paul. "Talk of the Town: Not in Our Front Yard," *New Yorker* (Aug. 7, 2000): 27.

Goode, James. *Capital Losses: A Cultural History of Washington's Destroyed Buildings.* 2nd ed. Washington, D.C.: Smithsonian Institution, 2003.

Gowans, Alan. *Styles and Types of North American Architecture.* New York: Harper Collins, 1992.

Green, Constance McLaughlin. *The Secret City: A History of Race Relations in the National Capitol.* Princeton, N.J.: Princeton University Press, 1967.

Greenberg, Allan. *George Washington: Architect.* London: Andreas Papadakis Press, 1999.

Greenough, Horatio. *Form and Function: Remarks on Art, Design, and Architecture.* Berkeley: University of California Press, 1947.

Gutheim, Frederick. *The Grand Design.* Washington, D.C.: Library of Congress, 1967.

Habermas, Jürgen. *The Structural Transformation of the Public Sphere: An Inquiry into a Category of Bourgeois Society.* Trans. Thomas Burger and Frederick Lawrence. Cambridge, Mass.: MIT Press, 1991.

"Hallowed Ground in Jeopardy—Keep the Mall as It Is." Editorial. *New York Times,* July 4, 1997: A18.

Hamilton, Alexander. *The Papers of Alexander Hamilton, Vol. 8.* Ed. Harold C. Syrett. New York: Columbia University Press, 1965.

Hamilton, Alexander, James Madison, and John Jay [Publius]. *The Federalist Papers.* New York: Mentor-New American Library, 1961.

Hamlin, Talbot. *Greek Revival Architecture in America.* London: Oxford University Press, 1944.

Harley, Sharon. "A Study of the Preservation and Administration of 'Cedar Hill': The Home of Frederick Douglass." U.S. Department of the Interior: National Park Service Publication, Frederick Douglass National Historic Site, undated.

Harris, C. M. "Washington's Gamble, L'Enfant's Dream: Politics, Design, and the Founding of the National Capital." *William and Mary Quarterly,* 3rd series, 56.3 (July 1999): 527–64.

Harrison, Eliza Cope, ed. *Philadelphia Merchant: The Diary of Thomas P. Cope, 1800–1851.* South Bend, Ind.: Gateway Editions, 1978.

Harvey, David. *Consciousness and the Urban Experience.* Baltimore: Johns Hopkins University Press, 1985.

Hawthorne, Nathaniel. "Custom House Sketch." In *The Norton Anthology of American Literature, Vol. 1,* ed. Nina Baym et al. 5th ed. New York: Norton, 1998.

Hay, John. *At Lincoln's Side: John Hay's Civil War Correspondence and Selected Writings.* Ed. Michael Burlingame. Carbondale: Southern Illinois University Press, 2000.

Hines, Thomas. "The Imperial Mall: The City Beautiful Movement and the Washington Plan of 1901–1902." In *The Mall In Washington, 1791–1991,* ed. Richard Longstreth. 2nd ed. New Haven: Yale University Press, 2002. 79–99.

Hitchcock, Henry Russell. *The Architecture of H. H. Richardson and His Times.* 1936. Cambridge, Mass.: MIT Press, 1970.

Holmes, Oliver W. "Suter's Tavern: Birthplace of the Federal City." *Records of the Columbia Historical Society* 49 (1973–74): 1–34.

Hutchinson, Louise Daniel. *The Anacostia Story: 1608–1930.* Washington, D.C.: Smithsonian Institution Press, 1977.

Irving, Washington. *Letters of Jonathan Oldstyle, Gent. & Salamagundi or the Whig-whams and Opinions of Launcelot Langstaff, Esq. & Others.* In *The Complete Works of Washington Irving,* ed. Bruce I. Granger and Martha Hartzog. Boston: Twayne Publishers, 1977.

Jacobs, Allan B., Elizabeth MacDonald, and Yodan Rofé. *The Boulevard Book.* Cambridge, Mass.: MIT Press, 2002.

Jacobs, Jane. *The Death and Life of Great American Cities*. New York: Random House, 1961.

Jacobson, Joanne. *Authority and Alliance in the Letters of Henry Adams*. Madison: University of Wisconsin Press, 1992.

James, Henry. *The American Scene*. 1907. New York: Scribners, 1946.

———. "Pandora." In *The Novels and Tales of Henry James: New York Edition, Vol. 18*. New York: Scribners, 1909. 95–168.

———. *Wings of the Dove*. 1902. New York: Penguin, 1986.

Jefferson, Thomas. *Notes on the State of Virginia*. Ed. Frank Shuffelton. New York: Penguin, 1999.

———. *The Papers of Thomas Jefferson, Vol. 17*. Ed. Julian P. Boyd. Princeton, N.J.: Princeton University Press, 1965.

Johnson, Thomas R. "The City on the Hill: Race Relations in Washington, 1865–1885." Ph.D. diss., University of Maryland, 1975.

Jones, Edward P. *Lost in the City*. 1992. New York: Harper Collins, 2002.

Jordy, William H. *Henry Adams: Scientific Historian*. New Haven: Yale University Press, 1952.

Kaledin, Eugenia. *The Education of Mrs. Henry Adams*. Philadelphia: Temple University Press, 1981.

Kaplan, Amy. "Manifest Domesticity." *American Literature* 70.3 (Sept. 1998): 581–606.

———. *The Social Construction of American Realism*. Chicago: University of Chicago Press, 1988.

Kaplan, Justin. *Walt Whitman: A Life*. New York: Simon & Schuster, 1980.

Keckley, Elizabeth. *Behind the Scenes*. New York: G. W. Carleton & Co., 1868.

Ketcham, Sally Johnson. Cedar Hill: The Frederick Douglass Home: Furnishing Plan, Section D. Unpublished ms. Washington, D.C.: Frederick Douglass National Historic Site, December 1971.

Kiley, Daniel Urban. "A Critical Look at the McMillan Plan." In *The Mall In Washington, 1791–1991*, ed. Richard Longstreth. 2nd ed. New Haven: Yale University Press, 2002. 296–303.

Kinney, Katherine. "Making Capital: War, Labor, and Whitman in Washington, D.C." In *Breaking Bounds: Whitman and American Cultural Studies*, ed. Betsy Erkkila and Jay Grossman. New York: Oxford University Press, 1996. 174–89.

Kismaric, Susan. *American Politicians: Photographs from 1843 to 1993*. New York: Museum of Modern Art, 1994.

Kite, Elizabeth S. *L'Enfant and Washington, 1791–1792*. Baltimore: Johns Hopkins Press, 1929.

Kramer, Michael P. *Imagining Language in America*. Princeton, N.J.: Princeton University Press, 1992.

Kunhardt Jr., Philip B., Philip B. Kunhardt III, and Peter W. Kunhardt. *Lincoln: An Illustrated Biography*. New York: Knopf, 1992.

Lears, T. J. Jackson. *No Place of Grace: Antimodernism and the Transformation of American Culture, 1880–1920.* New York: Pantheon, 1981.

Lee, Richard M. *Mr. Lincoln's City: An Illustrated Guide to the Civil War Sites of Washington.* McClean, Va.: EPM Publications, 1981.

Leech, Margaret. *Reveille in Washington: 1860–1865.* New York: Time Inc., 1941.

Lincoln, Abraham. *The Collected Works of Abraham Lincoln.* 9 vols. Ed. Roy P. Basler. New Brunswick, N.J.: Rutgers University Press, 1955.

———. *Abraham Lincoln: His Speeches and Writings.* 1946. Ed. Roy P. Basler. New York: Da Capo, 1990.

Longstreth, Richard, ed. *The Mall In Washington, 1791–1991.* 2nd ed. New Haven: Yale University Press, 2002.

———. "Introduction: Change and Continuity on the Mall, 1791–1991." In *The Mall In Washington, 1791–1991,* ed. Richard Longstreth. 2nd ed. New Haven: Yale University Press, 2002. 11–17.

Lowenfels, Walter. *Walt Whitman's Civil War.* New York: Knopf, 1960.

McCue, George. *The Octagon: Being an Account of a Famous Washington Residence: Its Great Years, Decline and Restoration* (Washington, D.C.: American Inst. of Architects, 1976).

McCullough, David. *John Adams.* New York: Simon & Schuster, 2001.

McFeely, William S. *Frederick Douglass.* New York: Norton, 1991.

McLaughlin, Jack. *Jefferson and Monticello: The Biography of a Builder.* New York: Henry Holt, 1988.

McPherson, James M. *Ordeal by Fire: The Civil War and Reconstruction.* New York: Knopf, 1982.

Meinig, D. W. *The Shaping of America: Geographical Perspective on 500 Years of History, Vol. 3.* New Haven: Yale University Press, 1998.

Miller, Angela. *The Empire of the Eye: Landscape Representation and American Cultural Politics, 1825–1875.* Ithaca: Cornell University Press, 1993.

Mitgang, Herbert, ed. *Abraham Lincoln: A Press Portrait.* Athens, Ga.: University of Georgia Press, 1989.

———. *Lincoln as They Saw Him.* New York: Rinehart & Co, 1956.

Montesquieu, Baron de. *The Spirit of Laws.* Trans. Thomas Nugent. New York: Hafner Press, 1949.

Moore, Charles. "The Improvement of Washington City." *Century Magazine* (Feb. 1902): 621–28.

Moore, Charles, ed. *The Improvement of the Park System of the District of Columbia.* 57th Congress, 1st session, Senate Report no. 166. Washington, D.C.: U.S. Govt. Printing Office, 1902.

Mumford, Lewis. *The City in History: Its Origins, Its Transformations, and Its Prospects.* New York: Harcourt, Brace and World, 1961.

Murray, Martin G. "Traveling with the Wounded: Walt Whitman and Washington's Civil War Hospitals." *Washington History* 8.2 (fall/winter 1996–97): 58–73.

National Capital Region and National Capital Office of Design and Construction. Historic Structures Report, Part I: Frederick Douglass Home, Washington, D.C. Unpublished ms. Washington, D.C.: Frederick Douglass National Historic Site, February 1965.

National Park Service. "Frederick Douglass Home Feasibility Study." Washington, D.C.: Frederick Douglass National Historic Site, 1985.

——. "Frederick Douglass's Property Investments." Unpublished ms. Frederick Douglass National Historic Site, Washington, D.C.

——. Dept. of the Interior. *Washington: The Nation's Capital*. Washington, D.C.: U.S. Govt. Printing Office, 2000.

Nicolay, John G., and John Hay. *Abraham Lincoln: A History*. 10 vols. New York: The Century Co., 1890.

Oates, Stephen B. *With Malice Toward None: The Life of Abraham Lincoln*. New York: Harper & Row, 1977.

Ochsner, Jeffrey Karl. *H. H. Richardson: The Complete Architectural Works*. Cambridge, Mass.: MIT Press, 1982.

O'Gorman, James F. *H. H. Richardson: Architectural Forms for an American Society*. Chicago: University of Chicago Press, 1987.

——. *H. H. Richardson and His Office: Selected Drawings*. Boston: Harvard University and David Godine, 1974.

Olmsted Jr., Frederick Law. "Landscape in Connection with Public Buildings in Washington." In *Papers Relating to the Improvement of the City of Washington, District of Columbia*. Comp. Glenn Brown. Washington, D.C.: U.S. Government Printing Office, 1901. 22–34.

Osthaus, Carl R. *Freedmen, Philanthropy, and Fraud*. Urbana: University of Illinois Press, 1976.

O'Toole, Patricia. *The Five of Hearts: An Intimate Portrait of Henry Adams and His Friends, 1880–1918*. New York: Clarkson Potter, 1990.

Owen, Robert Dale. *Hints on Public Architecture*. 1849. New York: Da Capo, 1978.

Ozouf, Mona. *Festivals and the French Revolution*. Trans. Alan Sheridan. Cambridge, Mass.: Harvard University Press, 1988.

Padover, Saul K., ed. *Thomas Jefferson and the National Capital*. Washington, D.C.: U.S. Govt. Printing Office, 1946.

Paine, Thomas. *The Rights of Man*. 1791–92. New York: Anchor, 1973.

Partridge, William T. "L'Enfant's Methods and Features of His Plan for the Federal City." Reports and Plans: Washington Region, National Capital Park and Planning Commission. *Annual Report: Supplementary Technical Data*. Washington, D.C.: U.S. Govt. Printing Office, 1930.

Peets, Elbert. *On the Art of Designing Cities: Selected Essays of Elbert Peets*. Ed. Paul D. Spreiregen. Cambridge, Mass.: MIT Press, 1968.

Perry, Frederika Douglass. "Recollections of Her Grandfather." Hologram. Manuscript Division, Howard University Library, Washington, D.C.

Peterson, Jon A. "The Mall, The McMillan Plan, and the Origins of American City Planning." In *The Mall in Washington, 1791–1991*. ed. Richard Longstreth. 2nd ed. New Haven: Yale University Press, 2002. 100–115.

———. "The Nation's First Comprehensive City Plan." *Journal of the American Planning Association* 5.2 (1985): 134–50.

Peterson, Merrill D., ed. *The Portable Thomas Jefferson*. New York: Penguin, 1977.

Pierson, William H., Jr. *American Buildings and Their Architects: Vol. I: The Colonial and Neoclassical Styles*. New York: Oxford University Press, 1970.

"The Price of Light." Editorial. *The Economist* (October 22–28, 1994): 84.

Rasmussen, William M. S., and Robert S. Tilton. *George Washington, D.C.: The Man Behind the Myths* (Charlottesville: University of Virginia Press, 1999.

Remini, Robert V. *Henry Clay: Statesman for the Union*. New York: Norton, 1991.

Reps, John W. *Monumental Washington, D.C.: The Planning and Development of the Capital Center*. Princeton, N.J.: Princeton University Press, 1967.

———. *Washington on View: The Nation's Capital since 1790*. Chapel Hill: University of North Carolina Press, 1991.

Reynolds, David. *Walt Whitman's America: A Cultural Biography*. New York: Knopf, 1995.

Ridout, Orlando, V. *Building the Octagon*. Washington, D.C.: American Institute of Architects Press, 1989.

Romero, Lora. *Home Fronts: Domesticity and Its Critics in the Antebellum United States*. Durham, N.C.: Duke University Press, 1997.

Saltz, Laura. "Clover Adams's Dark Room: Photography and Writing, Exposure and Erasure." *Prospects* 24 (1999): 449–90.

Samuels, Ernest. *Henry Adams*. Cambridge, Mass.: Belknap—Harvard University Press, 1989.

Scheyer, Ernst. "Henry Adams and Henry Hobson Richardson." *Journal of the Society of Architectural Historians* (Mar. 1953): 7–12.

Schuyler, David. Letter to the author. Aug. 25, 2004.

———. *The New Urban Landscape*. Baltimore: Johns Hopkins University Press, 1986.

Scott, Pamela. *Temple of Liberty*. New York: Oxford University Press, 1995.

———. "'This Vast Empire': The Iconography of the Mall, 1791–1848." In *The Mall in Washington, 1791–1991*, ed. Richard Longstreth. 2nd ed. New Haven: Yale University Press, 2002. 37–58.

Seelye, John. *Beautiful Machine: Rivers and the Republican Plan, 1755–1825*. New York: Oxford University Press, 1991.

Shakespeare, William. *The Complete Pelican Shakespeare*. Ed. Alfred Harbage. New York: Viking, 1969.

Skowronek, Stephen. *Building a New American State: The Expansion of National Administrative Capacities, 1877–1920.* Cambridge: Cambridge University Press, 1982.

Sprague, Rosetta Douglass. "My Mother as I Recall Her." Frederick Douglass Collection, Library of Congress, reel 1.

Starr, John W., Jr. *Lincoln and the Railroads.* New York: Arno Press, 1981.

Stern, Robert M., with Raymond W. Gastil. "A Temenos for Democracy: The Mall in Washington and Its Influence." In *The Mall In Washington, 1791–1991.* ed. Richard Longstreth. 2nd ed. New Haven: Yale University Press, 2002. 262–77.

Steuben, Baron von. *Regulations, Order and Discipline for the Troops of the United States, 1779.* Hartford, Conn.: Nathaniel Patten, 1792. Evans Microprints, First Series: Item 24919.

Streatfield, David C. "The Olmsteds and the Landscape of the Mall." In *The Mall In Washington, 1791–1991.* ed. Richard Longstreth. 2nd ed. New Haven: Yale University Press, 2002. 117–41.

Sundquist, Eric, ed. *Frederick Douglass: New Literary and Historical Essays.* Cambridge: Cambridge University Press, 1990.

Teitelman, S. Robert. *Birch's Views of Philadelphia.* Philadelphia: Free Library of Phila.—University of Pennsylvania Press, 1983.

Thomas, Emory M. *Robert E. Lee: A Biography.* New York: Norton, 1995.

Thoreau, Henry David. *Walden.* Roslyn, N.Y.: Walter J. Black, 1942.

Trachtenberg, Alan. *The Incorporation of America: Culture and Society in the Gilded Age.* New York: Hill and Wang, 1982.

———. "Whitman's Lesson of the City." In *Breaking Bounds: Whitman and American Cultural Studies,* ed. Betsy Erkkila and Jay Grossman. New York: Oxford University Press, 1996. 163–73.

Traubel, Horace. *With Walt Whitman in Camden.* New York: Appleton, 1908.

Twain, Mark, and Charles Dudley Warner. *The Gilded Age.* New York: Meridian, 1994.

Upton, Dell. *Architecture in the United States.* New York: Oxford University Press, 1998.

Van Zanten, David. *Building Paris: Architectural Institutions and the Transformation of the French Capital, 1830–1870.* Cambridge: Cambridge University Press, 1994.

Washington, George. *The Diaries of George Washington, Vol. 4, 1748–1799.* Ed. John C. Fitzpatrick. Boston: Houghton Mifflin, 1925.

"Washington: Symbol and City." Permanent Exhibition. The National Building Museum, Washington, D.C.

Webster, Daniel. *The Papers of Daniel Webster: Correspondence, Vol. 2, 1825–1829.* Ed. Charles M. Wiltse. Assoc. ed. Harold D. Moser. Hanover, N.H.: University Press of New England, 1976.

———. *The Papers of Daniel Webster: Speeches and Formal Writings, Vol. 1, 1800–1833.* Ed. Charles M. Wiltse. Asst. ed. Alan R. Berolzheimer. Hanover, N.H.: University Press of New England, 1988.

West, Cornell. *The American Evasion of Philosophy.* Madison: University of Wisconsin Press, 1989.

White, Claire. "'Lost' Speech by Washington Is Found." *Daily Telegraph,* May 30, 1996: 7.

Whitman, Walt. *Complete Poetry and Collected Prose.* New York: Library of America, 1982.

———. *The Correspondence, Vol. 1.* Ed. Edwin Haviland Miller. New York: NYU Press, 1961.

———. *Memoranda During the War [&] Death of Abraham Lincoln.* Camden, N.J., 1875. (facsimile edition) Ed. by Roy P. Basler. Bloomington: Indiana University Press, 1962.

———. *Notebooks and Unpublished Prose Manuscripts, Vol. 2.* Ed. Edward F. Grier. New York: NYU Press, 1961.

Wills, Garry. *Lincoln at Gettysburg: The Words that Remade America.* New York: Simon & Schuster, 1992.

Wolf, Gary. *Wired: A Romance.* New York: Random House, 2003.

Wolin, Sheldon S. "The People's Two Bodies: The Declaration and the Constitution." In *The United States Constitution,* ed. Bertell Ollman and Jonathan Birnbaum. New York: NYU Press, 1990. 130–37.

Wood, Gordon S. "The Would-Be Gentleman." Review of *William Cooper's Town,* Alan Taylor. *New York Review of Books* 43 (Aug. 8, 1996): 36–39.

Works Progress Administration. *The WPA Guide to Washington, D.C.* 1942. New York: Pantheon, 1983.

"World War II Memorial Defaces a National Treasure." Editorial. National Coalition to Save Our Mall, June 24, 2004. http://www.savethemall.org/wwii/index.html.

Young, James Sterling. *The Washington Community, 1800–1828.* New York: Columbia University Press, 1966.

Index

Page numbers in **bold** indicate illustrations.

Abraham Lincoln: A History (Hay), 106
Abraham Lincoln: Last Sitting (photograph by Gardner), 58–60, **60**
access, routes of, xxvi–xxvii
Adams, Charles Francis, 77, 103, 111, 142
Adams, Clover. *See* Adams, Marian Hooper
Adams, Henry, xxv, xxvi, 99–142; as lobbyist, 110–11; as speculator, 99, 171 n. H3;
  property of (*see also* Hay-Adams houses): 1501 H Street, 113, 115, 119, 155; 1603 H Street (Richardson house with Hay), 101–7, **107**, 128–37; 1607 H Street (little White House), 106, **108**, 115, 129–30, 133, 139; Pitch Pine Hill (Beverly, Massachusetts), 112–13, **114**, 129;
  works: *Democracy*, 100–101, 105–6, 111, 113–19, 126, 141; *The Education of Henry Adams*, xxviii, 101, 106, 108–9, 128, 141–42; *Esther*, 105–6, 113, 119–25; *A History of the United States during the Administrations of Jefferson and Madison*, 106, 130; *Mont Saint Michel and Chartres*, 105, 106, 119; "The New York Gold Conspiracy," 99, 100–101
Adams, Marian Hooper, 106, 108, 112, 119; grave of, 107–10, **109**, 113, 128–30; as photographer, 113, **114**, 117, 131–32, **132**, 172 n. 34; suicide of, 108, 133
Adams, John Quincy, on roll call vote, 166 n. 23

Adams, Louisa Catherine, 33
Adams family, 111
Agassiz, Louis, 122
Allen, William C., 166–67 n. 43
Allgor, Catherine, 10, 33, 158 n. 14
Anacostia River, 27, 146
Anthony, Susan B., 93
Arlington Cemetery, 68, 115, 148
Arlington House (Custis Lee Mansion), 53–54, **54**, 68, 115–17, 148, 167 n. 46
Arnebeck, Bob, 3, 4
avenues, xxiii, 6, 12, 18, 27–31, 40–41, 143–44; Walt Whitman on, 63

Baltimore and Pacific Railroad terminal, 144–45, 149
Bancroft, George, 126
Bayard Smith, Margaret, 33–34
Bentham, Jeremy, 10
Berlant, Lauren, xxix, 158–59 n. 18
Berlin, Isaiah, 42
Birch, William, *An Unfinished House in Chestnut Street, Philadelphia* (1800 engraving), 35–37, **36**
Blaine, James G., 126
Bleak House (Dickens), 92
Boston, 120, 176 n. 21
Bowling, Kenneth, 160 n. 6
Breadwinners, The (Hay), 172 n. 35
Breitweiser, Mitchell, 18, 25
Brookings Institution, 140
Brooks, Phillips, 173 n. 52
Brown, Gillian, 80, 159 n. 19
Brown, J. Carter, 150–51

Bruce, Blanche, 93
Burke, Edmund, 16–17, 20, 163 n. 40
Burnham, Daniel, 137–38, 139, 145, 152–54, 177 n. 45

Calhoun, Floride, 33
Cameron, Donald, 126, 128, 136
Cameron, Elizabeth, 126, 128, 173 n. 52
Capitol, U.S., 6, **48**, 63, 64, 100, 144, 146–47, 148; cartoon of, 49–50, **50**; dome, 43, 47–53, **49**, **51**, 147, 166–67 n. 43; H. Adams on, 105, 116
Capitol Hill, 125, 169 n. 29, 176 n. 27
Carrolsburgh, 19
Champs Elysées, 145–46, 147
Chancellor, Edward, 3, 41, 100
Chartres Cathedral, 105
Chesapeake and Ohio Canal, 30
circulation, xxvi–xxvii, 14, 18–19, 31, 33–34, 37, 41–42, 43–45, 144, 147–55; and domesticity, 66–67. See also infrastructure, physical
Civil Rights Act (1866), 83
Civil Rights March (1963), 151
Civil War: effect on Washington, D.C., 42–43; and speculation, 38–40
Clay, Henry, 34, 42, 44–45, 126
Cleveland, Grover, 100, 128, 130
communication, routes of, xxvi
Compton, Frances Snow (pseudonym for Henry Adams), 120
Constitution, U.S., 152, 161 n. 21; embodied in plan of Washington, xxi, xxii, 6–7, 10, 18
Cope, Thomas P., 35–36
Corcoran, William, 126, 139
Cosmos Club, 110–11
"Crossing Brooklyn Ferry" (Whitman), 61
Custis, George Washington Parke, 167 n. 46
Custis Lee Mansion. See Arlington House

Davis, Jefferson, 53
Decker, William, 103, 120
de Certeau, Michel, 68
de Crèvecoeur, J. Hector, 10–11
Democracy (Adams), 100–101, 105–6, 111, 113–19, 126, 141

domesticity: in Democracy, 116–19; and hospitals, 64–67; national, xxvi, 31–34, 56, 66–67; speculative, 35; in Washington, D.C., 9–10
Douglass, Anna Murray, 82
Douglass, Charles, 170 n. 32
Douglass, Frederick, xxv, xxix, 71–98, **98**; and domesticity, xxvii–xxviii, 78–98; grandmother of, 90–1; mother of, 90, 92; properties of: A Street, 81–82, 84–86, **85**; Cedar Hill, 73–74, 79, 81–82, 84, 87–98, **89**, **92**, **93**, **94**, **95**, **96**, **97**, **98**; other, 168–69 n. 4; 17th Street, 84, 169–70 n. 29, 170 n. 30, 170 n. 31; works: My Bondage and My Freedom, 76, 81; Narrative of the Life of Frederick Douglass, 79, 80
Douglass, Frederick, Jr., 170 n. 32
Douglass, Helen Pitts, 97–98
Douglass, Lewis, 82–83, 170 n. 32
Downing, Andrew Jackson, 127, 144

Earmon, Cynthia, 158 n. 14
Education of Henry Adams, The (Adams), xxviii, 101, 106, 108–9, 128, 141–42
Elkins, Stanley, 9
Emerson, Ralph Waldo, 44
Erkkila, Betsy, 168 n. 74
Esther (Adams), 105–6, 113, 119–25
Evenson, Norma, 143, 145–46, 147

federalism, 4, 5–6, 13, 18–20
federalists, debate with republicans over design of national capital, 21–29
Federalist, The, xxvi, 6, 14, 20–1, 22
"Five of Hearts, The," 113, 172 n. 35
Foner, Eric, 38
Franklin, Benjamin, and real estate speculation, 159 n. H4
Franklin, Wayne, xxviii–xxix
Fredrickson, George, 75
Freedman's Savings and Trust Company, 71–74
Free Soil Party, 111
French Revolution, 43, 150
Fryd, Vivien, 58

Gallatin, Albert, 30, 40–41, 111
Gallatin, Hannah, 33
Gardner, Alexander, *Abraham Lincoln: Last Sitting* (photograph), 58–60, **60**
Garnet, Henry Highland, 93
Garrison, William Lloyd, 93, 171 n. 54
Georgetown, 19
George Washington (Greenough, statue), 58, **59**
George Washington Esq. President of the United States (Savage, portrait), 25–27, **26**
Gilded Age, The (Twain and Warner), xxi, 99–100
Girard College, 57
Goldberger, Paul, 150, 152
Gowans, Alan, 53, 167 n. 46
Grant, Ulysses S., 126; statue of, 148
Greenleaf, James, 4–5
Greenough, Horatio, 57, 58; statue of George Washington, 58, **59**
Gurney, Ellen Hooper, 123

Habermas, Jürgen, 31
Hamilton, Alexander, 6, 14, 16, 20–21, 22, 157 n. 7
"Handkerchief Maps," 14, 161 n. 25
Harris, C. M., 6, 160 n. 6, 160–61 n. 18
Harrison, Benjamin, 128
Harvey, David, xxix, 14
Haussmann, Georges Eugène, 14, 68
Hawthorne, Nathaniel, on literary romance, 13, 144
Hay, Clara, 113
Hay, John, 47–48, 114, 133–34, 139; death of, 140; friendship with H. Adams, xxviii, 106, 113, 127, 128, 131; and Lincoln's first inaugural address, 52; works: *Abraham Lincoln: A History*, 106; *The Breadwinners*, 172 n. 35
Hay-Adams Hotel, 141, **141**
Hay-Adams houses, xxix, 106–7, **107**, 113, 123–24, 133–35, **135**, 174 n. 93; building of, 174 n. 85; cost of, 174 n. 91; and Clarence King, 174 n. 85; razing of, 140–41; as speculation, 141
Henry, Patrick, and real estate investments, 159 n. H4
Hines, Thomas, 176 n. 21, 177 n. 45

Hints on Public Architecture (Owen), 57
History of the United States during the Administrations of Jefferson and Madison, A (Adams), 106, 130
Hitchcock, Henry Russell, 174 n. 93
Hooper, Robert William, 120, 122, 124–25; death of, 133
hospitals, xxvii, **65**; and circulation, 64; Whitman on, 63–66

infrastructure, physical, xxvi, 40–45, 147–49; and Whitman, 34–40, 60–67. *See also* avenues; circulation
Irving, Washington, 11–12

Jackson, Andrew, 126; monument to, 126, **127**
Jacobs, Jane, 68
James, Henry, 146; "Pandora," 106–7, 118, 127
Jefferson, Thomas, 5, 16, 17–18, 163–64 n. 59, 164 n. 63, 164 n. 64; *Notes on the State of Virginia*, 25; plan for a capital city, 6, **7**, 13, 21–25; republicanism of, 22–29

Kaplan, Amy, xxvi
Kennedy, John F., 140
Kiley, Dan, 150
King, Ada Todd, 174 n. 85
King, Clarence, 113, 114, 122, 128, 173 n. 52; secret wife of, 174 n. 85
Kinney, Katherine, xxix, 43, 62, 64, 158 n. 18
Kramer, Michael, 161 n. 21

La Farge, John, 113, 172 n. 35, 173 n. 52
La Farge, Mabel Hooper, watercolor of Henry Adams, 136, **137**
Lafayette Square, 73, 103–4, 125–28, 139–40, 173 n. 71, 175 n. 116; and Bernard Baruch, 140; and John F. Kennedy, 140; and Renwick Museum, 140
Law, Thomas, 4
Latrobe, Benjamin Henry, 9, 13, 16, 120
Lee, Mary Custis, 53
Lee, Robert E., 53–54, 115, 148
L'Enfant, Peter Charles, 18–19, 22–23, 25, 27–31, 68, 137, 141, 153; dismissed

L'Enfant, Peter Charles *(continued)*
from planning Federal City, 163 n. 49;
as federalist, 14, 138; grave of, 68; on
Jefferson's plan, 22; and Robert
Morris house, 35–37; name of, 160
n. 4; and Versailles, 12–13, 160 n. 4
L'Enfant plan for a federal city, 6–15, **8**,
18–19, 22–31, 41, 102, 104, 143–46,
148, 152–55, 159–60 n. 3, 162 n. 32,
175–76 n. 2; and the Constitution,
6–7, 10; melding federalism and republicanism, 134
Le Nôtre, André, 175–76 n. 2
Lincoln, Abraham, xxv, xxx, 38–60;
inaugural addresses of, 43, 46, 47;
first inaugural address, 50–54; and
infrastructure, xxvi–xxvii, 38–40, 42,
46–53; as orator, 45–47; second inaugural address, 54–56, 66; as speculator, 39–40
Lincoln, William, 46
Lincoln Memorial, 68, 148, 150, 152
little White House (Adams home at
1607 H Street), 106, **108**, 115, 129–30,
133, 139
Lodge, Henry Cabot, 128, 136
Longstreth, Richard, 150

Madison, Dolley, 33; house of, 111, 126
Madison, James, 21, 44
Maison Carrée, 22, **23**
Mall, National, 37, 40, 53, 56–57, 68,
143–52, 154–55, 175–76 n. 2; as specu-
lative space, 143–44
Marx, Karl, 10
McClean, John, 126
McKim, Charles, 145
McKitrick, Eric, 9
McMillan Plan of 1902, 139, **140**,
143–55. *See also* Senate Park
Commission
Meinig, D. W., xxvi, 44
Memorial Bridge, 148
Metropolitan Club, 111
Miller, Angela, xxiv
Mills, Clark, monument to Andrew
Jackson, 126, **127**
Mills, Robert, 48–49
Monticello, 5
Mont Saint Michel and Chartres
(Adams), 105, 106, 119

monuments: Peets on, 151; Goldberger
on, 152
Moore, Charles, 148
Morgan, J. Pierpont, 39
Morris, Robert, 4–5, 14; Philadelphia
house of, 35–37, **36**, 141
Mount Vernon, 148
Mumford, Lewis, 27
My Bondage and My Freedom
(Douglass), 76, 81

*Narrative of the Life of Frederick
Douglass* (Douglass), 79, 80
National Capital Planning Commis-
sion, 151
National Mall. *See* Mall, National
New York City, 11–12
"New York Gold Conspiracy, The"
(Adams), 99, 100–101
Niagara Falls, 120–22
Nicholson, John, 4–5
Notes on the State of Virginia (Jeffer-
son), 25

Octagon House, 31–32
Ogle, Anne, 31–32
O'Gorman, James, 122, 130
Olmsted, Frederick Law, Jr., 145, 147,
148, 149, 176 n. 21
Olmsted, Frederick Law, Sr., 148, 149,
176 n. 21
Osthaus, Carl, 72, 73
Othello (engraving by C. Becker),
87–88, **88**
Othello (Shakespeare), 87–88, 170 n. 36
O'Toole, Patricia, 107
Owen, Robert, 56–57; *Hints on Public
Architecture*, 57
Ozouf, Mona, 12, 17, 43, 150, 162–63 n. 39

Paine, Thomas, 16, 17
"Pandora" (James), 106–7, 118, 127
Panopticon, 10
Patent Office, 43, 56, 63, 64, 105
"Patowmack Company," 4, 159 n. H4
Peets, Elbert, 10, 127, 139, 144, 146, 151,
160 n. 4
Pennsylvania Avenue, xxiii, 66–67, 148
Peterson, Jon A., 153
Philadelphia, 11–12, 35
Phillips, Wendell, 93, 94

Pitch Pine Hill, 112–13, **114**, 129
Potomac River, 24, 27, 41, 146, 148
Powers, Hiram, statue of a Greek slave, 95–96, **97**

racial equality, 71, 74–79; and domesticity, 78–98; in Washington, D.C., 82–83
railroads, 38–40, 105; and segregation, 76–78
Randolph, Martha Jefferson, 33
Reconstruction, xxvii, 74–75
Regulations, Order, and Discipline for the Troops of the United States (1779), 30
Reps, John W., xxvi, 3, 12, 161 n. 20
republicanism, 11–12, 13, 17–18; debate with federalists over design of a national capital, 21–29
Rice, Cecil Spring, 128
Richardson, Henry Hobson, xxix, 103, 106, 111, 113, 122, 128, 129; Henry Adams house, 101–7, **107**, 128–37, 174 n. 93; Ames Gate House, 122–23; Ephraim W. Gurney house, 123, **123**; Trinity Church, 113, 120, 124. *See also* Hay-Adams houses
Rohrbach, Augusta, 158 n. 12
Romero, Lora, xxvi
Roosevelt, Theodore, 128, 172 n. 35
routes of communication. *See* infrastructure, physical

Saint-Gaudens, Augustus, 105, **109**, 113, 138, 145, 172 n. 35; and statue for Adams grave, 107–9, 113
Saint John's Church (Lafayette Square), 120, 124–25, **124**, 131, 139
San Marco, Piazza (Venice), 146, 147
Savage, Edward, *George Washington Esq. President of the United States* (engraving), 25–27, **26**
scale, 21–25
Saltz, Laura, 132
Schurz, Carl, 112
Schuyler, David, 9
Scott, Pamela, xxi, 12–13
Seelye, John, xxvi, 43, 165 n. 12
segregation, 76–78, 82–83, 88–90
Senate Park Commission, 138, 139, 143, 151, 152–54, 175 n. 2, 177, n. 43; members of, 145. *See also* McMillan Plan of 1902

Seward, William, 51
Shaw, Robert Gould, 172 n. 35
slavery, 32, 79–81, 90–92, 111
Slidell House. *See* little White House
Smith, Adam: and speculation, 162 n. 27; *Wealth of Nations*, xxii, 19–20
Smith, Margaret Bayard, 33–34
Smithsonian Institution, 56–58, 144
Specimen Days (Whitman), 65, 168 n. 74
speculation, xxv, xxx–xxxi, 3–5, 14–16, 18–19, 19–20, 38–40, 53–54, 72–74, 99–101, 152–55; defined, xxii–xxiii; 161–62 n. 27; real estate, xxiii–xxiv, 19–20, 158 n. 11
Stanton, Elizabeth Cady, 88, 93
Steiner, Michael, xxviii–xxix
Stevens, Thaddeus, 75
Stowe, Harriet Beecher: on Abraham Lincoln, 47; *Uncle Tom's Cabin*, xxx, 81
Streatfield, David, 151, 176 n. 21, 176 n. 27
suffrage, black, 75
Sumner, Charles, 94, 111, 126

Tayloe, John, II, 31–32
Taylor, Alan, *William Cooper's Town*, 158 n. 17
Thoreau, Henry David, *Walden*, xxv, xxx, 43, 158 n. 12
Thornton, William, 31
Trachtenberg, Alan, 61, 64, 137, 153
Tyber Canal, 24

Uncle Tom's Cabin (Stowe), 81
Union Pacific railroad, 72
Union Square, 148
Upton, Dell, 5, 63, 157 n. 3, 157 n. 7, 171 n. 49
U.S. Chamber of Commerce, 139
utopianism, 12

Vanderbilt, William H., 39
Vaux, Calvert, 149
Versailles, 12, **13**, 160 n. 4, 162 n. 32
Virginia State Capitol, 22, 23, **24**

Walden (Thoreau), xxv, xxx, 43, 158 n. 12
Walker, George, 22
Walter, Thomas U., 57

War of 1812, 32

Washington, D.C., population of, 32, 184

Washington, George, xxiii, xxvi–xxvii, 3–37, 58, **59**, 101, 153, 157 n. 7; first inaugural address of, 162 n. 32; and L'Enfant Plan, 5–10, 160–61 n. 18, 162 n. 32; portraits of, 164 n. 67; and Potomac River development, 4, 159 n. H4, 163 n. 47; as speculator, 3–5, 30–31; statue of, 144

Washington Casino, 111

Washington City Canal, 41

Washington Monument, 104–5, 144, 147, 148, 150, 151, 152

Wealth of Nations (Smith), xxii, 19–20, 162 n. 27

Webster, Daniel, 42, 111, 126; on Clay's Cumberland Road speech, 45

Webster-Hayne debate, 34, 44

West, Cornell, 44

"When Lilacs Last in the Dooryard Bloom'd" (Whitman), 67

White, Stanford, 172 n. 35

White, William, 78–79

White City (Columbian Exposition) 137–38, 145, 153; H. Adams and, 138

White House, 73, 139; H. Adams and, 103, 115, 117

Whitman, Walt, xxv, xxvii, xxx, 42, 60–67; and circulation, 42; on hospitals, 63–6; and infrastructure, 39–40, 60–7; on Lincoln, 59–60, 66; plan for yearbook 1863, 61–62; works: "Crossing Brooklyn Ferry," 61; *Specimen Days*, 65, 168 n. 74; "When Lilacs Last in the Dooryard Bloom'd," 67; "Wound Dresser " 65–66

William Cooper's Tavern (Taylor), 158 n. 17

Wills, Garry, 39, 46–47, 50–51, 57

Wolf, Gary, 154–55, 177 n. 49

women, role in fostering national domesticity, 33–34

Wood, Gordon, 5

World War II memorial, 152

"Wound Dresser," 65–66

Wye House, 90

Young, James Sterling, xxi, 18